CHICANO:
THE BEGINNINGS
OF
BRONZE POWER

CHICANO:

THE BEGINNINGS
OF
BRONZE POWER

Renato Rosaldo   Robert A. Calvert   Gustav L. Seligmann

Abridged Edition

WILLIAM MORROW & COMPANY, INC., NEW YORK, 1974

ACKNOWLEDGMENTS

A note of thanks is also due to Sherry DeMatteo,
Dolores Snyder, Dean Ragland, Ellen Small, Ray Gill,
Dorothea Autilio, Mary Klein, and Dr. Kenneth L.
Culver. Each has made a contribution of time and talent
toward the publication of this volume.

First Morrow Paperback Editions printing 1974

Abridged edition

Printed in the United States of America.
Library of Congress Catalog Card Number 74-16917

ISBN 0-688-07878-8

1   2   3   4   5   78   77   76   75   74

AUTHORS ACKNOWLEDGMENTS

For a volume of this size the editors obviously run up a series of debts that never fully can be paid. Tradition, however, lets us escape by acknowledging them by name. They know and we know that this is only a token; yet we offer it and it is accepted, because both sides know that no other payment can be made. We owe two general types of debts; the first are intellectual and the second, more prosaic but equally valuable, are administrative. Ward Albro of Texas A&I University and Leo Estrada and Nef Garcia of North Texas State and Abraham Hoffman of the University of Oklahoma made very useful comments not all of which were taken. We were probably wrong. Sharon O'Brien and Trisha Rainwater performed yeowomen service in preparing this volume. Mrs. Shirley Taylor and Isaura Tijerina brought order out of the chaos of our handwriting and typed neat rough drafts for us to mess up again. Lastly we must thank our editor Clifford Snyder—he knows when to push and when to wait. This makes him invaluable to his authors.

CONTENTS

CHICANO:

THE BEGINNINGS
OF
BRONZE POWER

INTRODUCTION

Most Americans view the various geographical regions of their nation in stereotyped images. The concept once held of the Southwest blends together a desert landscape and the sleeping Mexican—sombrero tilted to the noonday sun. Like most folk wisdom, this picture contains an element of truth. The scarcity of water has shaped the section's economy, and the presence of a large, culturally distinct minority has given it a unique charm. But the shy mañana-seeking Mexican is a cultural phenomenon created by Anglo fantasy and not by Chicano behavior.

Moreover, even this Anglo fantasy is collapsing rapidly before the assault of a number of Bronze Power movements that have arisen to challenge the sleepy Mexican image. The challenge came from the Southwest, but it did not come overnight. It emerged slowly from the an-

guish of a subjugated people. But before we turn to the present revolution, it might be well to look briefly at Bronze Power antecedents, remembering that to arrange any history, particularly that of a social movement, into chronological periods results in oversimplifications and the glossing over of exceptions to the rigid time periods selected.

Furthermore the image of the sleeping Mexican implied that all Brown people are alike, a racist concept that presently many Americans rightfully hold up to ridicule. Yet, otherwise perceptive observers of and sympathizers with the Bronze Power movement still toss all the revolutionaries into the same melting pot and try to render their varied geographical heritages into a single cultural broth. As whites lumped together Malcolm X, Black Power, and Martin Luther King, Anglos frequently speak of a varied

1

Bronze Power only in terms of one movement such as César Chávez or Brown Berets or *La Raza Unida.*

The road to Mexican American cultural unity has been arduous, twisted, and has not yet been attained. Much like the Black revolution, Bronze Power must draw its adherents from people in different environments. Both movements find their cadre divided along rural and urban lines. These different experiences established different goals and varying degrees of militancy in the movements, but the Brown Power movement differed from the Black revolution in that its rural constituency had different heritages, too, based upon state boundaries rather than regional ones. Therefore one may speak of rural southern Blacks or northern ghetto dwellers and divide the Black revolt thusly, but a historian must speak of California or Texas Chicanos as well as *barrio* dwellers and rural *peons.* Furthermore, unlike the Blacks, Brown people have received constant cultural renewal through intermittent immigration. The periodic influx of immigrants invigorated cultural concepts but slowed the attainment of various goals because, historically, newcomers were less likely to challenge the oppressors.

What homogenizes a heterogeneous group into a national identity of Bronze Power or Black Power is racial injustice. Injustice, then, turned the varied geographic heritage of Chicanos into movements such as *La Raza Unida,* a term that cannot be translated adequately into English. It is a cultural concept as well as a political threat to established political parties in the Southwest. It is only one goal of Bronze Power, but this cultural and political unity announces that the Chicano can no longer be taken lightly by either major political party or by Anglos. After more than a century of living in the Southwest, the Mexican American has become a force to be reckoned with, too. In America Bronze Power, like Black Power, is here to stay.

The social climate that produced Bronze Power fell into two distinct epochs—1848–1932, which might be called the age of acquiescence, adjustment, and subjugation, and the period from 1933 through Viva Kennedy in 1960, a period of working within the system. Chicanos in each southwestern state reacted somewhat differently in each period. Generally, however, in the first age Mexican Americans tried to adapt somewhat to the more aggressive behavior patterns of the Anglo culture. Usually the Hispanic population neither accepted nor openly rejected Anglo mores, but ignored them or—in extreme cases—sacrificed material holdings to the new settlers in order to retain Mexican cultural values. Thus, in the first stage of the struggle to preserve their native culture before the assault of the *gringo,* Mexican Americans acquiesced when necessary, adjusted somewhat, but at all costs maintained their ethnic uniqueness. The result was poverty and subjugation.

The next epoch in Mexican American history, 1933–1960, stressed upward mobility within the Anglo system. During this twenty-year period, Chicanos tried to crack the system by political and economic methods. In the mid-1920's other Chicanos joined New Mexico *Hispaños,* who had retained the ballot after subjugation, in becoming more politically active. Sizable numbers of Mexican Americans realized by then that the "American Dream" of cultural diversity and material well-being had not included them. Rather than a multiracial culture, Anglos offered prejudice; rather than the expected prosperity, Mexican Americans found abject poverty. Thus throughout the Southwest they sought ways to crack the system and enter into the economic, social, and political mainstream.

"The system," however, asked for technological skills that few Mexican Americans possessed. Thus lack of training and racial antagonisms condemned most Chicanos either to the poverty of migrant farm labor or some other equally menial and unrewarding employment. One way to ameliorate such conditions came through strikes. These strikes had some successes when immediate demands were met, but long-range aspirations such as collective bargaining rights were not. Undoubtedly the strikes did aid in creating a feeling of class consciousness that

Bronze Power advocates would draw upon in the future. But strikes did not bring most Mexican Americans into the "American Dream."

Other activities besides strikes expressed the discontent of Chicanos. The young particularly resented the blatant prejudice all around them, but they had not received enough cultural security to help them cope with racism. One result, for example, was the *Pachuco* phenomenon of the mid-1940's, where rootless young Mexican Americans tried to create a subculture that gave them prestige in an hostile Anglo world. Other Chicanos reacted more traditionally, seizing the ballot and building a political base that allowed a few individuals to obtain successes.

Yet as a class Chicanos failed to "crack the system," even though a talented few could succeed by traditional means. The slowness of this sort of success, if it came at all, grated upon the more militant. Furthermore, to many it seemed that the best way to crack the system was to become a cultural "Anglo." In short, one made it faster if he obliterated his past. To many Chicanos the cost was too dear, particularly since white hyphenated groups had not paid it.

Then came the "Viva Kennedy Clubs." Here Chicanos ran a political campaign without Anglo leadership, in their own language, among their own people. These "Clubs" gave confidence to young Chicanos, trained men in leadership techniques, and offered them political experiences. Their cadre came from the young: Chicanos tired of trying to crack the system slowly, and having to become acculturated Anglos. These young came from rural and urban *barrios* of the Southwest, where poverty and prejudice created anger. They looked to leaders from the *barrios*, who were in training in poverty programs and had felt the inflexibility of Anglo prejudice. They modeled their revolt on the Black Power movement, and they demanded that American wealth be extended to Brown people without sacrificing the unique heritage of Mexican Americans. That is, Bronze Power.

But Bronze Power meant that nearly all Mexican Americans at all levels must identify with not only the frustration and anger caused by Anglo prejudice but also with the goals of the young. As pointed out earlier, however, Mexican Americans came from different environments with different problems. Consequently Bronze Power will take different guises, will boast of many leaders, and will advocate more than a few goals. The historical past will create this Bronze heterogeneity. To deal with specific examples of the past and to examine the heterogeneity of the movement let us take our historical periodization and apply it to the southwestern states.

Between 1848 and 1932, a massive influx of Anglos poured into California, spurred first by the gold rush and then by climate, farming and those other intangibles that have made the Golden State what it is today. These new settlers overwhelmed the old, and by 1890 the *Californios* had been subjugated. This loss of dominance was not painless, but from 1848 to 1850 a hundred thousand Anglos came to the gold fields and drove out the native miners. Violence occurred. Anglos, primarily, used intimidation and murder to force Mexicans to the small village of Los Angeles or back to Mexico and even to South America. *Californios* fought back, in some cases, such as Joaquin Murrieta, in a fruitless defense of their status.

Then, in the early twentieth century, large numbers of Mexicans and some Spanish-speaking Americans from other states in the Southwest migrated to California. In the case of both of these groups the compelling force was improvement of their lot. Southwesterners, antedating the Oakies, went to the Imperial Valley and picked crops or looked for their own kind in Los Angeles, hunting for menial tasks in an urban *barrio*. Mexican immigrants had similar goals, but after 1910 revolutionary struggles disrupted the life-style of the poor, too. Most historians of the Mexican Revolution have emphasized rightly the improvements the revolution brought to the *peon*. They have ignored, however, the large number of *peons* who fled north to avoid the struggle; many went to California, joining Mexican Americans in the fields and city slums.

These new immigrants augmented old ones in trying to crack the system with the strikes that began in the Imperial Valley in 1928 and continued through the Del Monte berry-pickers' strike of 1933. The gains were short-term ones. Migrant workers continued to work for starvation wages. Some did succeed, like Edward R. Roybal, who won a council seat in Los Angeles, in 1948, but for nascent Bronze Power advocates such victories were too little and too late.

To complicate further the lot of California's Chicanos, the Anglos stole their past. The small native, pastoral existence was quickly and completely overrun by the Anglos in 1848; population figures demonstrate the completeness of the invasion. In 1848 the non-Indian population was estimated to be around 14,000. Mestizo or Spanish numbered 7,500. In 1850 the population increased twelvefold and then grew to 1.5 million by 1900. The original inhabitants became an insignificant minority who spoke a *foreign* language and had strange customs; the *Californio* became a foreigner in his own land.

Once he was no threat, he could be romanticized. Beginning with the leadership of Charles Lummis and building upon the romanticism of Helen Hunt Jackson, Anglo Californians fantasized about and popularized their Spanish heritage. Historical societies refurbished missions, the swallows of Capistrano were immortalized, and Anglos moved to the suburbs and romanticized about *rancheros*. Californians, though, were speaking of Spanish, not Mexican, culture, and they despised and discriminated against the members of the new immigration. Thus while Father Serra was pushed for canonization, Juan Sanchez remained a dirty Mexican. Leo Carillo, the movie actor and bona fide descendant of a pre-Anglo ranching family, rode a white horse in the Rose Bowl parades, while Mexican restaurants on *El Camino Real* posted "No Mexicans Allowed" signs. Anglos ground under the native society then resurrected it with a romance and legends of their own.

The romance and legend did not concern the unskilled Mexican and Chicano who moved to the state at the turn of the century and settled in rural California as farm workers or in urban Los Angeles as unskilled laborers. These were Mexicans, not Spaniards. It is the sons of the *Pachucos* and the poor, not the descendants of the original inhabitants, who currently lead the revolt in California. César Chávez and the Brown Berets are neither Zorro nor his descendants. They must rediscover and create their own past. They must define the goals of their movement too, in terms of new immigrants to California.

The story in Colorado and Arizona paralleled that of California. Acquired, like California, by the Treaty of Guadalupe Hidalgo, neither state had a large population in 1848. When miners came to southern Colorado and to a lesser extent to Arizona, they found few non-Indians to overwhelm. Anglos soon dominated both areas. Tucson, Arizona, for example, had about a thousand inhabitants in the 1850's and grew slowly until the twentieth century, even though it was the state's largest city and its cultural center. Thus there was no Spanish-Mexican culture to overwhelm and few Anglos to overwhelm it. That did not mean that Arizonan Anglos accepted Mexican Americans readily, however. For example, when in 1904, the New York Foundling Hospital tried to place forty of its charges in foster homes of Mexican Americans in the Clifton-Morenci area of Arizona, Anglos literally took up arms. Better to be an orphan than to be reared a Mexican. Subjugation thus was complete. The influx of Mexican Americans and Mexican nationals at the turn of the century went first to the mining areas, then to irrigated farming areas, where they served as laborers, and finally to the unskilled jobs of the cities—Denver, Phoenix and Tucson. There the Mexican met the same sort of prejudice of Southern California Anglos. And in 1943, George I. Sanchez, the author and director of the Center for International Studies at the University of Texas, noted that the *Pachuco* phenomenon of California appeared in Arizona and Colorado. At least in Arizona and Colorado the prejudice of California is not accented by the irony of the glorification of the oppressed's culture. In Arizona and Colorado the non-Anglo past that the state celebrates is that of the Indian. The leaders of Bronze Power in those two states, like California, rootless, come from the twentieth-century migrations.

The New Mexico Chicano's heritage differed from his western neighbors'. Anglos came to New Mexico not for gold but for land. Throughout the state, specifically in the northern third, they found the good land held by *Hispaños*. Through a series of legal and quasi-legal maneuvers, Anglos wrested the old land grants away from the original owners. Native New Mexicans, practitioners of Roman law, neither understood the new law code nor the English language. Their lands were easy prey to legal sharks. When the law failed, Anglo entrepreneurs used the territorial government, controlled by the Santa Fe Ring, to manipulate the law or legal codes to suit their purposes. The issue for *Hispaños* would be always land.

Ironically control of the Territory by the Santa Fe Ring rested on *Hispaños'* votes. That was one way to crack the system. Political *patrons*, such as Thomas B. Catron and Solomon Luna, delivered with regularity the *Hispaño* vote to the candidate of their choice, always a Republican. Thus, unlike Southern California or some areas of Texas, the twentieth century did not see the *Hispaño* disenfranchised, only "voted." It was to break this control of the native vote that the Democrats in 1916 nominated Ezequiel Cabeza de Baca, who died during his first month in office, and the Republicans, in 1918, in a like maneuver, nominated Octaviano Larrazolo, who became the second Spanish surnamed Governor elected in the United States.

Larrazolo was a true Mexican American, born in Mexico and reared in New Mexico, while de Baca was a native New Mexican. It is not clear whether these men really cracked the system or were simply used by it, for when in 1920 it appeared that the Republicans needed neither Larrazolo nor his principal supporter, Bronson M. Cutting, the Old Guard dumped them both with almost indecent haste. However, Dennis Chavez became Senator in 1935 and won reelection in 1940, 1946, 1952, and 1958, thus giving *Hispaños* continuing representation at the highest level of the state's political hierarchy. The talented few went to the top with the New Deal.

For Bronze Power advocates in New Mexico there were too few Chavezes. Like Chicanos in California, they remained mostly in a condition of poverty, but their historical development was entirely different from California. In New Mexico the relatively large population of small landowners was not overrun numerically by the Anglos. The population influx from Mexico in the twentieth century settled in the southern part of the state or in urban areas and augmented the ranks of the original inhabitants. These new immigrants accepted the older traditions of the *Hispaños*, giving to New Mexican Chicanos a sense of roots and traditions. In New Mexico there were no *Pachuco* riots or strikes in the period from the New Deal to Viva Kennedy.

Instead, the center of Bronze Power first came, not from the *barrios* of Albuquerque, but from the land claims of Tierra Amarilla. This rural culture, quaint and romanticized by some Anglo writers, fell before twentieth-century technology. Television, paved roads, and automobiles destroyed the descendants of the original settlers and rekindled their political activism in its often violent forms. Note the verb "rekindled." In the late nineteenth century organizations such as *Los Gorras Blañcas*, men wearing white masks fought *gringos* in San Miguel County rather than lose their land. In the late 1960's, as the economic situation in the remote villages deteriorated and Anglo technology eroded *Hispaño* village culture, Chicanos like Reies Tijerina came forward to reclaim the land and to protect their heritage. Of equal importance for the future of Bronze Power, Tierra Amarilla, New Mexico, is not Delano, California, and Reies Tijerina is not César Chávez. The two movements have different causes, different needs, different leaders, and elicit different responses from their followers.

Texas gave us yet a third pattern in the heterogeneity of the Mexican American experience. Overall the period of subjugation hardened racial attitudes on the part of both Anglos and

Chicanos. The native population, a very small one, was overwhelmed by Anglo migrations in the nineteenth century. When a hundred years later the *peons* migrated north, anxious to escape the revolutions in Mexico, they were met by Anglo hostility. Texas Rangers and local law officers had harassed Chicanos with regularity, particularly in South Texas along the Rio Grande border. In turn Mexican border raiders, such as Juan Cortina, met this Anglo terror with raids of their own. It was out of this history of terror, counterterror, and despair that the quixotic *Plan de San Diego* grew in 1915.

The Plan was simplicity itself. At 2 A.M. February 20, 1915, the Mexican American population of Texas, New Mexico, Arizona, Colorado, and California would rise up, slaughter the Anglos, and establish a separate republic. The plan came from Texas Chicanos, frustrated, alienated, and enraged, who hoped for racial stirrings among the oppressed peoples of all five states. The plan failed, of course, when Basilio Ramos was captured near Alice, Texas. But in July, 1915, groups of Chicanos did battle Rangers and Anglo vigilantes. The irredentist movement collapsed before Anglo violence in the fall of that year, and the Plan of San Diego passed into history. Many Texas historians maintain that 1915–1917 was a watershed for Mexican Americans in Texas. After the violence of San Diego and other uprisings in the Rio Grande Valley, Mexican Americans chose assimilation. By 1927 for example, the LULAC organization (League of United Latin American Citizens) advocated assimilation by becoming "the most perfect and loyal citizen of the United States of America." With organizations like LULAC the Mexican conceded that the Texas revolution had ended.

The reason that Chicanos of the other four southwestern states did not rally to the *Plan de San Diego* was that their experiences differed from Texas Chicanos. In Texas Chicanos faced three problems: they were culturally and linguistically different from the majority population; they were poor, landless, and had to depend upon Anglos for economic well-being; and most importantly Texans remembered the Alamo. They have forgotten the Spanish surnames inside the walls but never the ones outside. In the Anglo consciousness Chicanos descended from and were the enemy. It was this concept of "the enemy" that finally drove Mexican Americans to force, and that allowed Valley Chicanos to see, Anglos as "the enemy," too. The concept was uniquely Texas; the *Plan de San Diego* was the natural outgrowth of this uniqueness.

Unfortunately, thus, for Texas Chicanos, Santa Anna lives in the hearts and minds of Texans. Anglo-Texas created a stereotype as a result of the Meir Expedition, the Alamo, and Goliad. The Anglo-Texan legend is that the Mexican, cruel by nature, responds only to force. Since he is cowardly and treacherous, he attacks without warning, is by nature a sneak thief, and because of mixed blood is a degenerate. The Mexican, lacking any desirable characteristics, does recognize, however, the superior qualities of Anglo-Texans and looks to them for leadership.

Instead of a rosy, romanticized past—as glorified in California—the atrocities of the Alamo and Goliad make up the Anglo-Texans' historical consciousness. Instead of identifying the Chicanos with the much publicized charm of the native mountain villages of the Rio Arriba country of New Mexico, that Anglo-Texans see on their vacations, they identify them with the urban squalor of "Mextown" or the rural squalor of an adobe shack. In short, in Texas the Mexican American past is frequently a thing of loathing, and its present lacks charm and character. Crystal City, then, differs from Tierra Amarilla and Delano, California; José Angel Gutierrez is neither César Chávez nor Reies Tijerina.

The concept of the enemy within made cracking the system difficult in Texas. The pecan shellers of San Antonio, for example, struck at the beginning of this historical period. The strike ended with less than a complete victory for either side but was more successful for Texas Chicanos than were the California strikes of the same historical period. Politically the situation changed little until after World War II. Political bosses in the Valley paid poll taxes for Mexican Americans and voted their "Mexicans" with impunity. Following the war, returning veterans challenged the *status quo*. Organizations such as the G.I. Forum developed grass-roots movements, by hard and dangerous proselytizing efforts, that would emerge as political threats to established Anglo institutions in the next decade. The election of Henry Gonzales to the United States Congress from San Antonio and Raymond Telles' successful campaign for Mayor of El Paso in the late 1950's are manifestations of this Chicano political power. For Bronze Power this was not enough.

Change has come to Texas as to all the other southwestern states. Anglo-Texas anxiously recruited new industries and brought outside influences into the state. Not that the new people are *per se* better, or more liberal on racial matters (newcomers adapt to and then adopt local mores quickly) but the industrial, national organizations freed Chicanos from local bonds.

The Del Monte plant in Crystal City, Texas, may well be a microstudy of the impact of a new economic unit upon a local Texas community. This plant unionized, hired Mexican Americans and made most Chicanos no longer dependent upon local Anglos for survival. These newly freed Chicanos, either union officials or Del Monte workers, challenged the local politicos and won at least some political rights. Texans could have mustered a formidable array of wea-

pons and crushed the union, but such actions on the part of the state or the community could lead to strikes or boycotts where the unions are stronger than in Crystal City. Del Monte would suffer, the appeal of Texas for new industries would diminish, and the economy of Crystal City and the Anglos' pocketbooks would flatten. The old order in Crystal City, Texas, and elsewhere in the United States is crumbling.

And that's what Bronze Power is all about: the pulling down of the old racist order. To do this the young have seized upon the metaphysical concept of *La Raza,* the Bronze equivalent of soul. But before *La Raza* emerges Chicanos will have to blend their historical differences. César Chávez is not a significant leader in upstate New Mexico, where *Hispaño* ranchers and farmers do not react favorably to paying union dues to farm laborers. Nor is a twentieth-century immigrant in the *barrio* of Los Angeles moved to violence by the news that an Anglo lawyer cheated a Chicano out of the Tierra Amarilla land grant in the nineteenth century. Tijerina faces the same sort of problem, in South Texas, where Chávez's appeals make sense to migrant workers. Yet movements such as the grape boycott failed essentially in Texas urban centers such as Dallas or Fort Worth. It will be a while before Chicanos can present a unified front to the Anglo establishment. Bronze Power, then, offers many solutions, aims for many goals, and boasts of numerous leaders. It is only beginning, as the following essays show.

GLOSSARY FOR INTRODUCTION

Anglo—Short for Anglo-American. Usually it is used in the Southwest to designate anyone with a non-Mexican heritage.

Barrios—Mexican American sections of town; usually lower-class housing.

Brown Berets—Militant groups of Chicano youths; they usually wear brown berets as an identifying feature.

Californios—Name given to the Spanish or Mexican inhabitants of California at the time of U.S. acquisition.

El Camino Real—The King's Highway—name of the highway through the Central Valley of California

César Chávez—Leader of the National Farm Workers Association and Chicano activist.

Chicano—Probably a truncated form of *Mexicano* and originally a pejorative term. Today it has implications of a belief in strong ethnic nationalism and political activism.

Crystal City—Small town in Southwest Texas. Site of the first major political victories of non-urban, Texas Mexican Americans.

Juan Cortina—A Texas border rancher who shot a Texas marshal who was beating a *peon*. Cortina fled to Mexico and formed a force which raided into Texas. He was a strong advocate of protecting Texas Mexican Americans, and he was eventually appointed Governor of the Mexican state of Tamaulipas.

Delano, California—Farming community and center of the agricultural strikes led by César Chávez.

9

Goliäd—Site of a battle in the Texas Revolution. As he did at the Alamo, Santa Anna had most of the captured Texans killed.

Los Gorras Blañcas—"The White Caps." A night-riding group in San Miguel County, New Mexico, who burned fences and tried to drive Anglos off the Las Vegas community land grant.

Gringo—Pejorative term for Anglos. It was probably derived from *griego*, "Greek," hence foreigner.

José Angel Gutierrez—Crystal City resident and founder of the *La Raza Unida* political party.

Hispaño—New Mexican of Spanish or Mexican origin, whose family predates Anglo occupation. Hispaños usually live in the northern third of the state.

La Raza—Literally "The Race"; general term embodying culture, language, and heritage of Spanish-speaking people.

La Raza Unida—Literally "The United Race"; political party founded in Crystal City, Texas, in 1970 by Chicanos.

Mestizo—mixed—blood—Spanish or Mexican and Indian.

Mexican American—An inhabitant of the United States of Mexican origin. Politically this term denotes a person more conservative than a "Chicano."

Mier Expedition—In 1842, in retaliation for a Mexican invasion, around two hundred Texans invaded Mexico, and eventually surrendered to a larger Mexican force at Mier on the lower Rio Grande. The captives were forced to draw lots (black beans for death, white ones for life) to see which were executed for the invasion.

Joaquin Murrieta—California bandit (partly legendary) who resisted the Anglo miners and oppressors.

Pachuco—A movement among California Mexican American teen-agers in the mid-1940's. The group wore zoot suits. Antagonism between servicemen and this group led to the zoot-suit riots of the 1940's in Los Angeles.

Patron—A large landowner who has *peons* working for him.

Peon—A worker usually tied to the land or to a patron by debt and custom.

Rancheros—Owners of ranches.

Rio Arriba—A county in upper New Mexico and also a name given to New Mexico north of Santa Fe.

San Miguel County—County in north central New Mexico. Las Vegas is the county seat. Center of *Los Gorras Blañcas.*

Tierra Amarilla—County seat of Tierra Amarilla County in New Mexico. Center of Reies Tijerina and the *Alianza* activities.

Reies Tijerina—Founder of the *Alianza Federal de Mercedes* (Federal Alliance of Land Grants) in 1963. The *Alianza's* goal is the return of the New Mexico land grants to their original *Hispaño* owners.

Treaty of Guadalupe Hidalgo (1848)—Treaty that ended the Mexican war and ceded New Mexico, Arizona, California, Colorado, Utah, and Nevada to the United States.

Viva Kennedy Clubs—Political clubs organized in *barrio* areas by the Kennedy campaign staff in the 1960 election.

Zorro—Fictional depiction of a *Californio ranchero.*

GLOSSARY FOR BOOK

Aztlan—Mythical home of the Aztec Indians.

Bracero—A Mexican national hired to work in the United States as a farm worker.

Campesino—A Mexican agricultural laborer.

Cantina—Spanish for bar or tavern.

La Cause—Literally "The Cause." The term usually refers to the California labor strikes of the late 1960's.

La Huelga—Literally "The Strike." The term usually refers to the grape and lettuce strikes in California in the late 1960's.

Jefe—A local leader. Political leaders are often referred to as "jefe politicos."

La Raza Cosmica—Literally "The Cosmic Race." A term José Vasconcelos, a Mexican educator and philosopher, uses to designate all *Hispaño* peoples.

Machismo—Derived from *Macho*, "male." A term used to connote virile masculinity.

Patria Chica—Hispanic concept of loyalty to and identification with a localized region.

Politico—A political leader.

Troquero—In migrant worker circles this can refer to the owner of the truck they travel in.

Virgen de Guadalupe—Our Lady of Guadalupe; the patron saint of Mexican independence.

1.

THE BEGINNINGS OF BRONZE POWER

VOTE POR CHAVEZ!

Guy Smalley

FeRNANdo PeÑAlOSA

*Fernando Peñalosa (Professor of Sociology at California State
College at Long Beach), has long been concerned with the
differences between the concept of Mexican Americans held
by sociologists and the reality of the life situation of
Chicanos. In two articles, reprinted from SOCIOLOGY AND
SOCIAL RESEARCH, Professor Peñalosa first builds a model
to refute the usual textbook picture of a Mexican American
minority as being largely unskilled farm laborers. He argues,
instead, that the Anglo-Mexican cast system was breaking
down as a result of increased opportunities. Three years later
in 1970, the emergence of Chicano militancy in the barrios
forced him to re-think his earlier position. He articulates his
new view in the second article. The student should note not
only the changing position of Dr. Peñalosa, but the historical
perspective that these essays give to the Chicano movement.
From SOCIOLOGY AND SOCIAL RESEARCH, Vol. 51,
(July, 1967).*

The Changing Mexican American In Southern California

INTRODUCTION[1]

One of the hazards of any empirical science such as sociology is the constant temptation to reify what is essentially a statistical concept or a theoretical construct of the researcher. When such a model is essentially homologous with empirical reality, little theoretical or practical harm may come from reification. But when the model is essentially static, while the empirical reality with which the model is putatively homologous is in fact in a process of dynamic change, either the theoretical or the practical consequences, or both, may be unfortunate. It may safely be asserted that the concept or construct "Mexican-American population" as ordinarily found in the sociological lit-

[1]The practical definition which has been used by the writer in his researches in southern California is as follows: A Mexican-American is considered to be any person permanently residing in the United States who is descended from Spanish-speaking persons permanently residing in Mexico, and who in childhood and youth was enculturated into Mexican-American subculture.

15

erature frequently manifests a significant gap with empirical reality.

The most often used, and undoubtedly the best, approximation to the parameters of this population relies on a count of the Spanish-surname population, particularly in the states of the Southwest. But while the term "Spanish-surname population" is operationally definable, the terms "Mexican-American population" or "Mexican-American community" are not so easily controlled. Existentially there is no Mexican-American community as such, nor is there such a "thing" as Mexican-American culture. The group is fragmentized socially, culturally, ideologically, and organizationally. It is characterized by extremely important social-class, regional, and rural-urban differences. Partially because of the great regional variations of this ethnic group, this paper will be concerned primarily with southern California, one of the areas of greatest concentration of this population in the Southwest.

THE MEXICAN-AMERICAN POPULATION

Despite or perhaps because of its extreme fragmentation, there is significant evidence of increased self-consciousness of the group as it struggles through a crisis for self-identity. A perennial topic of discussion in Mexican organizations, as well as in talks given by Mexican-American leaders before Anglo groups is, "What shall we call ourselves?" In various regional and personal contexts this minority group is often called "Spanish-Americans," "Spanish," "Spanish-speaking people," "Latin-Americans," "Latinos," "Hispanos," etc. In southern California the most prevalent term used is "Mexican-American." This term, however, has little currency outside of southern California, and even in the latter area there is some dissatisfaction with the term. In recent years there has been an increase in use of the expression "Americans of Mexican descent" at the expense of the term "Mexican-American." Yet these terms are not in any strict sense synonymous, but realistically represent two quite different segments of the population under discussion. Persons of Mexican descent who were not at one time enculturated into the subculture of some Mexican-American

neighborhood are best labelled "Americans of Mexican descent" rather than "Mexican-Americans." The former do not constitute an ethnic minority group as do the latter. Another recent trend is that the attempt to disguise Mexican ethnic origin by self-identification as "Spanish" appears to be on the wane.

At the present time, in southern California as in the Southwest as a whole, the Mexican-American population is increasing more rapidly than the white population as a whole and only slightly less rapidly than the Negro population. In southern California the Spanish surname population increased 92.3 percent between 1950 and 1960, but more than 100 percent in Los Angeles (100.5) and nearby Orange (122.0) counties. The result is that the Mexican-American continues to be the largest minority group in southern California. In 1960 there were 870,600 Mexican-Americans in the eight southern California counties. It is probably now well over 1,000,000. This population is 78.8 percent native-born. The fact that immigrants from Mexico during 1955–60 accounted for 5.1 percent of California's Spanish surname population five years and over in 1960 indicates that natural increase is not the only significant factor contributing to the population's growth. Since 78.0 percent of the Mexican-Americans in southern California in 1960 were under the age of 35, this young population has a very high growth potential. Undoubtedly this fast growing segment of California's population will become numerically and proportionally even more important in the future.

ATTENUATION OF TRADITIONAL CULTURE PATTERNS

The standard accounts of Mexican-Americans stress their relatively high degree of cultural conservatism. This population is partially indigenous to the region, since it was largely responsible for settling the Southwest before its acquisition by the United States from Mexico in 1848. The continuing waves of immigrants, largely rural lower-class in background, from Mexico have been of much larger dimensions than the flow of acculturated individuals into the mainstream of American life.

Thus it has been that persons of Mexican descent have resided in southern California for almost two hundred years and many have largely retained their language and culture over this long span of time.

The primary reasons would seem to be the nearness of the country of emigration and the failure of the public school system to teach an adequate command of the English language and the other skills necessary for successful entry into the occupational world. As a result Mexican-Americans have had to compete economically with a continuous incoming supply of cheap Mexican national labor. The latest waves of the latter were those of the braceros and of the hundreds of thousands of "wetbacks" who have played their part in the continuing low average economic status of the Mexican-American population.

Despite great obstacles, this population as a whole is clearly moving further away from lower-class Mexican traditional culture and toward Anglo-American middle-class culture, so that both its cultural status and its social-class status are changing. It is true that immigrants in many ways reinforce the traditional patterns locally, but they are coming from a changing Mexico much more urbanized and industrialized than the Mexico known to the immigrant of two, three, or four decades ago. The latest waves of immigration have come from socioeconomically higher, more urbanized strata of Mexican society. Mexican-American migrants also come in important numbers from other states of the Southwest, particularly from Texas and New Mexico. The communities from which they have come are generally more traditionally oriented than southern California Mexican-American communities. On the other hand, in the latter, particularly the urban ones, intermarriage and normal social relations among the various subtypes of Mexican-Americans are promoting their merger into a more homogeneous population.

MEXICAN-AMERICAN HETEROGENEITY

There have been no recent major published studies specifically concerning southern California Mexican-Americans, but the tacit assumption of

general works or of studies of communities in other areas is that their conclusions apply with equal force to the former. Many reports have either concentrated on limited aspects of the group, or used source materials two or more decades old, or both.

The most competent documentations of traditional Mexican folk culture in both Mexico and in the United States often make the assumption that understanding this culture is somehow the key to understanding Mexican-American culture. The latter is frequently dealt with as if it were a variety of Mexican folk culture. The rejection of such an oversimplification does not imply, of course, that there is no value in understanding this "folk" or "preindustrial" culture with its close ties to the land, its different sense of time, its lack of emphasis on formal education, and a social structure based primarily on personal rather than impersonal relationships. At the same time, such concepts should not constitute a perceptual screen with which to view the current situation. It is important to note in this connection that in recent years Mexican-Americans in southern California have been categorized along with a number of other ethnic groups and social strata as "culturally deprived" or "economically disadvantaged." It is patent that the nature of the "cultural deprivation" or "economic disadvantage" of this ethnic group is primarily a handicap of class and not of culture, unless we specify lower-class culture. This point has been frequently missed by a number of observers. Kluckhohn, for example, has asserted that "Mexican orientations ... *in our system* secure very little for individuals except a lack of mobility and a general lower-class status. Indeed the other group in America which has orientations most similar to the Mexican is the non-aspiring, generalized lower-class group." It is clear from the context, though not explicitly stated, that Kluckhohn is referring specifically to traditional Mexican lower-class culture. The middle-class Mexican immigrant and his descendants have not been ordinarily "culturally deprived" or "economically disadvantaged," unless they gravitate to a Mexican-American *barrio* with its particular culture. If they move into a predominantly Anglo neighborhood, as they usually do, their problems are normally no greater than those of middle class immigrants from other countries. Mexican middle class persons are more like American middle class persons in their general way of life and basic outlook than they are like lower class persons from their own country.

There is a reaction among educated Mexican-Americans and among some informed social scientists against the characterizations of Mexican-American culture to be found in authoritative books and articles on the subject. They feel that these sources tend to create stereotypes by which even well-trained and well-meaning Anglos will tend to perceive the group, not taking account of individual differences and achievements. Pride and sensitivity about the collective image remain important traits even among the most highly acculturated Mexican-Americans.

The type of characterization which is most unsatisfactory revolves about concepts of the Mexican-American population as largely engaged in migratory agricultural labor. The impression is given in a recent textbook on ethnic relations that the Mexican-American population is concentrated in rural areas: "Although there are great variations in the background and social position of the Mexican population in the United States, many Mexican families are concentrated in rural areas in the West and Southwest where a considerable number of them earn livelihoods as migratory laborers." The same authors cite a 1952 Broom and Shevky article to the effect that "Many of them work in homogeneous gangs, with few contacts with non-Mexicans: the kind of casual labor which they usually find means migration, unemployment, isolation in labor camps; the language barrier reinforces the other problems." Another recent text is even more definite on this point: "Their low incomes and low educational status is due, at least in part, to their principal occupational status ... migratory farm laborers." The same text makes the statement that "Mexican-American children that do manage to attend school often do poor work ..." This statement is supported by citing a book published in 1946.

Such broad generalizations as those quoted tend to blur the lines of distinction among the various social classes among Mexican-Americans. They further fail to differentiate clearly among a number of interrelated factors: the lower class, rural origins of the immigrants; the low average occupational status of Mexican-Americans at the present time; and the ways in which their present day problems are shared by the members of lower class groups, ethnic or otherwise. They further fail to take into consideration the broad rural-urban, class, occupational, educational, and regional differences of the Mexican-American population. A homogeneity is postulated or inferred where none exists. Even if we confine our attention to one broad geographical area, such as southern California, and examine the culture and social structure of this population, the homogeneity fails to appear.

The Mexican-American subculture in its most common variant is probably best regarded and understood as a variant of American working-lower class culture. This culture is, of course, affected by all the limitations of lower status in a predominantly middle-class society. The group's way of life is further conditioned by the effects of the reaction of the group to discrimination. If we accept the concept of Mexican-American culture, at least in its southern California variety, as a variant of the United States working class subculture, but influenced to a lesser or stronger degree by traditional Mexican folk culture, it follows that these people should be regarded as partially Mexicanized Americans rather than as partially Americanized Mexicans. No one who has carefully observed the way of life of rural and of urban lower-class people in Mexico, which would represent the original roots of most Mexican-Americans, would make the mistake of considering them the reverse.

RECENT SOCIOCULTURAL CHANGE

The forces of acculturation and assimilation working over a period of three or more generations have brought about the present situation. Most of the change has been slow and barely perceptible to many of the most-quoted authors in the field. Nevertheless, there was a major breakthrough during World War II of forces promoting change and the solution of problems confronting the Mexican-American community. At this time there was a great flow of people out of the *barrio* or Mexican-American neighborhood. Young Mexican-Americans took industrial jobs in increasing numbers, went off to war, traveled around the world, and were treated as individuals, some for the first time. During World War II Mexican-Americans volunteered in greater numbers and won more Congressional Medals of Honor per capita than any other ethnic group. Veterans especially returned to find themselves dissatisfied with the old ways, and many went to college under the provisions of the G. I. Bill. Occupational skills were upgraded because of wartime industrial experience, and because of the additional educational opportunities made available to younger members of the group.

Social change involves of course not only a realignment of individual perceptions, attitudes and actions, but also a reorganization of structural relationships within the community. It is important to note that the types of American communities, both rural and urban, into which Mexican immigrants and interstate migrants of yesterday and today have moved form a most heterogeneous congeries. Some of the differences found from one Mexican-American community to another are undoubtedly due to the varying natures of the several Anglo-American matrices in which the Mexican-American communities are imbedded. The rate of sociocultural change therefore varies widely from one southern California community to another.

Before World War II the Mexican-American population in the Southwest was largely rural, but by 1950 it was two-thirds urban, and by 1960 it was four-fifths urban. In southern California this population was 83.7 percent urban in 1960. With the tremendous rate of urbanization and metropolitanization of the region many communities that were rural towns or semi-isolated suburbs have now become thoroughly urbanized, with a consequent further urbanization of the resident Mexican-American populations.

One significant phenomenon occurring in these newly urbanized areas has been an attenuation of formerly very rigid interethnic lines of stratification. The older studies characterized Mexican-Anglo relations in southern California as of a caste or semicaste nature, with virtually separate Anglo-American and Mexican-American castes in the communities studied. The World War II and postwar periods promoted occupational and geographical mobility to such an extent that rigid caste barriers against intermarriage and equality of employment and housing opportunities have all but disappeared, particularly in urban areas.

Changes in the employment pattern in the Mexican-American work force appear to lie at the very confluence of forces promoting changes in this population. Closely related to the fact of increasing urbanization has been the shift from rural to urban occupations and the shift from unskilled to skilled jobs. These shifts have affected primarily the younger generation. Just over a decade ago Broom and Shevky had phrased the problem of studying Mexican-American social differentiation as one of determining to what extent people had left migratory labor and become occupationally differentiated. But California as a whole no longer has a Mexican-American population which to any significant extent engages in migratory agricultural labor. Only 14.9 percent of the Mexican-American labor force is engaged in agriculture, forestry, or fisheries, and only 12.2 percent are employed as farm laborers or foremen. Mexican-American field hands were largely displaced during the World War II and postwar periods by the huge influx of contract laborers from Mexico, the *braceros*. Having been displaced from agriculture, Mexican-Americans are not likely to return to this type of employment in large numbers now that the *bracero* program has almost completely been suspended.

From a preponderance of unskilled employment, Mexican-Americans in California have since World War II been concentrated primarily in blue-collar work of a semiskilled or skilled nature (46.3 percent) as compared to the total number of unskilled (farm laborers and foremen, other laborers, and private household workers: 23.4 percent). A significant proportion for the first time are now found also in entrepreneurial, professional, and other white-collar occupations (22.2 percent). Especially important has been the entry of Mexican-Americans into types of professional employment where they are in a position to assist in the efforts to solve the manifold problems confronting Mexican-Americans in southern California urban centers. Because to assert that Mexican-Americans have largely left behind the problems associated with migratory agricultural labor is not to say that they have no problems. It is rather that now their problems have become those of an underprivileged urban minority group.

CONTINUING PROBLEMS

The most serious problem undoubtedly lies within the area of education. In this connection it is important to recognize that Mexican-American children are not necessarily any more "culturally deprived" than are children of other low-income families. School authorities in southern California generally consider "bilingualism" as a handicap. Some teachers and administrators consider it as virtually tantamount to mental retardation. This is, of course, a misreading of the true meaning of bilingualism, which is equal fluency in two languages. The problem is obviously a lack of command of English, and not the ability to speak Spanish. Yet all poor and underprivileged people speak poorly and with an accent because they have not enough contact with the majority. True bilingualism, a potential asset in an increasingly international world, is actually discouraged, or at least it is not fostered, by the public schools.

Educational progress of the group as a whole has been relatively slow. Between the last two censuses of 1950 and 1960 the average number of years of schooling of the Mexican-American population in California increased by a little over one year (from 7.6 and 8.0 to 8.9 and 9.2 for males and females respectively). It is only in long range perspective that any impressive educational progress can be seen, e.g., the percentage of Mexican-Americans in Los Angeles who were completing junior college in 1957 was as large as the percentage of those completing the eighth grade in 1927.

Another focus for change among southern California Mexican-Americans lies in family structure. In urban areas of southern California at least, the traditional extended family group including siblings and their children is no longer found to any significant extent. The *compadrazgo* or ritual co-parenthood relation no longer has any significance as a fictive kinship relation. Related to the increased emphasis on individualism is the move away from traditional Mexican values and toward the Anglo-American values of achievement, activity, efficiency, and emphasis on the future.

The breakdown of traditional Mexican family structure appears to be related to a relatively high incidence of juvenile delinquency for the group. At the same time, Mexican-American delinquency is on the downgrade because many of the neighborhoods which contributed to such conditions are slowly disappearing as a result of urban renewal and freeway construction. As a proportion of total state commitments, Mexican-American delinquents dropped from 25 percent in 1959 to 17 percent in 1965.

Housing discrimination has eased considerably in southern California urban areas and Mexican-Americans can now purchase or rent housing in many desirable areas formerly closed to them. This is not to deny that widespread discrimination still exists. It is ironic, therefore, that analysis of voting results in precincts with high proportions of Spanish surname individuals showed that in the November 1964 state election Mexican-Americans voted heavily in favor of the controversial Proposition 14. The latter, which passed, (although recently ruled unconstitutional by the California Supreme Court) put a provision into the state constitution outlawing antidiscrimination legislation in the housing field. Mexican-Americans apparently failed to realize that the measure was directed against them as well as against the Negro. Their political leaders had simply assumed that Mexican-Americans would vote against a measure which was self-evidently against their own interests. They had failed to reckon with the Mexican-American fear of Negro competition for housing, and the latent hostility between the two groups in some residential areas.

Some Mexican-American neighborhoods have disappeared through forced urban renewal, that is, without the consent of the persons displaced. Some Mexican-Americans have come to refer cynically to urban renewal as "Mexican removal," since for the families concerned no problems are solved by urban renewal. In a number of southern California communities in the past two or three years, Mexican-American leaders (notably in Pico-Rivera in 1964) have been able to muster enough political power, with the assistance of sympathetic outsiders, to prevent urban renewal programs from uprooting them from their homes to higher priced housing elsewhere. It is now unlikely that a situation, such as that of Chavez Ravine, will be repeated. The latter was taken over several years ago by the city of Los Angeles for a housing project, but sold for $1.00 to the Los Angeles Dodgers for a baseball stadium. The highly publicized forcible removal of several Mexican-American families from the ravine left an indelible impression on the public, Mexican and Anglo alike.

Anglo professionals tend to perceive Mexican-American problems as connected with various forms of social disorganization. Mexican-Americans, on the other hand, perceive their problems primarily in terms of the blocking of their aspirations. While biculturalism and bilingualism are viewed by most Anglos as problems, they are not so viewed by most Mexican-Americans. On the other hand, these two characteristics do in fact lead to problems in a society ostensibly committed to cultural pluralism but in reality sustaining the melting pot ideology. There have always been cleavages and factionalism in Mexican-American communities, but never before has the issue of whether to assimilate or not to assimilate been so clearly placed before Mexican-American public opinion.

SOCIAL AND POLITICAL ACTION

The major goal now presented to the Mexican-American community by its leaders is no longer simply the abolition of discrimination as it was in the nineteen-thirties and nineteen-forties, but rather of allowing the Mexican-American to make the best use of his abilities, including the opportunity to capitalize on his bilingualism. Formerly the community was drained of talent as trained, professional people left the ethnic enclave and became integrated into the dominant society.

Now they are finding that by moving professionally back into the *barrio* and working on Mexican-American problems they can advance their own careers and become recognized as community leaders. The community is therefore no longer losing its potential leadership as it once did. The old conservative Mexico-oriented leadership has been giving way to a new leadership of college educated professionals who are thoroughly at home in the Anglo world, but who have retained their ethnic roots.

Current changes appear to indicate a metamorphosis of the group from a lower ethnic caste to a minority group resembling a European immigrant group of a generation or two ago such as, for example, the Italian-Americans in New York, Boston, or San Francisco. Thus, for the first time since the 1850s Mexicans in southern California were appointed to public policy-making positions during the recent administration of Governor Edmund G. Brown. These political appointees in state and local government have been in a position to help open up employment opportunities to other Mexican-Americans and have also provided for better communication between various state agencies and the people. Similarly, Mexican-Americans now have their own political organizations such as The Mexican-American Political Association (MAPA) and have emerged as a political force in their own right. At election time the Anglo-American power structure has become increasingly cognizant of this new political force. Mexican-Americans for their part have learned that if they want such benefits as streets paved and kept in good repair, street lighting, adequate schools, Mexican-Americans on teaching staffs and on the police force, they have to make their power felt at the polls. As a result, a significant number of officials have been elected. There are at latest count 15 mayors, 56 city councilmen and 20 school board members of Mexican-American origin throughout the state, the great majority in southern California.

Another indication of increasing Mexican-American political strength was the recent defeat of the bracero program, for which Mexican-Americans are taking a great deal of the credit. Their leaders had long fought this program which they felt had undermined efforts to establish minimum wages, adequate housing, and schooling for farm workers and their families.

On the national level, one result of the 1960 and 1964 campaigns was that numerous political patronage opportunities were opened up to professional Mexican-Americans in the Peace Corps, the Alliance for Progress, AID, and in the War on Poverty. Mexican-American leaders are increasingly becoming concerned not only by what they can do for their own ethnic group but also for their country as a whole. They are especially eager to utilize their unique abilities and skills in promoting United States goals in Latin America, to which area they will no doubt continue to be sent in increasing numbers. Southern California, where the largest urban concentration of Mexican-Americans in the country is found, has produced and no doubt will continue to produce more than its share of such leaders, as this population as a whole moves ever closer to the mainstream of American life.

Fernando Peñalosa

From SOCIOLOGY AND SOCIAL RESEARCH *Vol. 55,*
(October, 1970).

Recent Changes Among The Chicanos

The term "Chicano" is rapidly replacing the term "Mexican American" as the self-chosen term for the group especially among its more militant and better informed members. A stronger sense of community is developing among the Chicanos, at the same time that pride in the *barrio* subculture is increasing and a renewed interest is manifested in Mexico's scientific and humanistic achievements. Social and political action is taking more militant forms. Some of the most significant recent gains have been in higher education, with the increase in Mexican American enrollment and the institution of Chicano studies programs.

Introduction. Recent changes among the Mexican American population in southern California and elsewhere have made necessary the modification or even invalidation of certain conclusions arrived at by the author in an article published in this journal three years ago.

Pending receipt of the results of the 1970 United States Census, it is difficult to quantify some of the changes that have been taking place, although the most significant new developments are more qualitative than quantitative in any case. These changes will be discussed under a number of headings: (1) terminology, (2) sense of community, (3) Mexican American subculture and assimilation, (4) social and political action.

Terminology. One term referring to the Mexican American population which has now gained considerable ground among the more militant and more articulate leaders of this ethnic group is "Chicano." This term is used as a mark of ethnic pride and is considered preferable by those who stress its use for reasons among which are its

23

popular origin and the fact that it was chosen by members of the group itself. That is, it was not imposed on the group by Anglo-Americans, as were such terms as "Mexican American" or "Spanish American." The parallel between the differing uses and connotations of "black" vs. "Negro" is of course obvious. A somewhat less strong tendency is the use of "brown" and of "La Raza," both with their connotations of pride in a mestizo racial heritage. The somewhat circumlocutious and euphemistic Census Bureau term "White persons of Spanish surname" on the other hand currently strikes many Chicano leaders as amusing.

The tides of change are reaching even that stronghold of resistance to Mexican identification, New Mexico. Nancie Gonzáles found it necessary to add to the second edition of her *Spanish Americans of New Mexico* a new chapter titled "Activism in New Mexico, 1966-1969." Mrs. Gonzáles indicates that the terms "Mexican American" and "Chicano" are used with increasing frequency in that state.

The new Chicano leadership has been drawn from what the author previously distinguished as "Mexican Americans" (those enculturated in the barrio or ethnic enclave) and "Americans of Mexican descent" (those brought up in a largely Anglo environment). This distinction however is increasingly hard to justify as the level of ethnic consciousness and participation rises in both groups.

Sense of Community.   While the postulation of the "existence" of a Mexican American community may be tantamount to reification of the concept, it is apparent nevertheless that a sense of such community "existing" is increasing among Chicanos. This is manifested by an increase in the public use of the terms "Chicano community" or "Mexican American community," the increasing number of persons identified as "community" leaders, the increasing use of collective action and mutual help in such situations as confrontations with school authorities in Los Angeles and Pomona or in the Coachella Valley grape strike, demands of Chicano college students that their education be made relevant to and productive of social change in their community, and increasing intercommunity and interstate visits and

activities of leaders, which receive wide publicity. Furthermore, a recent study carried out by the author revealed that 50.9 percent of a random sample of persons of Mexican descent in San Bernardino, California, felt themselves to be a part of the Mexican American community "very strongly" or "for the most part."

Subculture and Assimilation.   The direction of cultural change among Mexican Americans is no longer entirely certain, if indeed it ever was. It is becoming clearer, however, that for many persons upward social mobility does not require a complete shedding of ethnicity. As a matter of fact some of those who are now experiencing the most rapidly possible upward mobility (i.e., in government or higher education where ethnicity has suddenly become a valuable asset) are among those most assertive of their pride in their own subculture. They would maintain that it is no longer necessary to become a "Tío Taco" (brown equivalent of "Uncle Tom") to get ahead.

On the other hand, the relationship between the resurgence of Mexican American ethnicity and the steady erosion of linguistic assimilation on the use of Spanish in this population is theoretically and pragmatically a highly problematic phenomenon. Thus, for example, the survey mentioned above showed that 11.1 percent of the first generation adults spoke "mostly English" to their children, 67.6 percent of the second generation, and 81.8 percent of the third. Furthermore, 30.2 percent of the children spoke "mostly English" to their parents of the first generation, 81.6 percent to second-generation parents, and 93.8 to third-generation parents.

In another important development, Anglo educators and others are gradually learning to use the term "culturally different" rather than the offensive (to minority groups) "culturally deprived." Chicano leaders of both lower class and middle class family origins are increasingly prone to affirm their similarities rather than their differences, and at least symbolic loyalty to the barrio *subculture.* To assert that Mexican Americans "should be regarded as partially Mexicanized Americans rather than as partially Americanized

Mexicans," as the author did in the previous paper is at best a gross oversimplification.

There is a current resurgence of interest in the culture of Mexico (in the nonsocial science sense) with the sharp upturn in Chicano enrollments in colleges and universities largely due to the recent inauguration of special admittance and assistance programs such as E.O.P. (Educational Opportunities Program), and with the burgeoning development of Chicano or Mexican American studies departments and curricula, particularly in California. Young Chicanos are reaching out beyond the barrio subculture to learn about the history of Mexico, its architecture, its literature, its classical and modern music, its philosophers and historians, and its world-famous achievements in tropical medicine, cardiac medicine, fundamental education, and mural art. Mexican intellectual and artistic heroes such as José Vasconcelos, Alfonso Caso, Diego Rivera, Carlos Fuentes, and Carlos Chávez are being added to the pantheon which includes such Chicano militant heroes as George I. Sánchez, Ernesto Galarza, Julian Nava, César Chávez, Reies López Tijerina and Rodolfo "Corky" Gonzáles.

Furthermore, there has been an accelerating cultivation of barrio art, literature, music and drama (e.g., the *Teatro Campesino* and the *Teatro Urbano*). In the forefront of this resynthesis of barrio and Mexican culture have been the dozen or so "underground" newspapers, members of the Chicano Press Association, published in various cities of the United States, and the activities of Quinto Sol Publications in Berkeley, California, particularly its intellectual journal *El Grito; a Journal of Contemporary Mexican American Thought.*

Social and Political Action. While many of the targets of social and political action, and much of the strategy and tactics remain the same, the past few years have brought about a change in the rhetoric and in the demands which can best be summed up in the phrase "Chicano liberation." This refers to the idea that Chicanos should have control over the institutions which affect them most closely, or at least to have an active role in the relevant decision making processes. Spokesmen for the movement reject what they consider

mere concessions made to them or favors doled out to them by the majority society.

Recent examples of the new trend include such activities as the high school walk-out led by Sal Castro in Los Angeles in 1968 demanding greater community control over the type of education given the Los Angeles Chicano school population, the largest in the nation. Another concerns the 1970 public demonstrations of *Los Católicos por la Raza* in an attempt to force the Catholic church to relate more relevantly to the concerns and problems of the Mexican American community. Then largely as a result of the agitation and plain hard work of student organizations such as UMAS (United Mexican American Students), MECHA (Movimiento Estudiantil Chicano de Aztlán), and the Brown Berets, Mexican Americans Centers and/or Mexican American or Chicano Studies Departments have been set up or are in the process of being established in every major college and university in California, as well as in a number of smaller colleges and junior colleges. These centers and departments are being administered and staffed by Chicanos with wide experience in social action programs, academic work or both.

A group called the "Chicano Coordinating Council of Higher Education," which consists of Chicano student and faculty representatives for institutions of higher education throughout California, has recently issued an ambitious plan for Chicano higher education. This volume consists of a collection of working papers describing the desiderata for Chicano studies programs, recruitment, admission and support of Chicano students, political action, and community involvement. It might be claimed that more than equality is demanded. For example, more autonomy is demanded for Chicano studies than is normally enjoyed by other academic departments. Furthermore a quota system is suggested: "Institutions must immediately accept and establish the principle of proportional representation for Chicanos— students, faculty, staff, and employees—in all areas and all levels of higher education. For example, the percentage of Chicano students enrolled at those institutions located in areas with a significant Chicano population must equal the percentage of school-age Chicanos in those areas ... Those colleges and universities situated in areas with few or no Chicanos must refer to the percentage of Chicanos in the state to determine the percentage of Chicanos students they must enroll. Presently, the Chicano student-age population in the state of California is approximately seventeen percent." Such a policy would of course result in numerical over-representation.

As curricula are being developed for Mexican American studies programs, existing text materials are being carefully scrutinized, with the result among others that the works of Anglo sociologists and anthropologists are being carefully reevaluated, with highly critical conclusions. Such works as Celia Heller's *Mexican American Youth* and William Madsen's *Mexican Americans of South*

Texas have been singled for especially stringent criticism, as well as some studies sponsored by the University of California at Los Angeles Graduate School of Education. No longer may Anglo sociologists study Mexican Americans and expect to enjoy immunity from criticism by their subjects. Chicano sociologists have learned well what their Anglo Professors taught concerning ethnocentrism and are now beginning to turn upon their former mentors with some very penetrating questions about the validity of existing sociological studies of the Mexican American. Anglo sociologists have not yet begun to respond, but the resulting interchange should prove most healthy in forcing all concerned to reexamine their unstated, unconscious, theoretical, and ideological assumptions.

FRANCES L. SWADESH

Frances Leon Swadesh (Curator of Ethnology, Museum of New Mexico Research Laboratory, Sante Fe) has had a varied career in both academic and government service. Dr. Swadesh has published two articles dealing with the Alianza movement as well as a number of other articles in scholarly journals. In 1968 she delivered this paper on the Alianza at the annual meeting of the American Ethnological Society and it later appeared in that organization's PROCEEDINGS. In this article Dr. Swadesh evaluates the Alianza as a native cultural phenomenon.

By permission of the author and the University of Washington Press.

The Alianza Movement: Catalyst For Social Change In New Mexico

A series of dramatic incidents, set in the spectacular surroundings of some tiny mountain communities of northern New Mexico, have made familiar to countless people in the United States, Mexico and other countries such terms as "Tierra Amarilla," "Canjilon," "Coyote," "The Alianza" and "Reies López Tijerina."

These terms first burst into front-page headlines on June 5, 1967, when some twenty men entered the Rio Arriba County courthouse at Tierra Amarilla, bent on making a "citizens' arrest" of Alfonso Sanchez, district attorney of New Mexico's first judicial district. Grounds for the attempted arrest were that Sanchez had banned a public meeting at Coyote, where land-grant heirs were gathering for a fresh assertion of their claims to lands granted their ancestors by the governments of Colonial Spain and Mexico. Sanchez had arrested a number of leaders and members of the Alianza (renamed "Confederation of Free City States" but still better known by the original name), which is the main organization of land-grant heirs. He had arrested these people both in Coyote and on the highway, and had seized Alianza records and called Alianza leaders "Communists."

Alfonso Sanchez was not found in the courthouse at Tierra Amarilla, but the wrathful men who sought him held the courthouse for two hours. They shot and wounded a state policeman and a jailor, drove a judge and various county employees into closed rooms and shot out many of the courthouse windows before they departed. The last men to leave loaded two hostages into a police car and made a spectacular getaway.

That same day, 350 New Mexico Guardsmen, 250 State Policemen, 35 members of the Mounted Patrol, with horses, tanks and helicopters, mobilized for a historic manhunt. Eventually, thirty people were charged with crimes, including kidnaping, a capital offense. At preliminary hearings on these charges in early 1968, charges were dropped against all but eleven and the kidnaping charge was reduced to "false arrest," a fourth degree felony.

The accused, however, were not all rounded up for a number of months. The first targets of the manhunt were women, children and elderly members of the Alianza, who were camped out near Canjilon. They were seized and held overnight at the point of bayonets, under conditions of physical hardship and personal indignity.

News photographs of mothers with babies in their arms, teenagers and elderly cripples being herded by the National Guardsmen drew swift intervention by the Human Rights Commission and by the New Mexico Civil Liberties Union. Liberal Anglos became uncomfortably aware that the Spanish-speaking people of their state might have some cause for feeling rebellious.

Behind the sensational headlines of June, 1967, and the even more sensational headlines which have announced subsequent events in northern New Mexico, there is an ongoing process of social change, constantly accelerating, of which the Alianza is the chief catalyst. This process has been described as a "movement fully within the category of those described elsewhere as nativistic cult movements" by Nancie González. This interpretation follows the analysis of revitalization movements made by Anthony Wallace in his 1956 article of that title. Dr. González, throughout her report, refers to Reies Tijerina as the "prophet" of the nativistic movement and stresses all revelational and dream-inspired aspects of his rise to leadership among the grant heirs.

THE PROBLEM

The question is, does the Alianza actually fit within Wallace's revitalization concept? It is my contention that, despite many early developments in the organization which lend themselves to that interpretation and the strikingly charismatic nature of its leader, the answer is no, on the following grounds:

(1) Revitalization movements described by Wallace share with other movements for social change such a characteristic as deliberate innovation functioning as their principal motor force, rather than the chain reaction effect of evolution, drift, diffusion, historical change or acculturation.

(2) On the other hand, the principal goal of a revitalization movement is to transform the culture, to make it more satisfying. Such a process is largely internal, whereas other movements for innovative change strive to change the conditions of existence of subordinated groups by directly challenging the controls exercised by the dominant group. Such a process is largely external.

For instance although the Ghost Dance Religion had the expressed goal among others, of causing the White Man to disappear, the focus of the movement was internal and the steps taken to achieve the above goal were symbolic rather than practical. On the other hand, the mystique of the American Revolution was not unlike that of a revitalization movement, yet its main objective was to challenge control exercised by the British Empire.

(3) The dynamics of revitalization movements, their directional processes vary from those of other innovative movements. Even Christianity, one of the most widely influential movements cited by Wallace, involved a process of cultural divergence, the splitting off of the first Christians

from the Judaic tradition. The Alianza, on the other hand, while originally a movement of divergence, early embraced principles and organizational methods which changed its direction, and brought it into participation in a much larger movement.

(4) The principal revitalization movements cited by Wallace were religious movements. In assessing the Alianza, the pervasive religiosity of New Mexico's Hispanos is evident. In the Alianza, however, religion does not affect the motor force for change, in fact the dynamic for change, as I shall demonstrate in a later paragraph, operates *despite* religious factors.

(5) Finally, Wallace lists six revitalization types: Nativistic, Revivalistic, Cargo, Vitalistic, Millenarian and Messianic. If the Alianza really is a nativistic cult movement or any other revitalization type, how is it possible to explain its vital part in a new cross-ethnic alignment of subordinated groups in the United States whose declared intention is to challenge domination by the "White-Anglo-Saxon-Protestant" system? It should be added that this is not a movement of cultural or racial exclusiveness, as many "WASPS" are a part of it.

Below is a documentation of the innovative characteristics of the Alianza as they have emerged in its brief history. Each is linked with the problems they have been forced to solve and with the results of the innovative experience.

INTRODUCTION: CHANGES DESIRED BY HISPANOS

The Alianza was founded to deal with grievances which are wide-spread and deep-seated among the Hispanos of New Mexico. Specifically, these grievances stem from alleged violations of the Treaty of Guadalupe Hidalgo. Under that treaty, signed in 1848, Hispanos became citizens of the United States, but citizens with special rights acquired through previous governments, such as the right to their grant lands. Historical evidence supports the allegation that citizenship has been only nominal and that deprivation of the grant lands has forced a large percentage of Hispanos into chronic poverty. Economic loss has been accompanied by loss of cultural rights, especially the right to use the Spanish language in the environment of the school and the State Legislature.

The grievances are founded on facts, and many interested observers of the early 1960s conceded that something ought to be done about them. The prevailing opinion about the Alianza in its formative years, however, was: "Those people won't get anywhere."

The reason for this scepticism was the isolated and rustic character of the Hispano communities. New Mexico's 269,000 Hispanos constitute only 30 percent of the total state population, and are the most isolated and atypical of the more than four million Spanish-speaking people dwelling in five southwestern states. Despite occasional published opinions that the Hispanos are politically the most active of all Spanish-speaking groups and that, in the counties where they constitute a majority, they have "complete control of the power structure," the reverse is more nearly the case.

What passes for "Hispano political activity" is largely the activity of a handful of precinct leaders and henchmen who are deeply involved in the power structure but are far from controlling it. Any small base of power, in a social setting where so many are impoverished and powerless, can be used to control voting and other political behavior with a minimum of promises, bribes, threats and sanctions.

This is an attenuated continuation of the semi-colonial system originated during New Mexico's prolonged Territorial period. Hand-picked Hispanos served in the Legislature as junior partners to those who really held the reins. Their official task was to represent the overwhelming majority of the population, but in practice they helped keep this majority under control.

Control is still maintained, much as in the late nineteenth century, by garbling as much as possible the information which reaches Hispano communities and by taking advantage of the extended kin system to control entire groups by controlling their key members. This system is today the foundation of precinct politics in Albuquerque, a city of some 300,000, in every precinct with a high percentage of Hispano residents. Leaders and candidates build their influence through their relatives, affines and compadres and win support of other kin groups by extending small favors or handing a few dollars to key members.

In communities where the tendency for social enclavement is strong, the plea of ethnicity is useful as a last resort. Of many a Hispano incumbent who has proven himself incompetent or worse, the saying goes, "He's a bastard, but he's *our* bastard," since it is assumed that any Anglo in his place would be worse. To satisfy this sentiment, the New Mexico power structure allots certain slots to Hispanos whom they can control.

Along with this system goes widespread factionalism, dividing the smallest as well as the largest communities, mainly into rival kin groups. While this system can decide the vote in counties where the Hispanos constitute a majority, and is important in counties where their united vote can constitute a balance of power, it provides them with little say on the issues and with very narrow choice in candidates. Political lag will continue in New Mexico, along with its regressive system of taxation upon the backs of the poor, until Hispanos learn to form coalitions around issues of common concern with other ethnic groups.

SCHEDULE OF INNOVATIVE CHANGES

The Alianza has existed as a formal organization since 1963, but its organizational roots go back somewhat further:

1959

Reies Tijerina was invited to give his views on the land-grant problem to a meeting of the Abiquiu Corporation of Tierra Amarilla Grant heirs. The meeting was broken up by fighting between factions of the Corporation, some insisting that non-members had no right to speak. Tijerina, assisted from time to time by his brothers and other supporters, spent much time during the next five years collecting data on the Spanish and Mexican land grants of the Southwest in the National Archives of Mexico.

1963

Having completed his researches in Mexico, Tijerina returned to New Mexico and promptly founded the *Alianza Federal de Mercedes* (Federated Alliance of Land Grants), whose first annual convention held during the Labor Day weekend, was attended by some 800 delegates. The Alianza was incorporated under Federal and State laws as a non-profit, non-political organization. Its constitution, adopted by the convention, represented a new approach to the grievances of the Hispanos.

a) *United Action:* Most previous efforts to press land grant claims had been initiated on behalf of individuals, families or factions on a single grant, often in opposition to other heirs. Never before had representatives of many grants united to press their claims.

b) *The Common Lands:* Common, or *ejido,* lands constituted the greatest acreage by far of all community land grants. The principle of *ejido* has been no less dynamic in New Mexico than in Post-Revolutionary Mexico, where it continues to serve as the basis for land reform and the establishment of producers' cooperatives. Until the Alianza raised the issue, however, the very existence of *ejido* lands in the southwest had been obscured.

A large percentage of the New Mexico *ejido* lands had been assigned to the Public Domain by the Surveyors General of the period 1854–1880, because they paid no attention to claims other than those made on behalf of individuals. Some of the *ejido* lands were later opened up for Homestead entry, but a much larger acreage was incorporated into National Forest lands in the early years of the twentieth century.

The heirs were largely unaware of these transactions, due to isolation and the language barrier, and only reacted when fences were erected on these lands, cutting off their access to grazing and firewood. The history of violence in New Mexico is closely linked with the fencing off of *ejido* lands, from the Lincoln County outbreaks in 1876 to those on the Sangre de Cristo Grant at the Colorado-New Mexico border in 1963.

c) *New Legal Strategy:* Previous to the formation of the Alianza, heirs had repeatedly sought relief through the courts. There, case after case had been lost while the lawyers reaped fortunes. For instance, the lawyer who represented the heirs of the Canyon de San Diego in 1904, managed to get confirmation of 80 percent of the original 110,000 acres, then took half the acreage as his fee. A quiet-title suit on behalf of some Tierra Amarilla heirs undertaken by Alfonso Sanchez shortly before he became district attorney won nothing for the heirs but brought Sanchez into ownership of some Tierra Amarilla real estate.

The Alianza took the position that no competent legal decision on the grant lands could be made below the level of the Supreme Court. Early efforts were made to persuade the Attorney General of the United States and the New Mexico Senators to work for a Congressional bill to investigate the facts. In case this tactic should fail, recourse to the United Nations was mentioned in the Constitution of the Alianza. The Constitution also invited the moral support of all individuals and organizations with a disinterested concern for human rights.

1964

By the time of its second annual convention, the Alianza claimed a membership of 6,000 land grant heirs from the five states of New Mexico, Colorado, California, Texas and Utah. Some out-of-state delegates attended the convention, giving New Mexicans the sense of a common cause beyond their individual and community problems.

a) *Contact with Indians:* Friendly contact with members of several Indian Pueblos developed following the 1964 convention. The potential for joint efforts with the Pueblos began to be considered, since the documentary basis for both Hispano and Peublo land claims was the Spanish and Mexican Archives. With this thought in mind, when Taos Pueblo began to press its claim to the Blue Lake area, the Alianza voiced its support. By so doing, it lost potential supporters among the Hispano population of the Taos area, due to the attitude of envy which has characterized the His-

pano view of Indian gains in this century. Having once taken this position, the Alianza has continued to seek further for friendly relations with Indians, and the number of Pueblos represented has risen with each annual convention.

b) *Direct Action:* Some Alianza members had scant hope that Congressional action would be taken, despite continuing efforts toward the introduction of a bill. Some Tierra Amarilla Grant heirs began posting notices against "trespassers" on what used to be the Tierra Amarilla ejido lands, by which they meant Anglo ranchers who had bought tracts, built ranches and claimed ownership of these lands. A new *Mano Negra* scare was born.

Ever since 1912, when fencing was begun on the Tierra Amarilla common lands, a vigilante organization called the *Mano Negra* (Black Hand) had intermittently cut fences, slashed livestock and set fire to barns and haystacks. Lately, it has been rumored that some ranchers have set fire to their own premises so that they could whip up sentiment against the *Mano Negra* and, by implication, the Alianza, while collecting insurance on the damages.

Hispanos have had to resort to vigilante action whenever they have lost hope of securing justice through the government or the courts. Most Hispanos will not condone vigilante action, neither will they condemn it under certain circumstances.

1966

This was a year of accelerated change for the Alianza. Many of the older members were hesitant about making the changes, but in this year the total membership claimed for the Alianza rose to 20,000.

a) *New Leadership-Membership Relations:* One of the reasons the Alianza has been described as the core of a Hispano nativistic movement is the personality and background of its founder and leader, Reies López Tijerina. His charisma, rhetoric and visionary references to dreams all fit neatly into Wallace's portrayal of the "prophet" of such a movement. His background as a travelling preacher of the Assembly of God sect, during his years as a migrant worker, only adds to the image for the outside observer.

Focusing on the attitude of the Alianza membership toward their leader, one is forced to a differing view. This point first came to attention when Tijerina went to Spain in the spring of 1966, to study colonial archives in Seville. Long before he was due to return, many members began to be so fearful that he had taken his travel money and disappeared for good that they went to Alianza headquarters every day to check on the news. In view of the fact that Tijerina's bride of a few months had been left at home, such a likelihood appeared remote.

Conversation with some of the members revealed that, since Tijerina was Texas-born and a Protestant to boot, many of his Catholic New Mexico followers accorded him the distrust with which they meet "outsiders." Even his rhetoric, while greatly admired, was often not fully believed. Distrust was so deep that the Alianza membership had voted to put Tijerina on a very slim budget which often failed to cover expenses. Sometimes, a concerned member would buy his groceries.

When Tijerina returned from Spain in the early summer of 1966, he assessed the mood of the membership and resolved to build confidence by deeds rather than by words. He turned to a program of action and participation which placed him in the position of a participant-leader and began to develop leadership skills among the more promising members.

This tactic was productive. While no other Alianza leader compares with Tijerina as a public speaker, the pace of work continues during his increasingly lengthy absences, whether out of state or in jail. The Alianza has become a functioning organization, although its style of work is too spontaneous to impress outsiders as anything but chaotic.

b) *Self-Identity:* Over the 1966 Fourth of July weekend, a large delegation of Alianza members marched from Albuquerque to Santa Fe, many camping by the roadside at night and 125 assembling in Santa Fe to seek an audience with Governor Campbell. After a long wait, the delegation was able to present the Governor a petition asking his support for a Congressional bill to investigate their land-grant grievances. On this occasion, the inaction of Senator Montoya was criticized openly for the first time. For many Alianza members, this was their first taste of group demonstrative action.

Although the official purpose of the march fell short of accomplishment, in that no substantial help came from the Governor, its enduring effect on the membership was to change their perception of themselves. Through the public action they had jointly taken, they affirmed their identity as members of "La Raza," or what Reies Tijerina calls "a new breed," the people of New World Hispanic culture with its many increments from indigenous sources.

This broadening and firming-up of group self-identity gave Alianza members pride and tranquil self-confidence to a degree which is uncommon among Hispanos of today. Like members of other groups who are subject to lifelong social discrimination, maddeningly covert when it is not blatantly overt, Hispanos have tended to feel painfully ambivalent about themselves. Questionnaires which they have to fill in our prevalently racist land leave them wondering whether they are "white" or "other non-white." The language question is a constant thorn, since few of today's adults have escaped the ordeal of initiation into a school system where the use of English is forced upon pupils who can often barely understand it, let alone speak it. Such situations feed feelings of inadequacy and timidity—and also burning resentment against the dominant Anglos.

c) *Changing Role of Women:* Women, from the start, had been devoted members of the Alianza. The fund-raising dinners they prepared and served were vital supporting activities, yet no women had assumed a public role in the organization until the march to Santa Fe. Since then, their activist role has unfolded, sharpened by the experience of arrest, of the jailing of their husbands for weeks at a time and of visits by FBI agents. More and more women have taken these events in their stride and have emerged as fluent spokesmen for their organization.

d) *Youth Roles:* No formal youth group has been formed in the Alianza yet, informally, the teenage and young adult sons and daughters of active Alianza members have made a place for themselves in the organization. Many of them participated in the July, 1966, march to Santa Fe and an increasing number have participated in subsequent activities of the organization. In addition to the arrests which followed the Tierra Amarilla uprising, some very young people were charged in the original indictment. Perhaps because of the stresses voluntarily incorporated into their lives, these young people appear more poised and purposeful than is common for their age-group. Despite the police surveillance with which they are surrounded, none of these youth have been mentioned in the records of pick-ups for marihuana and drug use which are constant among youth of their income level. Disorder and brawling at Alianza dances are unknown.

e) *Renewal of Community Ethic:* In October, 1966, convinced that only by direct acts of civil disobedience could they force official attention to the land issue, Alianza members began to spend weekends in a National Forest campground located on *ejido* land of the *San Joaquin del Rio de Chama* (or Chama Canyon) Grant. Its area totalled some one-half million acres bestowed upon a group of settlers in 1806. The land shark, Thomas Burns, won his claim to the entire grant in the Court of Private Land Claims in 1904, but Congressional confirmation was denied because the Carson National Forest was created at this time and included the San Joaquin Grant area.

The heirs to the grant continued to live there, mainly in Canjilon at the northeast corner. For years, they were unaware that their grant had been taken away from them.

The Alianza campers took possession of the campground in the name of the San Joaquin Corporation, whose legal existence as the governing body they proclaimed. They refused to buy the required camping permits, cut a few trees for firewood and forbade the Forest Rangers to trespass on their grant.

Not all the campers were heirs to this particular grant. Some had come from as far away as California to participate in the "test case." On the other hand, the San Joaquin Corporation was real enough. This corporation had been re-activated under a constitution dated February 9, 1940, and

for twenty-seven years had been dedicated to the following goals:

> ... to protect the society which is encompassed by said Corporation against the injustices and tricks of tyrants and despots, of those who insult us and seize our lands; to seek Law and Justice; to initiate lawsuits; to acquire, hold, possess and distribute through proper legal channels the rights, privileges, tracts of land, wood, water and minerals which were deeded to, and bequeathed by our ancestors, the heirs and assigns of the Grant of the Corporation of *San Joaquin del Rio de Chama* (ms, translation by F. L. S.).

On October 26, the Forest Service proceeded against the Alianza by placing a stop sign at the campground entrance and stationing uniformed personnel there. When the Alianza caravan drove into the campground without stopping, the Rangers followed them and demanded that they pay up or vacate. At this point, the Rangers were seized, their trucks and radios were impounded and a mock trial was conducted, in which they were charged with violation of the laws of the grant.

Participants in these proceedings who came from nearby communities and had deep-seated personal resentments against the Rangers would have preferred to carry matters much farther, but they were restrained by leading Alianza members. The Forest Service trucks and radios were returned and the Rangers were instructed to depart.

One year later, Reies and Cristobal Tijerina and three others were convicted in Federal Court of having "assaulted" Forest Rangers and of expropriating Government equipment. The verdict is being appealed.

The experience of living together under the community legal code and customary rules of their ancestors, often wistfully recollected by their grandparents, revived among Alianza members a sense of the vitality of their traditional value system. The feeling for solidary relations of the community, reaching beyond the ties of the extended kin group, was expressed by many Alianza members after the San Joaquin experience, and has become crystallized in strong ties of loyalty and affection among the members. These sentiments bring to mind the theme of Lope de Vega's great drama, "Fuente Ovejuna."

f) *Quest for an Alliance with Negroes:* While Alianza leaders had, in the past, stated that they did not intend to adopt the militant direct action methods of the Negro movement, their admiration for the organizational strength and effectiveness of this movement had grown with time and experience. Dr. Martin Luther King was invited to be a featured speaker at the 1966 annual convention of the Alianza. When he declined on the grounds of a previous commitment, Stokely Carmichael was invited. Carmichael accepted but was called elsewhere at the last moment.

A young Negro staff member of the local Poverty Program agreed to pinch hit. Despite his hastily prepared speech, delivered in broken Spanish, he was cordially thanked for his expression of Negro sympathy for Hispano aspirations.

Alianza members had hitherto been trying to win the sympathy of people in power for their slogan, "The land is our heritage: Justice our credo." Now they had come to realize that they would not be heard until they had the strength to force a hearing and that, to have this strength, they must seek allies among other subordinated peoples.

1967

The "uprising" at Tierra Amarilla has been described in the opening paragraphs of this report. What remains to be discussed are the innovative changes it produced:

a) *Recognition by Other Spanish-Speaking Groups:* Since June, 1967, "Tierra Amarilla" has become a rallying cry as well as a place name. From Denver came Rodolfo "Corky" Gonzales, leader of the Crusade for Justice, to hail the Alianza members for having "had the guts" to take their stand. A few weeks later, Bert Corona, leader of the Los Angeles Mexican-American Political Association ("MAPA"), made a like pilgrimage to Albuquerque. César Chávez, leader of the migrant farm workers of the Southwest, was in-

vited to Albuquerque to address liberal organizations, but took time out to attend a regular meeting of the Alianza. There, after an effusive greeting by the membership and a public embrace with Tijerina, Chávez announced that, if he were a New Mexico resident, he would sure be an Alianza member. He hoped all Hispanos of New Mexico would join, because the issue of the land is crucial to rural Mejicanos and reflects the cruel injustices to which they have been subjected. Chávez predicted no early victories, but spoke soulfully of the road of sacrifice that would have to be travelled by those who are committed to the struggle, sacrifice in atonement for the sins of others. The membership responded with heartfelt "Amens," for Chávez had touched the wellspring of Penitente thought which is still so alive in northern New Mexico.

b) *Partnership with Negroes:* The 1967 annual convention of the Alianza was attended by a busload of *Mejicano* and Negro activists from Los Angeles. The culminating point of the convention was a "Treaty of Peace, Harmony and Mutual Assistance" jointly signed by the Alianza leaders and leaders of SNCC, CORE, Black Panthers and other Black Power organizations. The members of the Alianza, with the ringing approval of all present at the convention, thus identified their movement with the objectives of Black Power, no longer on the basis of temporary and conditional "mutual self-interest," but in the context of "full brotherhood" (see center-page spread in *La Raza*, Los Angeles newspaper, 10/20/67).

1968

a) *Impact on Youth:* Partly inspired by the "Black Beret" and "Brown Beret" movement of Los Angeles activist Negro and *Mejicano* youth, the Alianza youth are starting to move out in new directions. In Albuquerque, it will be hard to build unity between "Black and Brown," as the two groups are now identified, because of the record of poor communication between the groups and of clashes between their youth. The coolness is partly the product of conservative trends in the local

Negro leadership which, in the future, is likely to be stimulated to new trends or else to be replaced.

On April 22, 1968, students of an Albuquerque junior high school called a strike. Under the slogan, "We want Education, not Contempt," the students charged that the educational curriculum of the school was adequate only for its few Anglo students, no effort being made to compensate for the educational handicaps of the Hispano majority and the Negro minority. Other student demands were an end to hitting the students, punishing them for speaking Spanish on school premises and displaying prejudice against Hispanos and Negroes. Forty of the students were arrested while marching to recruit students from other junior high and high schools to form a joint delegation to the School Board. Among those charged with "littering," "loitering" and "truancy" were two Tijerina offspring.

An ambitious plan has been written for a free summer workshop for fifty Spanish-speaking youth, to provide them with a background in all the knowledge of the world of today that they will need in order to become effective leaders. Included in the proposed curriculum are history, philosophy and the arts. Sponsorship and funding for the project are being sought.

b) *Leadership Role of the Alianza:* Paradoxical as it may seem, the relatively small Alianza with its widely scattered and largely rural membership occupies a central place in the regionwide united movement of minority groups. As such, the Alianza has become significant on a nationwide scale. The Tierra Amarilla episode so stirred the imagination that the Alianza has become standardbearer for the entire Southwest.

The authentic leadership of the Alianza in the ranks of the poor caused Dr. Martin Luther King to invite Reies Tijerina to the planning conference for the Poor People's March, held shortly before his assassination. King also chose Tijerina to be mobilization director for New Mexico and to be one of three leaders representing Mejicano-Chicano-Hispano demands in Washington.

Predictably, the implementation of these decisions produced hostile editorials in the New Mexico press and anguished wails from some liberals. While the mobilization commanded strong support from poor people and many middle-class liberals, measures to paralyze Tijerina's leadership were promptly taken.

On April 27, Reies and Cristobal Tijerina were arrested and warrants were out for the arrest of eleven other Alianza members on an indictment issued by the Rio Arriba County Grand Jury. The indictment reversed the decisions of the preliminary hearing on the "Tierra Amarilla Uprising" and reinstated the kidnapping and other charges which had been reduced or thrown out of the case by judicial decision. No new evidence was cited. Bond for most of the defendants was set at $24,-500.

The national leaders of the Poor People's March expressed their conviction that these arrests were an attack on the March itself. They demanded through the Justice Department's intervention release of the accused by writ of Habeas Corpus.

The State Attorney General and District Attorney Alfonso Sanchez, however, cling to the expressed belief that, once the Alianza leaders are behind bars for a long stay, the Hispanos will once more relapse into apathy. The State Attorney General has taken the position that the Alianza is part of a Communist plot and that elements at the University of New Mexico and in the Poverty Programs are in league with the plot. The State OEO director was dismissed as a result of the allegations, and covert investigations have been made of a number of Community Action programs. It is not known whether the recent firing of several University deans is connected in any way with the State Attorney General's campaign.

c) *Progress:* Despite the storm of controversy and accusation which surround the Alianza, it is considered a real political force in the upcoming elections. While no direct, overt concessions may be made on issues which the Alianza has raised, behind-the-scenes promises are expected, as in the gubernatorial elections of 1966. Very quietly, action is being taken to soften Hispano grievances and to still the protests. It is said that the Forest Service has opened grazing facilities to Hispanos to a greater extent than at any time since the 1930s. In addition, projects funded both publicly and privately are centering on the economic problems of the northern counties. Producers' cooperatives have been established in several communities, with promising results. Whether or not these concessions will still Hispano demands remains to be seen.

SUMMARY AND CONCLUSIONS

The development of the Alianza in less than five years since its foundation in 1963 is notable for the changes in the very process of change itself which can be traced. At the start, the organization had many of the characteristics of a nativistic cult; the charismatic leader, the goal of restoration of socioeconomic forms to a prior state, the search for ethnic identity and the renewal of the traditional community ethic. Had these been the only characteristics of the organization, the Alianza might have become a revitalization movement according to the definition of Anthony Wallace.

The main direction of such a process of change is toward cultural divergence or, in the evolutionary theory of Sahlins and Service (1960), "Specific Evolution." This apparently, is the main direction of many nativistic, cargo, messianic, etc. cults.

The Alianza, on the other hand, included from its inception innovative changes such as unity of purpose and action on a scale long unfamiliar to Hispanos, the linking of human, ethnic and political rights with those of property and, finally, the transformation of the action program from a base in traditional vigilantism to active participation in today's major national sweep for social change.

Here, I think, is an example of deliberate innovation that does not fit the revitalization concept. As an analogy, the emergence of a divergent sect of "Christian" Jews with a revitalized religious concept can be compared with the early Christian Church and its relation to the transformations between the time of the late Roman Empire and the emergence of the Medieval State. The latter changes seem to fit the stagewise advance to a higher level which Sahlins and Service call "General Evolution".

The Alianza movement is as yet very young, yet the changes it has stimulated make possible a new direction for the Hispano rural communities. Presently under severe stress of rapid acculturation and forced emigration for livelihood, they could restabilize if the conditions of existence for which the Alianza presses were met. It has already been noted that some avenues of economic development have been opened as a result of the Alianza's campaign. It should be added that those Hispano communities which have the resources for self-support (Chimayo, for example) possess both cultural stability and the flexibility to incorporate elements of the majority culture which are compatible with Hispano values.

Can it be said that cultural revitalization and social revolution are alternative aspects of the same process of deliberate innovative change? If so, it is logical that a revitalization movement may develop into a revolution, and that an aborted or detoured revolution may become a revitalization movement.

In setting criteria for predicting the success or failure of a revitalization movement, Anthony Wallace implies that "success" might be equivalent to social revolution:

> While a great deal of doctrine in every movement (and, indeed, in every person's mazeway) is extremely unrealistic in that predictions of events made on the basis of its assumptions will prove to be more or less in error, there is only one sphere of behavior in which such error is fatal to the success of a revitalization movement: prediction of the outcome of conflict situations. If the organization cannot predict successfully the consequences of its own mores and of its opponents' mores in a power struggle, its demise is very likely. If, on the other hand, it is canny about conflict, or if the amount of resistance is low, it can be extremely "unrealistic" or extremely unconventional in other matters without running much risk of early collapse.

While cultural change was not an objective of the Alianza, some cultural changes are occurring due to the easing of the cultural enclavement of the rural communities. This, then, is a by-product of the past struggles. Yet, within the movement that is sweeping the country, the greatest cultural change that is sought is one in the dominant culture. As Dr. Martin Luther King stated shortly before his death:

> The American people are infected with racism—that is the peril. Paradoxically, they are also infected with democratic ideals—that is the hope. While doing wrong, they have the potential to do right. But they do not have a millenium to make changes.

It is in the light of this national perspective that the social changes of which the Alianza is the catalyst should be viewed.

JOAN London + Henry ANDERSON

*Joan London (Publication Editor for the California Labor
Federation) and Henry Anderson (Farm Labor organizer and
presently employed by California Department of Public
Health) have both written about, and worked extensively for
the cause of California farm labor. Mr. Anderson has written
three books on migrant workers, and Ms. London is the
author of a biography of her father as well as numerous
pamphlets and articles on labor issues. They collaborated
upon SO SHALL YOU REAP (1970), and the following
selection about Ernesto Galarza and his early farm work for
AWOC comes from that book. This highly sympathetic
portrayal of Galarza outlines the continuous problems that
union representatives face in fighting an oppressive system
and in keeping in the vanguard of the movement.
From SO SHALL YE REAP by Joan London and Henry
Anderson, Copyright © 1970 by the authors and Thomas Y.
Crowell Company, Inc.*

Man Of Fire: Ernesto Galarza

Among the extraordinary persons who have
made the farm workers' cause their own, one of
the most exceptional is Ernesto Galarza, a wiry
man with a shock of graying hair and penetrating
eyes under full black eyebrows, a brilliant speaker
and writer, a doctor of philosophy from Columbia
University.

Galarza fought, at times simultaneously and almost single-handedly, the power of agribusiness,
federal and state governments, and Big Labor. In

the uneven contest, he may seem to have lost, as
the world usually reckons winning and losing. But
social movements have their own secret reckon-
ings. Galarza kept alive the embers of the farm
labor movement in California during a long night
in which they came close to being extinguished
altogether.

Ernesto Galarza was born in Tepic, Nayarit, on
Mexico's Pacific Coast, at about the time the Mexican revolution was being conceived in secret

38

meetings led by Francisco Madero and others. In 1910, the revolution reached the shooting stage; Galarza's parents fled the country. One of his earliest memories is of crouching on the floor of a train bearing them north to the border as bullets spattered on the outside.

The Galarzas settled in Sacramento, where Ernesto had the opportunity, denied many a Mexican child before and since, of attending school regularly. In the summers, he did farm labor of various types.

A group of his high school teachers insisted that he go on to college. The leader of this group was an alumnus of Occidental, a small liberal arts college in southern California, and Galarza was turned in that direction. He obtained an academic scholarship, and in 1923 entered Occidental College. Since his scholarship did not meet room, board, and incidental expenses, he waited on tables, mowed lawns, and did whatever other work he could find. Periodically, he drove to Sacramento in his Model A Ford to help with problems of his brothers and sisters; as the eldest, he had become head of the family upon the death of his parents.

He went to graduate school at Stanford University, where he majored in economics, but then and throughout his life, he creatively combined an interest in the humanities and the social sciences. When he writes on economics, "the Dismal Science," it is with a grace, wit, and style which are rare in any field.

During his year at Stanford, Galarza met and married Mae Taylor. After he received his master's degree, they left for Columbia University, where he had won a fellowship to pursue his doctorate. He was almost certainly influenced by the School of Education at Columbia University, although he did not study directly under John Dewey. His entire adult life has been marked by a special concern for education. It was no accident that when the time came to choose a title for himself in the farm labor movement, it was Director of Research and Education.

By 1934 Galarza had satisfied all the requirements for his doctor of philosophy degree except the dissertation. He needed full-time employment; by now, he and Mae had two daughters. For something over a year, he was employed by the Foreign Policy Association as a specialist in Latin affairs. Then, in 1936, he was offered a job with the Pan American Union as a research associate in education. He accepted gladly, since the position seemed an ideal outlet for several of his skills and interests, including his belief in education as an instrument of social change. Through his association with the Pan American Union, he hoped to help bring justice to the Spanish and Portuguese Americas without the kind of violent revolution he had witnessed in his childhood in Mexico.

During his years with the Pan American Union, Galarza worked on his dissertation, a study of the electric light and power industry in Mexico. It was completed in 1943, and Galarza received his doctorate from Columbia in 1944.

On Galarza's recommendation, a Division of Labor and Social Information was created within the Pan American Union in 1940, and he was made its first director. The job gave him a modest voice in policy recommendations, allowed him to travel rather extensively throughout the hemisphere, and supported his family in comfort. Later he said, "I would be there yet if I had been willing to turn to stone like the building we were housed in, and the diplomats who came there to keep us from accomplishing anything. Animated marble busts!"

In 1942, the World War II version of the *bracero* program was enacted. As a labor agreement between two member nations of the Pan American Union, it fell within Galarza's portfolio. He obtained permission to conduct an investigation of the program from the standpoint of its effect upon relations between the "good neighbors," Mexico and the United States.

Galarza bypassed the snares of bureaucracy and conducted the investigation in his own way. He went directly into the camps where braceros were housed and talked with them about their concerns: wages, food, medical care, recreation, their families, whatever. On the basis of visits to twenty camps, detailed interviews with two hundred of the workers, and brief discussions with hundreds more, he wrote a "Personal and Confidential Memorandum on Mexican Contract Workers in the United States." In effect, he concluded that the contract labor program, far from being administered as an instrument of neighborliness, was being used as an instrument through which the larger neighbor exploited the smaller.

Galarza stayed nearly eleven years with the Pan American Union. The break came in 1946, precipitated by an event which he summarized before a Senate committee six years later, in a characteristic mixture of anger, eloquence, high principle, and humor:

> I resigned voluntarily . . . on account of illness. I suffered a stroke of nausea when I observed at close quarters the betrayal of Bolivian miners and farm workers by the United States Department of State. This betrayal led to the installation in Bolivia of a coalition government composed of four parts tin barons, three parts corporation farmers, and two parts Communist Party. Sinister in its origin, hypocritical in its execution, and tragic in its ending, this obscure but significant diplomatic incident has yet to receive the attention it deserves.

For a time Galarza was "at liberty." He could have had any of a number of academic or bureaucratic positions, some of them paying handsomely, but he was looking for something which would permit him to come directly to grips with social justice, and he was willing to wait for the right opportunity.

For some years, Galarza had known of H. L. Mitchell and the Southern Tenant Farmers Union, which, in 1945, had become the AFL's National Farm Labor Union. In 1947, Mitchell received a grant which made it possible for the NFLU to move outside its base in the South into California. It soon became apparent that the drive in California needed a Spanish-speaking organizer; a coming-together of the man and the job took place. In 1948 Galarza and his family moved to California, where the long NFLU strike against the Di Giorgio Fruit Company was already in progress.

The Galarza family home was established in San Jose, but Ernesto spent most of his time in the field, familiarizing himself with the changes in California agriculture since he had last done farm labor in the early 1920s. He was the very model of diplomacy, staying in the background while the Di Giorgio strike director, Hank Hasiwar, continued the activities which were already in motion. When Galarza eventually became his own strike director, Hasiwar returned his consideration with a loyalty rare in organized labor.

By 1950, Galarza felt ready for a major move. He was the principal organizer of an NFLU local in the area of Tracy, San Joaquin County, where most of the canning tomatoes in California were grown. The membership and staff decided to call a strike in September, 1950, to protest a wage cut in tomato picking.

Perhaps as many as three thousand workers became involved. Other unions and community groups did not respond as generously as they had three years earlier in the Di Giorgio strike, but one man did: Father Thomas McCullough. Years later he recalled, "We all fell in love with Ernie. The rest of us had been kind of fumbling around with the problem, and here was a man who really knew what he was doing! Boy, we thought, this is it! He was so dynamic. Such a grasp of the field. And how he can capture an audience! We thought, here's the leader we've all been waiting for!"

Large numbers of wetbacks were employed by the tomato growers at that time, but Galarza felt he could deal with the problem. "Despite all their handicaps, wetbacks are freer than braceros," he said. "They can walk off their jobs. Braceros can't." Some observers felt that the refusal of Teamster truck drivers to respect the NFLU picket lines was the most crucial factor in breaking the strike, but Galarza did not agree. "It wouldn't have made any difference if they drove through our lines, if there had been nobody behind the lines picking the tomatoes. What broke us was two thousand braceros, sent in to pick under Highway Patrol and police escort."

By the spring of 1951, Galarza was ready to try again. In many ways, the Imperial Valley was the most improbable of places for a fledgling union to try to organize agricultural workers. It was just across the border from a practically inexhaustible supply of cheap labor, and it was the bastion of an especially lawless brand of union-busting. Even today, there are those in health, welfare, law, and other fields who shrug their shoulders and say, "Imperial County? It's not part of the United States. It's another country."

At the same time, there were good reasons for going into the Imperial Valley. For nearly a quarter-century an undercurrent of Mexican self-organization had existed there, and Galarza was now confident of his ability to galvanize the latent militancy of Spanish-speaking workers. An even more important reason for the move was later expressed by Galarza in this way:

> Theoretically, it may have seemed that we should have stayed in Tracy, but we weren't able to operate on the basis of neat logic. We had to be fluid; we had to move wherever the wetback or bracero tides were running the highest. If we hadn't shifted here and there, plugging this weak spot in the·dike, and then that, there wouldn't have been any dry land left anywhere in the state. By 1951, it was obvious that the major port of entry for the tide of Mexican nationals, legal and illegal, was Imperial County. The most useful thing we could do for the workers of the Tracy area, and every other part of the state, was to try to plug that hole.

The NFLU struck the Imperial Valley cantaloupe harvest in April, 1951. The immediate grievance was that the work, which had been done for years at piece rates, enabling skilled local crews to make fairly good earnings, had been shifted to a straight seventy cents an hour. Since Mexican nationals could survive on this, while American citizens could not, local workers were rapidly being forced out of the area.

When the U.S. Border Patrol proved lax in rounding up wetbacks, the union members made citizens' arrests of illegal entrants, and guarded the border to prevent their re-entry. Once again, however, the union underestimated the potentialities of the bracero system. On a number of ranches, braceros took the places of the wetbacks the union had removed; sometimes wetbacks were simply legalized on the spot by federal agents.

In the sense that the strike did not gain wage increases or contracts, it failed, but as Galarza explained:

> Many of our strikes had objectives other than the usual ones. If we talked in the usual terms, that was because the labor fakers back East didn't understand any other kind. In fact, the strike was quite successful in its underlying purpose, which was to get rid of the wetback traffic. The stink we raised played an important part in getting the Texas labor movement to pay attention to the problem, in getting a number of exposés published in national magazines, in getting some Congressional hearings, and in getting the entire Immigration and Naturalization Service reorganized in 1954.

In the summer of 1951, Congress enacted Public Law 78, placing the bracero system on a more permanent basis than before. The NFLU fought the law from its introduction at a Department of Labor conference in February, 1951, to its passage in July. Once the law was on the books, however, union strategists felt that until it came up for Congressional reconsideration in 1953, the best that could be done was to try to find ways to turn it to their advantage.

Galarza noted an obscure clause in the treaty with Mexico which implemented Public Law 78: "No Mexican workers shall be assigned to fill any job which is vacant because of a strike or lockout." He had confidence in a society of laws, and this treaty was part of the supreme law of the land.

With this confidence, Galarza returned to the Imperial Valley in May, 1952. He found the local farm labor force already almost decimated by the effects of Public Law 78. From nearly five thousand the year before, the number of local cantaloupe pickers had shrunk to fewer than a thousand. He did his best to rally those who remained, and proceeded with his test of the treaty between the United States and Mexico.

More than half of the local workers walked off the job. Under ordinary circumstances, this would have been economically effective. Public Law 78 was no ordinary circumstance, however. It was a simple matter for members of the growers' association who had more braceros than they could use —a common condition throughout the life of the system—to transfer their excess workers to fellow members who were being struck. Galarza complained to the authorities that this was a violation of the law. They promised to "investigate," but that was the last he heard of the matter. In June, the cantaloupe harvest was over; so were Galarza's illusions about government agencies, including those which were theoretically "labor-oriented."

During much of 1953 and 1954, Ernesto Galarza was in Louisiana helping to organize sugar-cane workers and small strawberry tenant farmers, whose earnings were often lower than those of argicultural workers in California.

The 1953 effort was defeated by court injunctions. California growers have often obtained, from judges who are sometimes growers themselves, injunctions which limit the number and location of pickets. In Louisiana, however, injunctions prohibiting all picketing were obtained by corporate agricultural interests from their friends on the bench. The union's painstaking work of organizing two thousand people, and inducing them to leave their jobs, was nullified overnight.

Although the injunctions could not be set aside in time to save the union's 1953 efforts, the union appealed, hoping to keep the legal precedent from being used against it at other times and in other places. The Louisiana Supreme Court upheld the injunctions with these memorable words: "The guarantee of freedom of speech, even if picketing and speech are held to be identical, cannot be maintained in the face of such irreparable injury to property." Lacking the resources to appeal the decision to the United States Supreme Court in the usual manner, the union filed a pauper's oath, and a volunteer attorney, Daniel Pollitt, handled the case. Two years later, the Supreme Court set aside the injunctions on First Amendment grounds, but the damage to the union could not be undone.

Subsequent organizing efforts in Louisiana were destroyed in an even more remarkable manner. The rural-dominated state legislature enacted a "right to work" law in 1954. It was evidently a reprisal against the Louisiana labor movement for having supported the 1953 agricultural strike. The newly merged state AFL-CIO organization launched a campaign to repeal the "right-to-work" act, with strong support from the now renamed National Agricultural Workers Union. A repeal bill was introduced in the spring of 1956.

Without the knowledge of the NAWU, an agreement was worked out between the state labor federation and representatives of the American Sugar Cane League: the League would use its powerful influence to repeal the 1954 act—and substitute one applying only to agriculture.

In the legislative process, grower lobbyists and their beholden legislators amended the definition of "agricultural labor" to include cotton ginning and compressing, rice milling, sugar refining, and other work not included in the original agreement. Despite even this, the state AFL-CIO called the amended law "good legislation."

As Galarza pointed out, this put Louisiana in a distinguished position. Many states had many kinds of discriminatory legislation against farm workers, but Louisiana alone had a "right to work" law applying exclusively to agriculture. Furthermore, Galarza wrote, it "is the only so-called 'right to work' law on the books of any state in the Union which carries the endorsement of organized labor, AFL-CIO."

Galarza and H. L. Mitchell sought to have the national AFL-CIO repudiate Louisiana labor's position. They journeyed to a resort in the Pocono Mountains of Pennsylvania, where the AFL-CIO executive council was meeting in the fall of 1956. From the standpoint of the embattled little farm workers' union, the resort, owned by the International Ladies Garment Workers Union, was ironically named: Unity House. The NAWU's appeal was rejected.

The president and executive council of the AFL-CIO appeared wedded to a philosophy of labor Darwinism, under which the rule, survival of the fittest, applies to the evolution of trade unions as well as organic species. Given this philosophy, the position of the Louisiana AFL-CIO seemed perfectly reasonable: It is our job to look out for the interests of workers who are already organized and paying their dues; it is not our job to look out for anyone else; if the weak lose out, it is too bad, but it is their own fault for being weak.

To speak of turning points in men or movements is always something of a falsification. Such moments are always preceded by an accretion of experiences which point toward the eventual change. If the scales had not fallen from Galarza's eyes at Unity House, they would have fallen before long somewhere else, just as his final disillusionment with the U. S. Department of Labor would have taken place sooner or later if it had not occurred in the Imperial Valley in 1952.

Galarza left the Pocono Mountains with a burden under which a lesser man would have buckled. He was convinced now that in the task of organizing agricultural workers, he and his relative handful of co-workers were confronted with no fewer than three major classes of obstacles: first and most obvious, agricultural employers; second, the U. S. Department of Labor and state public employment services, with their control of the bracero program giving them a kind of power in labor-management relations never before or since wielded by government in this country; and third, organized labor itself.

The last of these obstacles was the most galling. It was not that labor, by and large, was hostile to the organization of agricultural workers. Scores of resolutions containing eloquent words about the "plight of the farm worker" were passed at conventions representing millions of organized workers. This rhetoric, however, only irritated Galarza, because it was so much less than he felt he had a right to expect from avowed friends. " We don't want their fine words," he said in a 1957 interview. "We want their support: financial, political, moral. When we go before a Congressional committee, for instance, we want to know that we're not being traded away in the back cloakroom. . . . We do not have that kind of assurance now."

Galarza undertook, simultaneously, to destroy the alliance between growers and government bureaucrats, and to shake organized labor out of its complacency. All the while, insofar as he was able, he maintained contact with farm workers in the Imperial Valley and other areas where the union had established footholds. He had neither large numbers of supporters, nor finances, nor friends in high places. His weapons were highly personal: the shield of research and analytical thought, the sword of the written and spoken word. Armed with these, he set forth to do battle with the fortified feudal cities of the bracero system, and the indifference of organized labor.

His basic tactic was to document the flouting of laws—the abuses, the corruption, the debasement, the scandals inherent in the bracero system—and to publicize his findings as widely as possible. If the growers and the government fought back, so much the better. Keep the controversy going, keep the pot boiling, keep the issue in the public eye: that was the most that could be hoped for in the short run. As long as the issue was open, there was always the possibility that some scandal would prove so odious, some salvo so explosive, that public indignation would be aroused and the somnolent democratic conscience stirred into action.

To be truly effective, the technique of *j'accuse* requires that the accuser have enough "troops" that the accused must pay attention. But Galarza was caught in a cruel moral dilemma. He could have gone to any number of places throughout the state and induced the local farm workers to protest visibly against the bracero system. This would have strengthened his hand in the mass media, in the halls of Congress, and in labor circles. It would also have left those workers defenseless. Under the bracero system, there was no way a strike could be won. The strikers would lose working time, with neither strike fund nor unemployment insurance as a buffer, and when the strike was over they would find their jobs permanently filled by braceros.

Galarza resolved this moral dilemma in the only way his conscience would permit.

I made up my mind that, until the law was changed, I would never again ask a farm worker to stick his neck out where it could be chopped off by one stroke of the pen—a pen held in the hand of some bureaucrat in San Francisco or Washington, D. C.—certifying more braceros. For me to ask farm workers to go out on demonstration strikes that they could not possibly win would have been using them for other purposes. I would rather see the union die than use human beings in that way.

Now, if a group of workers asked me to come in and said they had already made up their minds they wanted to walk off the job, and wanted my advice, the situation was different. I would tell them, in full detail, the consequences of what they were doing, as I saw them. If they still insisted, I would give them all the assistance I could. There were situations like this now and then. The workers always lost, but there are times when men grow so desperate they would rather take actions they know will lose, than to continue to endure the unendurable.

Galarza consistently personalized his opposition, a technique which was not widely understood or accepted even by his friends. Unlike Father McCullough, he did not believe it was enough to belabor an abstraction, such as the "evil bracero system." In order to educate farm workers, and to arouse the general public, Galarza believed it was necessary to translate the abstractions into real acts by real individuals. Whenever he spoke of the abuses of the system, therefore, he tried to use as an illustration a specific bracero or a specific domestic worker who had undergone a specific type of treatment at the hands of a specific foreman or other official at a specific ranch on a specific date. Beyond that, he tried always to trace the abuses to the ultimate seats of responsibility: he named names of state and federal administrators he considered particularly culpable.

Unlike some critics of the system, Galarza did not believe that the bracero program was inherently unadministrable. Elimination of the program was the goal, but as long as it remained on the books he felt there was much latitude for administrators to make it better or worse. Convinced that administrators were systematically using this latitude to the detriment of agricultural workers, he reserved for these men a contempt beyond anything he felt toward growers, merchants, chiseling doctors, insurance companies, pushers, drivers, labor contractors, and others who took advantage of the helplessness of farm workers in general and braceros in particular. Although he despised it, he could understand the behavior of an agribusinessman whose motive was frankly to make as much money as possible. But he could not understand the public servants whose salaries were paid by American taxpayers, whose duty , by law, was to protect and advance the interests of American workers, but who (so it seemed to Galarza) betrayed their duty, not for money, but for the sake of betrayal itself.

Among the public officials he considered particularly responsible for the maladministration of the bracero system, Galarza identified Robert Goodwin, Director of the U. S. Bureau of Employment Security; Don Larin, Chief of the BES Farm Placement Service and later the California Department of Employment's highest farm labor official; Glenn Brockway, BES Administrator for the Western States; and Edward Hayes, head of the California Farm Placement Service. Hayes resigned in 1960, after the state Attorney General's office proved Farm Placement representatives had been discriminating against domestic workers and accepting gratuities from bracero users. He immediately became chief executive of the Imperial Valley Farmers Association, one of the nation's largest bracero-user groups.

Among those who have manipulated the fate of farm workers over the years, there is a game with generally well-understood rules. Heads of government agencies who administer foreign and domestic farm worker recruitment programs, and heads of labor groups who ritually criticize these programs, have far more in common with each other than either group has with agricultural workers. Within the rules of the game, it is tacitly understood that, whatever public pronouncements may be called for by the role of one or the other, there are no serious animosities, and it is bad form to hold a grudge. Established trade unions and the Department of Labor have a symbiotic relationship and neither is going to jeopardize it over an issue as peripheral to their traditional interests as farm labor.

Galarza understood this minuet, was repelled by it, and refused to dance to it. The following reminiscence is characteristic:

... I attended one of these conferences with state and federal people. You know the type. 'We're all interested in basically the same things here. Let's be reasonable.' The chairman was some unctuous bum who had made a career out of knifing farm workers in general and our union in particular. In a polite way, of course. He looked around the table and said, 'We can be on a first-name basis here. You call me So-and-so, and I'll call you Ernesto.' I said to him, 'You are quite mistaken, Mr. Chairman. I will call you Mister So-and-so, and you will call me *Mister* Galarza.'

The players of the game did not know how to deal with someone who refused to play by their rules. In the end, they had to choose between radically rethinking their assumptions or ejecting this maverick from the game. They chose to eject Ernesto Galarza, and had no trouble constructing justifications which they found entirely convincing.

Galarza fought back. As his personification of the opposition grew more refractory and his attacks more envenomed, some of his friends were unable to follow him. It seemed to them that his attacks were assuming the aspect of a vendetta. Galarza denied that it was a matter of personalities: "I may want to destroy a man's power in certain areas, but not the man himself. . . . It would be absurd for me to hound a person after he was removed from the kind of position in which he could make decisions harming farm workers."

From time to time, the president of the NAWU, H. L. Mitchell, whose headquarters were in Washington, D. C., asked Galarza to modify his attacks on government officials and labor bureaucrats: "After all, Ernie, I have to work with these guys back here." But Galarza felt that his candor made it easier for Mitchell to function: "Let me be the one they hate, Mitch. By comparison with me, you will be a model of sweet reasonableness."

The bracero program's administrators developed a standard tactic of turning the barbs back upon Galarza. In a radio interview in February, 1959, for instance, Secretary of Labor James Mitchell exemplified this technique: "Galarza is an able person and I may agree with some of his objectives, but he hurts his own cause with his extreme, unfounded allegations." Labor leaders who were stung by Galarza's shafts picked up the same patronizing line: "Too bad about Galarza. . . . "

Galarza continued to believe that his technique of trying to pinpoint responsibility for the bracero system was a sound use of his limited time and resources. But subsequent events showed that the system had a momentum of its own, sufficient to carry along with it anyone who might be in a given administrative position at a given moment. When Edward Hayes was removed from his key position, the newly elected governor, Pat Brown, put "liberals" in charge of the California Department of Employment and its farm labor functions. Yet throughout Brown's eight years in office, braceros remained in California. During the last two of those years, California was the only state in the Union to import any braceros at all.

Galarza's enemies carefully cultivated the legend that he was "Mr. Farm Labor"—that the farm labor movement began and ended with him—in the belief that if they could destroy his reputation the movement itself would be destroyed. One of their gambits was to smear him as a Communist. Galarza declined to honor this calumny with any reply. He assumed that his record would speak for itself. Throughout his adult life, he had been fighting all forms of totalitarianism, not with empty words, but by building democratic structures. He confided to a friend, almost in bewilderment, "Can't they see? I love this country in a way that people don't if they are born here, and take it for granted, and have never seen what things are like anywhere else. I love this country because, for all the things wrong, it comes close—close enough to glimpse what the good society might be like. The best way I can possibly imagine to show my respect and affection is to come closer yet—to help get over that remaining gap."

So long as the red-baiting was directed solely at him, Galarza remained silent. But when his wife was drawn into the smears, Galarza's chivalry and family pride compelled him to take steps.

After teaching in the San Jose school system for nearly three years, Mae Galaraza was abruptly told that her contract would not be renewed. Suspecting pressure from local growers, Galarza demanded the right to inspect his wife's personnel file. In the course of the controversy, the superintendent of the school district publicly called Galarza a "Red." Galarza brought suit, in one of the first actions of its kind; this was at the time Joseph McCarthy was still riding high. Galarza won the case. Although only token damages were awarded, the message was apparently passed along the growers' network. Ernesto and Mae Galarza were not publicly attacked in this particular way again. But Mrs. Galarza's job in the San Jose schools was never restored.

It would be an exaggeration to say that Galarza stood entirely alone during the middle 1950s. He had friends; he could not have done things he did without their help. He had friends in a Joint U.S.–Mexico Trade Union Committee, which included representatives of the AFL, the CIO, the independent United Mine Workers, and various railroad brotherhoods. He also had friends in the Fund for the Republic. Late in 1955, Galarza received a grant-in-aid from the Fund to write a report on the bracero system. For four months he gathered evidence, from the impoverished villages of Mexico to the rich fields and orchards of California.

A report of several hundred pages, illustrated by scores of photographs, was submitted to the Fund for the Republic. With the help of John Cogley, former editor of *Commonweal,* Galarza condensed this material into an eighty-page booklet, and in July, 1956, *Strangers in Our Fields* was published by the Joint U.S.-Mexico Trade Union Committee. It was the most damaging bombshell to hit the institution of braceroism up to that time.

The institution was hurt. There is no other way to explain the way in which its functionaries reacted. Rather than ignoring the report, as they had ignored other criticisms, they ordered field representatives of the California Farm Placement Service to search for evidence to discredit Galarza. This enterprise probably cost tens of thousands of tax dollars. The quibbles were sent to Ed Hayes and through him to Glenn Brockway. In

August, the San Francisco regional office of the Bureau of Employment Security mimeographed a long critique of *Strangers in Our Fields,* with every intention of making it public. At the last minute, however, Department of Labor officials in Washington concluded that it would be the better part of valor not to joust with Galarza openly.

In his field work, careful as he might be, Galarza was not always able to avoid receiving misinformation. For instance, he unearthed some check stubs which appeared to show that a bracero working for the Southern California Farmers Association had net earnings of $6.48, $6.03, and $2.88 for three consecutive weeks' work. These stubs were reproduced in the booklet, over a quote from one of Galarza's interviews with a bracero: "You work one day, and another—no. We spent much time counting the flies, as the saying is."

The government agencies had access to payroll records; Galarza did not. They found he had been misinformed. Each of the checks was for one *day's* work. With this and a handful of other discrepancies, the agencies sought to bring the entire work into disrepute and to paint its author as a shoddy researcher at best and perhaps even a deliberate liar.

As anyone walking through a bracero camp with his eyes open could have verified, braceros did indeed spend "much time counting the flies." For that matter, it is difficult to see how $2.88 for a full day's work is much more defensible than $2.88 for a week's work. By keeping the argument on their own terms, however, proponents of the system were able to persuade themselves and some innocent bystanders that Galarza was irresponsible.

Acutally, much of Galarza's treatment of the bracero system, then and later, was understated. In *Strangers in Our Fields,* he said almost nothing about "health insurance" which constituted one of the system's major rackets; almost nothing about the subsystem of so-called "specials" under which Lyndon Johnson and other favored employers were able to obtain "predesignated" braceros.

Galarza was fully aware of the need for factual accuracy and careful documentation. He knew that proponents of the system placed all the burden of proof on its critics. He knew that they would search exhaustively for some trivial misstatement in order to bring a carefully built edifice of research tumbling down. Even a professionally trained researcher like Galarza found it almost impossible to prove a charge against the bracero system beyond any cavil. Employers' records were closed to him. Wage and hour data were altered. Potential witnesses were hustled back to Mexico.

Nevertheless, *Strangers in Our Fields* proved one of the outstanding successes of Galarza's career. It received widespread publicity, even in media, such as the Los Angeles *Times,* which no one had ever accused of pro-labor prejudice. The booklet went through two editions and 10,000 copies. Condensations of much the same material appeared in at least three national magazines. Urban liberals were slowly being weaned from the misconception that the "farm labor problem" in California was still a matter of jalopies, and Joad families played by Jane Darwell and Henry Fonda.

Galarza's booklet also helped stir into wakefulness some elements of the labor movement. Early in 1957, the AFL-CIO's Industrial Union Department, headed by Walter Reuther, gave the National Agricultural Workers Union $25,000, with the understanding that about half of it would be used for organizing in California.

Pitiable as the amount was, this was the most money Galarza had ever had to work with. Husbanding it carefully, he made it last over a year. He opened offices, sometimes rent-free in private homes, in Yuba City, Tracy, Stockton, Modesto, Hollister, and San Jose and began to "develop local people." As he later put it: "Obviously, you aren't going to organize a statewide union with that kind of money. I looked upon it as a demonstration project. . . . I wanted to prove that Galarza wasn't the only potential organizer in California. Over the years, I would estimate that I have found at least two hundred people in this state—field workers—who would be first-rate organizers, given the chance."

The key problem facing Galarza was this: around what axis can you organize, when your members' jobs will almost certainly be filled by braceros if they try to rise above the braceros' wages and working conditions? To an extent, Galarza answered this question in the same way as Father McCullough and César Chávez, although

there was little exchange of ideas among the three. The union proved its value to its members by performing services they lacked the time or expertise to perform, and which did not involve a premature collision with employers. For instance, Galarza's San Jose local discovered that, although agricultural workers had become partially covered by the Social Security Act in 1955, growers and labor contractors often pocketed the payroll deductions rather than sending them to the Social Security Administration. One union member who had worked for a single employer all year, and had earned close to $2,400, was credited with only $427 by the SSA accounting office in Baltimore. A union representative was able to get the "error" corrected.

Galarza felt that an NAWU local should also perform a quite different type of function. In effect, he trained his cadres to operate as he himself was operating: as sleuths for abuses under the bracero program. He was still convinced that there was little point in ordinary union activities as long as Public Law 78 was intact, and that the best way to obtain its modification was to ferret out the most flagrant scandals and publicize them.

In August, 1957, Galarza was sure he had a case which would "blow the whole thing out of the water." Thousands of American fruit pickers were gathering in the northern end of the Sacramento Valley, around Marysville and Yuba City, in anticipation of the peach harvest. Due to unseasonably cold weather, the peaches ripened late. While waiting, the Americans looked for jobs as boxspreaders, limb-proppers, and whatever else might be available in the area. They found all such work being done by braceros, although this was contrary to the letter of the braceros contracts and to the spirit of Public Law 78.

Galarza had complained of this type of violation on many other occasions, only to be told in so many words, "Oh, really? Prove it." Under this peculiar institution the standards of evidence required of critics of the system would have taxed a Blackstone, but Galarza gleefully accepted the challenge on this occasion, because he felt the evidence was irrefutable. Accompanied by a notary public, he went along the ditch banks and under the bridges of Sutter and Yuba counties, and obtained nearly two hundred sworn affidavits, complete with names, dates, places, every detail, from American workers who had vainly sought employment in the pre-harvest period. The northern California press carried the story as front-page news for days. Galarza called for a withdrawal of braceros, and for an investigation of the entire Farm Placement Service.

Governor Goodwin J. Knight rode out the storm, saying that the state Department of Employment, parent agency of the Farm Placement Service, should "be given an opportunity to look over the situation." By the time the Director of Employment had conducted his "investigation," exonerated himself and his department, and declared Galarza's charges "completely without merit," the peach harvest was half finished, American pickers were either working or had drifted from the area, the media no longer considered the incident newsworthy, and Galarza's salvos was bursting in air unseen and unheard.

Galarza began writing a series of open letters to the Governor on the bracero scandal-of-the-week. He called them his "Knight letters." It is doubtful that the Governor ever read them; the letters were intended primarily for newsmen, church and political groups, and friends of the farm labor movement.

When Democratic victories in the 1958 elections ended the public career of Goodwin Knight, Galarza turned to writing straight press releases on the endless irregularities he and his representatives were uncovering in the field. A typical release began: "Death took a turn as compliance officer for the Department of Labor in Imperial Valley, pointing a bony finger at one more routine violation of Public Law 78 . . . "A bracero had been killed while driving a tractor, an activity prohibited under the master contract, but commonplace. The Department of Labor, in "an indecently hasty whitewash," alleged that the bracero was operating the tractor·only "as a special favor" to the regular driver, and as a consequence there was no violation. Galarza demanded a full investigation at once, "before the truth is lost forever under a cloud of malathion and bureaucratic servility." As usual, his eloquence was ignored.

In time, weary of researching, writing, mimeographing, and distributing releases which were seldom if ever used, Galarza turned to writing essays which were apparently more for his own pleasure than anything else, although he distributed them to a small circle of friends. These essays are worth reading not only for their content but for their sardonic wit and verbal felicities. In a representative example of the Galarza style, he characterized the government's disciplinary measures against violators of Public Law 78 as "ten lashes laid on with a half-cooked noodle."

An essay entitled "Labor's Back Yard" is especially significant. Galarza charged that labor leaders "offer only token opposition while [their] most solemn pledges on human decency and democracy are denied one large segment of the brotherhood of labor." In conclusion, he warned:

> If democracy, freedom of organization and collective bargaining are principles, they apply to all. The struggle to realize them must be pressed into every corner of the land, their enjoyment denied no worker, however destitute or ignorant he may be.
>
> Otherwise, Otherwise, labor's long, bitter and often tragic commitment to humanity becomes a game of odd-man-out. The odd man must always be the low man on the totem pole. Once the "right to work" men have laid the axe to the base . . . no trade unionist need ask: "For whom does the axe fall?" It falls for him.

Galarza's near-despair was understandable. He exhausted the small grant from the Industrial Union Department early in 1958. He prepared a careful proposal to the IUD, calling for $250,000. With that amount, he was sure he could build a self-sustaining agricultural workers' union in California. He said later, "They didn't even have the courtesy to reply. For eight months I waited. I made three trips to Washington trying to build a fire under them. I had to close some union offices, disband some locals, and borrow $3,000 from friends to keep the others going."

The principal reason for the mysterious silence from Washington was that wheels were beginning to turn at the highest echelons of the national AFL-CIO, with motive power altogether different from Galarza's $250,000 program. The decision-makers involved did not feel it necessary to seek the advice of the one man who had had most experience organizing agricultural workers in California or even to notify him that plans were under way. Convinced that farm labor had been forgotten, Galarza became increasingly caustic in his comments about the California Labor Federation and the national AFL-CIO. In one of his gentler anecdotes, he said:

"Why is it that labor fakers always look so well fed? One time I was at a meeting with three or four of them. It was at one of these plush motels. It would be beneath their dignity to gather in a working-man's place. There they were, around the pool, overflowing their swimming trunks, wallowing around in the water for all the world like a bunch of great white whales. I felt like Captain Ahab making the discovery of his life! If I had had a harpoon handy, I would not like to be responsible for what might have happened."

Galarza's verbal harpoons helped to ensure that when the plans of the national leadership were completed he would be denied any significant role in them.

In February and March, 1959, when Jack Livingston, AFL-CIO Director of Organization, was looking for someone to head the new Agricultural Workers Organizing Committee, Galarza was never seriously considered. To the extent that his name arose at all, the decision-makers in Washington invoked the usual incantation, "Too bad, but he's lost his effectiveness." The most logical choice for the directorship of the Agricultural Workers Organizing Committee was, with only H. L. Mitchell's voice raised in his behalf, bypassed in favor of Livingston's old crony, Norman Smith.

The situation was as unfair to Smith as it was to Galarza, but each tried in good faith to make the best of it. In AWOC's early days, many magazines and newspapers assigned reporters to the story of "Big Labor's all-out drive in agriculture." Many reporters went first to Galarza; he invariably referred them to Smith. For all the general public

might have divined from the resulting stories, the organizing drive was a one-man undertaking, with Norman Smith as the new "Mr. Farm Labor."

Giving the lie to those who said he was a "prima donna," constitutionally incapable of "playing on a team," Galarza functioned as a training officer for AWOC. Each day, he traveled to a different area—Stockton, Modesto, Hollister, Yuba City, other far-flung points—to preside at a staff meeting of local organizers and stewards, asking and answering questions, anticipating problems likely to arise in the field.

As time passed, it became clear to Galarza that Smith was strategically adrift, with no coherent idea of how agricultural workers might be organized. In addition, Galarza believed that Smith was wrong in many tactical details, such as a tendency to rely on the assurances of politicians, while Galarza mistrusted all of them. But he held his peace. The staff meetings continued through December, although in the absence of any organizing plan it became increasingly difficult to train a staff. The break came in January, 1960, precipitated by jurisdictional and philosophical problems which had long been simmering in the farm labor movement.

Norman Smith used to say in all seriousness, "I don't care if the Devil himself comes to earth to organize farm workers, as long as the job gets done." Although he might have drawn the line at the Devil, Father McCullough also subscribed to this general theory, on the assumption that even if the union were initially undemocratic or otherwise unsavory, it could later be reformed from within.

Ernesto Galarza did not accept the proposition that any farm labor union at all is preferable to none. Both principled and practical considerations influenced his position. The only proper objective of the labor movement, he felt, is "the kind of human being it produces." He was not interested in the kind of union which produces dependent, manipulable people, even if they are well paid and well fed. He was interested in a union which would help people become more autonomous, more responsible, better able to weigh alternatives and make decisions for themselves. He feared that such a potential for human development would be lost if farm workers were absorbed by some larger union.

At the more "practical" level, Galarza doubted that a merger of agricultural workers with any other union would serve even to "put pork chops on the table." He had long since concluded that established union leaders, no matter how sincerely they might try, could not think within a framework which was relevant to farm workers' problems. "Organized labor just doesn't have any answers to questions like 'What do you do about braceros?' " he pointed out, "because it has never had to deal with foreign contract labor in any other union."

Galarza could not resist noting, furthermore:

"There is no love for the NAWU in the labor movement. We are an embarrassing stepchild. We embarrass them simply by existing. We are a constant reminder to them of things they should have done, but did not do. . . .

"And I'll tell you another way we stand to embarrass the fakers. . . . If we succeed, we'll precipitate a political crisis in the State of California. There'll hardly be a politician in the state who'll be safe. We were instrumental in electing the first Mexican-American councilman in the history of Brawley when we were active in that area. We have upset well-entrenched regimes in the Arvin-Lamont area of Kern County and in Sutter County, And this was done on peanuts.

"If the AFL-CIO gives us the support we have been crying for all these years, we can stand the State of California on its ear. Naturally, this makes a lot of people nervous. Very nervous. Including a lot of people in the labor movement, who have worked out some very careful living arrangements with incumbents—in both parties."

Fairly early in the history of AWOC, Galarza and H. L. Mitchell began to suspect that AFL-CIO officials were bent on dismantling the NAWU in favor of the United Packinghouse Workers of American. In their efforts to preserve what they considered the legal and moral jurisdiction of the NAWU, Galarza and Mitchell said and did things which some observers interpreted as an attempt to bring down the whole farm labor movement in a general Götterdämmerung. Such an interpretation was as superficial as it was uncharitable. Some personal feelings were involved, to be sure. Galarza and Mitchell would have had to be immune to normal human emotion if, after holding the fort so long, they had felt no resentment at being elbowed aside by Johnny-come-latelies. Basically, however, they fought to preserve the jurisdiction of the NAWU because they felt it alone represented the best interests of agricultural field workers. They had serious misgivings about the political backgrounds of some UPWA leaders. But they would have been equally reluctant to see farm workers delivered into the hands of Teamster leaders whose politics were at the other end of the spectrum.

In an attempt to retain the integrity of the NAWU, Galarza and Mitchell clawed with tenacity. . . .

RENASCENCE OF FARM LABOR

Something of a renascence of the farm labor movement, and of Galarza's career within that movement, took place in 1963. On May 29, the House of Representatives unexpectedly voted to discontinue the bracero program. Although the action was rescinded a few months later, it was a serious blow to the aura of invincibility which Public Law 78 had long enjoyed, and it counteracted some of the despair into which many of the friends of farm labor had sunk.

Then, on September 17, the California farm labor movement was electrified, and the gloaming of braceroism was hastened, by the bloodiest in a long series of catastrophes traceable to the insensitive way in which foreign contract-labor gangs had always been handled. In this case, the driver of a rudely converted truck full of braceros drove into the path of a speeding Southern Pacific freight train near the tiny town of Chualar in the Salinas Valley. Thirty-two of the workers were killed.

The old fires flared again in Ernesto Galarza. It was the kind of scandal he had long believed could be used as the springboard for a full-scale Congressional investigation, which in turn might disgrace the bracero program's administrators and sound the death knell of the entire system. His cries for an official investigation had never come to fruition, but now he roused himself for a last effort. Bringing into play all his skills of speaking, writing, flattering, badgering, maneuvering, he persuaded the large Mexican-American population of San Jose to back him solidly in asking the House of Representatives Committee on Education and Labor to investigate the Chualar disaster and to appoint him as staff director.

In some respects, Galarza's luck was good, in others, bad. Fortune in both cases, revolved around the personality of the chairman of the Education and Labor Committee, Adam Clayton Powell. A more politic chairman would not have hired the " controversial" Galarza in the first place, or kept him on in the teeth of the gale which his appointment aroused. Congressman Charles Gubser, a grower and a major user of braceros, had represented Galarza's district for some years. Protected by Congressional immunity, Gubser took to the floor of the House with unprecedented personal attacks on both Ernesto and Mae Galarza. Ignoring the opposition, Powell told Galarza to proceed with his report and let the chips fall where they might. The report appeared in the spring of 1964: one of the most thoroughly researched and best-written reports ever to appear under the imprimatur of a committee of the United States Congress.

At this point, however, it became evident that Powell's commitment to agricultural labor was no more than skin-deep. There was no follow-up to any of Galarza's recommendations in terms of legislation, although in its documentation of employer negligence the report was useful to attorneys for the survivors of the dead braceros. Instead of the settlements of $1,000 to $1,500 which had initially been made, settlements totaling over $2 million were eventually obtained.

Powell's lack of any real interest in agricultural labor also worked against the realization of a dream Galarza had entertained for years. He was not given the authority to put under subpoena his old enemies, ask them the questions they had always ignored or evaded, and require

them to answer publicly from the witness stand under penalty of perjury. About a year later, though, acting on his own with the assistance of a volunteer attorney, James Murray, Galarza came close to realizing this long-standing desire.

The Di Giorgio Corporation, in 1960, had sued a number of AWOC officials for showing the old film, "Poverty in the Valley of Plenty," which allegedly libeled the corporation. Galarza had been named a defendant, although he not only had had nothing to do with the showing but was not even associated with AWOC at that time. Galarza filed a countersuit, claiming malicious prosecution. In the course of this countersuit, he and Murray were able to obtain a number of depositions revealing interconnections between agricultural corporations and the government agencies which supposedly regulated them.

The verdict, rendered late in 1964, was another partial victory or partial defeat, depending on the perspective. The jury found that Galarza had had nothing to do with the showing of the allegedly libelous film, but it awarded him none of the damages he had asked.

Galarza retired to his writing, completing his analysis of the bracero system, for which Alaska Senator Ernest Gruening, an old friend, wrote the foreword. As its title implies, *Merchants of Labor* is an account of that portion of the agribusiness complex which deals in workers, rather than growing or selling fruits and vegetables. In particular, it is the story of bracero-user associations and the government administrators who catered to them. Although 1964 was the climactic year in the political struggle over Public Law 78, publishers still considered Galarza's book "uncommercial." He borrowed $1,500, paid to have this book printed by a San Jose firm, and undertook his own publicity and distribution. Orders came in; the first printing was sold out. In time, there was a second printing.

Then things were quiet again. By now there was a definite economic as well as psychological pinch. With many a wry comment, Galarza found a job with the War on Poverty. It required that he move to Los Angeles, but he did not give up the house in San Jose. In a little more than a year he was back, living on savings again, free to say what he pleased on any subject.

He is in some demand as a consultant—to the Ford Foundation, for instance, on a project having to do with Mexican-Americans in the Southwest. He appears frequently as a speaker at "brown power" conferences, where increasingly politically conscious Mexican-Americans are attempting to formulate a philosophy and program around which they can rally. He has published another book, entitled *Spiders in the House and Workers in the Field,* dealing with the 1947-1950 strike against Di Giorgio, and its aftermaths—including the part played by then Congressman Richard Nixon.

Galarza's contact with the farm labor movement is now minimal. He has no illusions about returning to the movement in which he invested so much of his life. In January, 1967, he journeyed to Delano, but came back to report that César Chávez was too busy to see him. Other times, other leaders: that is the way of social movements. Ernesto Galarza—fiery, loyal, brilliant, proud, organizer and doctor of philosophy—would no doubt agree.

Luis Valdez

Luis Valdez (Chicano author) writes for many American publications, among them the New Left periodical, RAMPARTS. Mr. Valdez argues that the CAMPESINO and not the urban dweller will guide LA RAZA. Furthermore he firmly rejects the belief that the melting-pot is beneficial. He sees no advantage in denying one's heritage merely to blend with the faceless mass of anglo society. It is for this reason that those who still maintain their ethnic identity, the exploited workers of all races, will be the vanguard and the soul of the effort to revolutionize America. Copyright Noah's Ark, Inc. (for RAMPARTS MAGAZINE) 1971. By permission of the Editors.

The Tale Of The Raza

The revolt in Delano is more than a labor struggle. Mexican grape pickers did not march 300 miles to Sacramento, carrying the standard of the *Virgen de Guadalupe,* merely to dramatize economic grievances. Beyond unionization, beyond politics, there is the desire of a New World race to reconcile the conflicts of its 500-year-old history. *La Raza* is trying to find its place in the sun it once worshipped as a Supreme Being.

La Raza, the race, is the Mexican people. Sentimental and cynical, fierce and docile, faithful and treacherous, individualistic and herd-following, in love with life and obsessed with death, the personality of the *raza* encompasses all the complexity of our history. The conquest of Mexico was no conquest at all. It shattered our ancient Indian universe, but more of it was left above ground than beans and tortillas. Below the foundations of our Spanish culture, we still sense the ruins of an entirely different civilization.

Most of us know we are not European simply by looking in a mirror—the shape of the eyes, the curve of the nose, the color of skin, the texture of hair; these things belong to another time, another people. Together with a million little stubborn mannerisms, beliefs, myths, superstitions, words, thoughts—things not so easily detected—they fill our Spanish life with Indian contradictions. It is not enough to say we suffer an identity crisis, because that crisis has been our way of life for the last five centuries.

That we Mexicans speak of ourselves as a "race" is the biggest contradiction of them all. The *conquistadores,* of course, mated with their Indian women with customary abandon, creating a nation of bewildered half-breeds in countless shapes, colors and sizes. Unlike our fathers and mothers, unlike each other, we *mestizos* solved the problem with poetic license and called ourselves *la raza.* A Mexican's first loyalty—when one of us is threatened by strangers from the outside—is to that race. Either we recognize our total unity on the basis of *raza,* or the ghosts of a 100,000 feuding Indian tribes, bloods and mores will come back to haunt us.

Just 50 years ago the Revolution of 1910 unleashed such a terrible social upheaval that it took 10 years of insane slaughter to calm the ghosts of the past. The Revolution took Mexico from the hands of New World Spaniards (who in turn were selling it to American and British interests) and gave it, for the first time and at the price of a million murders, to the Mexicans.

Any Mexican deeply loves his *mestizo patria,* even those who, like myself, were born in the United States. At best, our cultural schizophrenia has led us to action through the all-encompassing poetry of religion, which is a fancy way of saying blind faith. The Virgin of Guadalupe, the supreme poetic expression of our Mexican desire to be one people, has inspired Mexicans more than once to social revolution. At worst, our two-sidedness has led us to inaction. The last divine Aztec emperor Cuauhtemoc was murdered in the jungles of Guatemala, and his descendants were put to work in the fields. We are still there, in dry, plain, American Delano.

It was the triple magnetism of *raza, patria,* and the Virgin of Guadalupe which organized the Mexican-American farm worker in Delano—that and César Chávez. Chávez was not a traditional bombastic Mexican revolutionary; nor was he a

gavacho, a gringo, a white social worker type. Both types had tried to organize the *raza* in America and failed. Here was César, burning with a patient fire, poor like us, dark like us, talking quietly, moving people to talk about their problems, attacking the little problems first, and suggesting, always suggesting—never more than that—solutions that seemed attainable. We didn't know it until we met him, but he was the leader we had been waiting for.

Although he sometimes reminds one of Benito Juarez, César is our first real *Mexican-American* leader. Used to hybrid forms, the *raza* includes all Mexicans, even hyphenated Mexican-Americans; but divergent histories are slowly making the *raza* in the United States different from the *raza* in Mexico. We who were born here missed out on the chief legacy of the Revolution: the chance to forge a nation true to all the forces that have molded us, to be one people. Now we must seek our own destiny, and Delano is only the beginning of our active search. For the last hundred years our revolutionary progress has not only been frustrated, it has been totally suppressed. This is a society largely hostile to our cultural values. There is no poetry about the United States. No depth, no faith, no allowance for human contrariness. No soul, no mariachi, no chili sauce, no pulque, no mysticism, no *chingaderas.*

Our *campesinos,* the farm-working *raza* find it difficult to participate in this alien North-American country. The acculturated Mexican-Americans in the cities, *ex-raza,* find it easier. They have solved their Mexican contradictions with a pungent dose of Americanism, and are more concerned with status, money and bad breath than with their ultimate destiny. In a generation or two they will melt into the American pot and be no more. But the farmworking *raza* will not disappear so easily.

The pilgramage to Sacramento was no mere publicity trick. The *raza* has a tradition of migrations, starting from the legend of the founding of Mexico. Nezahualcoyotl, a great Indian leader, advised his primitive *Chichimecas,* forerunners of the Aztecs, to begin a march to the south. In that march, he prophesied, the children would age and the old would die, but their grandchildren would come to a great lake. In that lake they would find an eagle devouring a serpent, and on that spot, they would begin to build a great nation. The nation was Aztec Mexico, and the eagle and the serpent are the symbols of the *patria.* They are emblazoned on the Mexican flag, which the marchers took to Sacramento with pride.

Then there is the other type of migration. When the migrant farm laborer followed the crops, he was only reacting to the way he saw the American *raza:* no unity, no representation, no roots. The pilgrimage was a truly religious act, a rejection of our past in this country and a symbol of our unity and new direction. It is of no lasting significance that Governor Brown was not at the Capitol to greet us. The unity of thousands of *raza* on the Capitol steps was reason enough for our march. Under the name of HUELGA we had created a Mexican-American *patria,* and César Chávez was our first *Presidente.*

Huelga means strike. With the poetic instinct of the *raza,* the Delano grape strikers have made it mean a dozen other things. It is a declaration, a challenge, a greeting, a feeling, a movement. We cried *Huelga!* to the scabs, *Huelga!* to the labor contractors, to the growers, to Governor Brown. With the Schenley and DiGiorgio boycotts, it was *Heulga!* to the whole country. It is the most significant word in our entire Mexican-American history. If the *raza* of Mexico believes in *La Patria,* we believe in *La Huelga.*

The route of the pilgrimage was planned so that the Huelga could reach all the farmworkers of the San Joaquin Valley. Dependent as we were on each farmworking town for food and shelter, we knew the *raza* would not turn us down. *"Mi casa es suya,"* is the precept of Mexican hospitality: "My house is yours."

The Virgin of Guadalupe was the first hint to farmworkers that the pilgrimage implied social revolution. During the Mexican Revolution, the peasant armies of Emiliano Zapata carried her standard, not only because they sought her divine protection, but because she symbolized the Mexico of the poor and humble. It was a simple Mexican Indian, Juan Diego, who first saw her in a vision at Guadalupe. Beautifully dark and Indian in feature, she was the New World version of the Mother of Christ. Even though some of her worshippers in Mexico still identify her with Tonatzin, an Aztec goddess, she is a Catholic saint of Indian creation—a Mexican. The people's response was immediate and reverent. They joined the march by the thousands, falling in line behind her standard. To the Catholic hypocrites against the pilgrimage and strike the Virgin said *Huelga!*

The struggle for better wages and better working conditions in Delano is but the first, realistic articulation of our need for unity. To emerge from the mire of our past in the United States, to leave behind the divisive, deadening influence of poverty, we must have unions. To the farmworkers who joined the pilgrimage, this cultural pride was revolutionary. There were old symbols—Zapata lapel buttons—and new symbols standing for new social protest and revolt; the red thunderbird flags of the NFWA, picket signs, arm bands.

There were also political rallies in the smallest towns of the San Joaquin Valley. Sometimes they were the biggest things that had ever happened in town. Every meeting included a reading of *El Plan de Delano,* a "plan of liberation" for all farmworkers in the language of the picket line: "... our path travels through a valley well known to all Mexican farmworkers. We know all of these towns ... because along this very same road, in this very same valley, the Mexican race has sacrificed itself for the last 100 years ... This is the beginning of a social movement in fact and not in pronouncements ... We shall unite ... We shall strike ... Our PILGRIMAGE is the MATCH that will light our cause for all farmworkers to see what is happening here, so that they may do as we have done ... VIVA LA CAUSE! VIVA LA HUELGA!"

The rallies were like religious revivals. At each new town, they were waiting to greet us and offer us their best—mariachis, embraces, words of encouragement for the strike, prayers, rosaries, sweet cakes, fruit and iced tea. Hundreds walked, ran or drove up to the march and donated what little money they could afford. The countless gestures of sympathy and solidarity was like nothing the *raza* had ever seen.

The NFWA is a radical union because it started, and continues to grow, as a community organization. Its store, cafeteria, clinic, garage, newspaper and weekly meeting have established a sense of community the Delano farmworkers will not relinquish. After years of isolation in the *barrios* of Great Valley slum towns like Delano, after years of living in labor camps and ranches at the mercy and caprice of growers and contractors, the Mexican-American farmworker is developing his own ideas about living in the United States. He wants to be equal with all the working men of the nation, and he does not mean by the standard middle-class route. We are repelled by the human disintegration of peoples and cultures as they fall apart in this Great Gringo Melting Pot, and determined that this will not happen to us. But there will always be a *raza* in this country. There are millions more where we came from, across the thousand miles of common border between Mexico and the United States. For millions of farmworkers, from the Mexicans and Philippinos of the West to the Afro-Americans of the South, the United States has come to a social, political and cultural impasse. Listen to these people, and you will hear the first murmurings of revolution.

CÉSAR CHÁVEZ

*César Chávez (labor leader and Director of United Farm
Workers Organizing Committee, AFL-CIO) has been
without doubt the most charismatic labor leader to appear
upon the American labor scene since Walter Reuther. In this
autobiographical sketch from* RAMPARTS MAGAZINE, *Mr.
Chávez recounts the early history of his career.
Copyright Noah's Ark, Inc. (for* RAMPARTS MAGAZINE)
1971. By permission of the Editors.

The Organizer's Tale

It really started for me 16 years ago in San Jose, California, when I was working on an apricot farm. We figured he was just another social worker doing a study of farm conditions, and I kept refusing to meet with him. But he was persistent. Finally, I got together some of the rough element in San Jose. We were going to have a little reception for him to teach the *gringo* a little bit of how we felt. There were about thirty of us in the house, young guys mostly. I was supposed to give them a signal —change my cigarette from my right hand to my left, and then we were going to give him a lot of hell. But he started talking and the more he talked, the more wide-eyed I became and the less inclined I was to give the signal. A couple of guys who were pretty drunk at the time still wanted to give the *gringo* the business, but we got rid of them. This fellow was making a lot of sense, and I wanted to hear what he had to say.

His name was Fred Ross, and he was an organizer for the Community Service Organization (CSO) which was working with Mexican-Americans in the cities. I became immediately really involved. Before long I was heading a voter registration drive. All the time I was observing the things Fred did, secretly, because I wanted to learn how to organize, to see how it was done. I was impressed with his patience and understanding of people. I thought this was a tool, one of the greatest things he had.

It was pretty rough for me at first. I was changing and had to take a lot of ridicule from the kids my age, the rough characters I worked with in the fields. They would say, "Hey, big shot. Now that you're a *politico,* why are you working here for 65 cents an hour?" I might add that our neighborhood had the highest percentage of San Quentin graduates. It was a game among the *pachucos* in the sense that we defended ourselves from outsiders, although inside the neighborhood there was not a lot of fighting.

After six months of working every night in San Jose, Fred assigned me to take over the CSO chapter in Decoto. It was a tough spot to fill. I would suggest something, and people would say, "No, let's wait till Fred gets back," or "Fred wouldn't do it that way." This is pretty much a pattern with people, I discovered, whether I was put in Fred's position, or later, when someone else was put in my position. After the Decoto assignment I was sent to start a new chapter in Oakland. Before I left, Fred came to a place in San Jose called the Hole-in-the-Wall and we talked for half an hour over coffee. He was in a rush to leave, but I wanted to keep him talking; I was that scared of my assignment.

There were hard times in Oakland. First of all, it was a big city and I'd get lost every time I went anywhere. Then I arranged a series of house meetings. I would get to the meeting early and drive back and forth past the house, too nervous to go in and face the people. Finally I would force myself to go inside and sit in a corner. I was quite thin then, and young, and most of the people were middle-aged. Someone would say, "Where's the organizer?" And I would pipe up, "Here I am." Then they would say in Spanish—these were very poor people and we hardly spoke anything but Spanish—"Ha! This *kid?*" Most of them said they were interested, but the hardest part was to get them to start pushing themselves, on their own initiative.

The idea was to set up a meeting and then get each attending person to call his own house meeting, inviting new people—a sort of chain letter effect. After a house meeting I would lie awake going over the whole thing, playing the tape back, trying to see why people laughed at one point, or why they were for one thing and against another. I was also learning to read and write, those late

evenings. I had left school in the 7th grade after attending sixty-seven different schools, and my reading wasn't the best.

At our first organizing meeting we had 368 people: I'll never forget it because it was very important to me. You eat your heart out; the meeting is called for 7 o'clock and you start to worry about 4. You wait. Will they show up? Then the first one arrives. By 7 there are only 20 people, you have everything in order, you have to look calm. But little by little they filter in and at a certain point you know it will be a success.

After four months in Oakland, I was transferred. The chapter was beginning to move on its own, so Fred assigned me to organize the San Joaquin Valley. Over the months I developed what I used to call schemes or tricks—now I call them techniques —of making initial contacts. The main thing in convincing someone is to spend time with him. It doesn't matter if he can read, write or even speak well. What is important is that he is a man and second, that he has shown some initial interest. One good way to develop leadership is to take a man with you in your car. And it works a lot better if you're doing the driving; that way you are in charge. You drive, he sits there, and you talk. These little things were very important to me; I was caught in a big game by then, figuring out what makes people work. I found that if you work hard enough you can usually shake people into working too, those who are concerned. You work harder and they work harder still, up to a point and then they pass you. Then, of course, they're on their own.

I also learned to keep away from the established groups and so-called leaders, and to guard against philosophizing. Working with low-income people is very different from working with the professionals, who like to sit around talking about how to play politics. When you're trying to recruit a farmworker, you have to paint a little picture, and then you have to color the picture in. We found out that the harder a guy is to convince, the better leader or member he becomes. When you exert yourself to convince him, you have his confidence and he has good motivation. A lot of people who say OK right away wind up hanging around the office, taking up the workers' time.

During the McCarthy era in one Valley town, I was subjected to a lot of redbaiting. We had been recruiting people for citizenship classes at the high school when we got into a quarrel with the naturalization examiner. He was rejecting people on the grounds that they were just parroting what they learned in citizenship class. One day we had a meeting about it in Fresno, and I took along some of the leaders of our local chapter. Some redbaiting official gave us a hard time, and the people got scared and took his side. They did it because it seemed easy at the moment, even though they knew that sticking with me was the right thing to do. It was disgusting. When we left the building they walked by themselves ahead of me as if I had some kind of communicable disease. I had been working with these people for three months and I was very sad to see that. It taught me a great lesson.

That night I learned that the chapter officers were holding a meeting to review my letters and printed materials to see if I really was a Communist. So I drove out there and walked right in on their meeting. I said, "I hear you've been discussing me, and I thought it would be nice if I was here to defend myself. Not that it matters that much to you or even to me, because as far as I'm concerned you are a bunch of cowards." At that they began to apologize. "Let's forget it," they said. "You're a nice guy." But I didn't want apologies. I wanted a full discussion. I told them I didn't give a damn, but that they had to learn to distinguish fact from what appeared to be a fact because of fear. I kept them there till two in the morning. Some of the women cried. I don't know if they investigated me any further, but I stayed on another few months and things worked out.

This was not an isolated case. Often when we'd leave people to themselves they would get frightened and draw back into their shells where they had been all the years. And I learned quickly that there is no real appreciation. Whatever you do, and no matter what reasons you may give to others, you do it because you want to see it done, or maybe because you want power. And there shouldn't be any appreciation, understandably. I know good organizers who were destroyed, washed out, because they expected people to ap-

preciate what they'd done. Anyone who comes in with the idea that farmworkers are free of sin and that the growers are all bastards, either has never dealt with the situation or is an idealist of the first order. Things don't work that way.

For more than ten years I worked for the CSO. As the organization grew, we found ourselves meeting in fancier and fancier motels and holding expensive conventions. Doctors, lawyers and politicians began joining. They would get elected to some office in the organization and then, for all practical purposes, leave. Intent on using the CSO for their own prestige purposes, these "leaders," many of them, lacked the urgency we had to have. When I became general director I began to press for a program to organize farmworkers into a union, an idea most of the leadership opposed. So I started a revolt within the CSO. I refused to sit at the head table at meetings, refused to wear a suit and tie, and finally I even refused to shave and cut my hair. It used to embarrass some of the professionals. At every meeting I got up and gave my standard speech: we shouldn't meet in fancy motels, we were getting away from the people, farmworkers had to be organized. But nothing happened. In March of '62 I resigned and came to Delano to begin organizing the Valley on my own.

By hand I drew a map of all the towns between Arvin and Stockton—86 of them, including farming camps—and decided to hit them all to get a small nucleus of people working in each. For six months I traveled around, planting an idea. We had a simple questionnaire, a little card with space for name, address and how much the worker thought he ought to be paid. My wife, Helen, mimeographed them, and we took our kids for two or three day jaunts to these towns, distributing the cards door-to-door and to camps and groceries.

Some 80,000 cards were sent back from eight Valley counties. I got a lot of contacts that way, but I was shocked at the wages the people were asking. The growers were paying $1 and $1.15, and maybe 95 percent of the people thought they should be getting only $1.25. Sometimes people scribbled messages on the cards: "I hope to God we win" or "Do you think we can win?" or "I'd like to know more." So I separated the cards with the pencilled notes, got in my car and went to those people.

We didn't have any money at all in those days, none for gas and hardly any for food. So I went to people and started asking for food. It turned out to be about the best thing I could have done, although at first it's hard on your pride. Some of our best members came in that way. If people give you their food, they'll give you their hearts. Several months and many meetings later we had a working organization, and this time the leaders were the people.

None of the farmworkers had collective bargaining contracts, and I thought it would take ten years before we got that first contract. I wanted desperately to get some color into the movement, to give people something they could identify with, like a flag. I was reading some books about how various leaders discovered what colors contrasted and stood out the best. The Egyptians had found that a red field with a white circle and a black emblem in the center crashed into your eyes like nothing else. I wanted to use the Aztec eagle in the center, as on the Mexican flag. So I told my cousin Manuel, "Draw an Aztec eagle." Manuel had a little trouble with it, so we modified the eagle to make it easier for people to draw.

The first big meeting of what we decided to call the National Farm Workers Association was held in September 1962, at Fresno, with 287 people. We had our huge red flag on the wall, with paper tacked over it. When the time came, Manuel pulled a cord ripping the paper off the flag and all of a sudden it hit the people. Some of them wondered if it was a Communist flag, and I said it probably looked more like a neo-Nazi emblem than anything else. But they wanted an explanation, so Manuel got up and said, "When that damn eagle flies—that's when the farmworkers' problems are going to be solved."

One of the first things I decided was that outside money wasn't going to organize people, at least not in the beginning. I even turned down a grant from a private group—$50,000 to go directly to organize farmworkers—for just this reason. Even when there are no strings attached, you are still compromised because you feel you have to produce immediate results. This is bad, because it takes a long time to build a movement, and your organization suffers if you get too far ahead of the people it belongs to. We set the dues at $42 a year per family, really a meaningful dues, but of the 212 we got to pay, only 12 remained by June of '63. We were discouraged at that, but not enough to make us quit.

Money was always a problem. Once we were facing a $180 gas bill on a credit card I'd got a long time ago and was about to lose. And we *had* to keep that credit card. One day my wife and I were picking cotton, pulling bolls, to make a little money to live on. Helen said to me, "Do you put all this in the bag, or just the cotton?" I thought she was kidding and told her to throw the whole boll in so that she had nothing but a sack of bolls at the weighing. The man said, "Whose sack is this?" I said, well, my wife's, and he told us we were fired. "Look at all that crap you brought in," he said. Helen and I started laughing. We were going anyway. We took the $4 we had earned and spent it at a grocery store where they were giving away a $100 prize. Each time you shopped they'd give you one of the letters of M-O-N-E-Y or a flag: you had to have M-O-N-E-Y plus the flag to win. Helen had already collected the letters and just needed the flag. Anyway, they gave her the ticket. She screamed, "A flag? I don't believe it," ran in and got the $100. She said, "Now we're going to eat steak." But I said no, we're going to pay the gas bill. I don't know if she cried, but I think she did.

It was rough in those early years. Helen was having babies and I was not there when she was at the hospital. But if you haven't got your wife behind you, you can't do many things. There's got to be peace at home. So I did, I think, a fairly good job of organizing her. When we were kids, she lived in Delano and I came to town as a migrant. Once on a date we had a bad experience about segregation at a movie theater, and I put up a fight. We were together then, and still are. I think I'm more of a pacifist than she is. Her father, Fabela, was a colonel with Pancho Villa in the Mexican Revolution. Sometimes she gets angry and tells me, "These scabs—you should deal with them sternly," and I kid her, "It must be too much of that Fabela blood in you."

The movement really caught on in '64. By August we had a thousand members. We'd had a beautiful 90-day drive in Corcoran, where they had the Battle of the Corcoran Farm Camp 30 years ago, and by November we had assets of $25,-000 in our credit union, which helped to stabilize the membership. I had gone without pay the whole of 1963. The next year the members voted me a $40 a week salary, after Helen had to quit working in the fields to manage the credit union.

Our first strike was in May of '65, a small one but it prepared us for the big one. A farmworker from McFarland named Epifanio Camacho came to see me. He said he was sick and tired of how people working the roses were being treated, and he was willing to "go the limit." I assigned Manuel and Gilbert Padilla to hold meetings at Camacho's house. The people wanted union recognition, but the real issue, as in most cases when you begin, was wages. They were promised $9 a thousand, but they were actually getting $6.50 and $7 for grafting roses. Most of them signed cards giving us the right to bargain for them. We chose the biggest company, with about 85 employees, not counting the irrigators and supervisors, and we held a series of meetings to prepare the strike and call the vote. There would be no picket line; everyone pledged on their honor not to break the strike.

Early on the first morning of the strike, we sent out ten cars to check the people's homes. We found lights in five or six homes and knocked on the doors. The men were getting up and we'd say, "Where are you going?" They would dodge, "Oh, uh . . . I was just getting up, you know." We'd say, "Well, you're not going to work, are you?" And they'd say no. Dolores Huerta, who was driving the green panel truck, saw a light in one house where four rose-workers lived. They told her they were going to work, even after she reminded them of their pledge. So she moved the truck so it blocked their driveway, turned off the key, put it in her purse and sat there alone.

That morning the company foreman was madder than hell and refused to talk to us. None of the grafters had shown up for work. At 10:30 we started to go to the company office, but it occurred to us that maybe a woman would have a better chance. So Dolores knocked on the office door, saying, "I'm Dolores Huerta from the National Farm Workers Association." "Get out!" the man said, "you Communist. Get out!" I guess they were expecting us, because as Dolores stood arguing with him the cops came and told her to leave. She left.

For two days the fields were idle. On Wednesday they recruited a group of Filipinos from out of town who knew nothing of the strike, maybe 35 of them. They drove through escorted by three sheriff's patrol cars, one in front, one in the middle and one at the rear with a dog. We didn't have a picket line, but we parked across the street and just watched them go through, not saying a word. All but seven stopped working after half an hour, and the rest had quit by mid-afternoon.

The company made an offer the evening of the fourth day, a package deal that amounted to a 120 percent wage increase, but no contract. We wanted to hold out for a contract and more benefits, but a majority of the rose-workers wanted to accept the offer and go back. We are a democratic union so we had to support what they wanted to do. They had a meeting and voted to settle. Then we had a problem with a few militants who wanted to hold out. We had to convince them to go back to work, as a united front, because otherwise they would be canned. So we worked—Tony Orendain and I, Dolores and Gilbert, Jim Drake and all the organizers—knocking on doors till two in the morning, telling people, "You have to go back or you'll lose your job." And they did. They worked.

Our second strike, and our last before the big one at Delano, was in the grapes at Martin's Ranch last summer. The people were getting a raw deal there, being pushed around pretty badly. Gilbert went out to the field, climbed on top of a car and took a strike vote. They voted unanimously to go out. Right away they started bringing in strikebreakers, so we launched a tough attack on the labor contractors, distributed leaflets portraying them as really low characters. We attacked one—Luis Campos—so badly that he just gave up the job, and he took twenty-seven of his men out with him. All he asked was that we distribute another leaflet reinstating him in the community. And we did. What was unusual was that the grower would talk to us. The grower kept saying, "I can't pay. I just haven't got the money." I guess he must have found the money somewhere, because we were asking $1.40 and we got it.

We had just finished the Martin strike when the Agricultural Workers Organizing Committee (AFL-CIO) started a strike against the grape growers, DiGiorgio, Schenley liquors and small growers, asking $1.40 an hour and 25 cents a box. There was a lot of pressure from our members for us to join the strike, but we had some misgivings. We didn't feel ready for a big strike like this one, one that was sure to last a long time. Having no money —just $87 in the strike fund—meant we'd have to depend on God knows who.

Eight days after the strike started—it takes time to get 1,200 people together from all over the Valley—we held a meeting in Delano and voted to go out. I asked the membership to release us from the pledge not to accept outside money, because we'd need it now, a lot of it. The help came. It started because of the close, and I would say even beautiful relationship that we've had with the Migrant Ministry for some years. They were the first to come to our rescue, financially and in every other way, and they spread the word to other benefactors.

We had planned, before, to start a labor school in November. It never happened, but we have the best labor school we could ever have, in the strike. The strike is only a temporary condition, however. We have over 3,000 members spread out over a wide area, and we have to service them when they have problems. We get letters from New Mexico, Colorado, Texas, California, from farmworkers saying, "We're getting together and we need an organizer." It kills you when you haven't got the personnel and resources. You feel badly about not sending an organizer because you look back and remember all the difficulty you had in getting two or three people together, and here *they're* to-

gether. Of course, we're training organizers, many of them younger than I was when I started in CSO. They can work 20 hours a day, sleep four and be ready to hit it again; when you get to be 39 it's a different story.

The people who took part in the strike and the march have something more than their material interest going for them. If it were only material, they wouldn't have stayed on the strike long enough to win. It is difficult to explain. But it flows out in the ordinary things they say. For instance, some of the younger guys are saying, "Where do you think's going to be the next strike?" I say, "Well, we have to win in Delano." They say, "We'll win, but where do we go next?" I say, "Maybe most of us will be working in the fields." They say, "No, I don't want to go and work in the fields. I want to organize. There are a lot of people that need our help." So I say, "You're going to be pretty poor then, because when you strike you don't have much money." They say they don't care about that.

And others are saying, "I have friends who are working in Texas. If we could only help them." It is bigger, certainly, than just a strike. And if this spirit grows within the farm labor movement, one day we can use the force that we have to help correct a lot of things that are wrong in this society. But that is for the future. Before you can run, you have to learn to walk.

There are vivid memories from my childhood— what we had to go through because of low wages and the conditions, basically because there was no union. I suppose if I wanted to be fair I could say that I'm trying to settle a personal score. I could dramatize it by saying that I want to bring social justice to farmworkers. But the truth is that I went through a lot of hell, and a lot of people did. If I can even the score a little for the workers then we are doing something. Besides, I don't know any other work I like to do better than this. I really don't, you know.

John Shockley

John Shockley (Danforth Intern, Earlham College) in these two original essays discusses the now-famous Crystal City affair. Professor Shockley tells of the coalition of Chicanos and teamsters that won control of the city council in 1963, and of events over the next seven years that strained this political alliance. Students should be interested in the rise of class-consciousness within the Chicano majority prompted by the electoral victory. Both essays by permission of the author.

Crystal City: Los Cinco Mexicanos

A six foot high statue of Popeye in the center of town reminds all that Crystal City is no ordinary community. It is "the Spinach Capital of the World." As such it is the center of the Winter Garden Area of Texas, rich not only in spinach but in a number of other winter vegetables that can be grown in the area. But Popeye is only one aspect of the town's uniqueness—a uniqueness that is the cause for this study. It was here that in 1963 a group of five undereducated and poor Mexican-Americans were swept into office as city councilmen. Backed by the Teamsters who had organized the Del Monte spinach plant on the outskirts of town and supported further by the San Antonio-based Political Association of Spanish-speaking

People, the all-Chicano slate defeated the old Anglo establishment which had run the town since its inception in 1907. At the time this happened, Crystal City was the only community in Texas, and perhaps in the Southwest, where Anglos had been ousted from decades of rule. This study will attempt to understand why this revolution occurred, why it failed, and why it was so rare. The Chicano takeover in Crystal City proved to be a false start, but it can and has provided valuable lessons for the Chicano movement to draw on in later years.

At the time of the 1963 revolution, Chicano enthusiasts were proclaiming that Crystal City was merely the beginning of what was to happen in all of South Texas and in other areas where Mexican-Americans were a majority of the populace. Instead of that happening, however, in the elections two years later the chicano slate was beaten. Not only had they failed to capture the rest of South Texas; they had failed to hold even their base of Crystal City. An examination of the situation and circumstances in the community, however, would have shown that the town was in several respects quite different from other communities in South Texas. These differences were absolutely crucial to the success of the movement in 1963. Because of the town's composition and because of particular historical and economic factors, the town was a powder keg of a unique kind.

First, the town was overwhelmingly Mexican-American to an extent that is not common even for South Texas. For the county of Zavala as a whole, the 1960 census showed 74.4 percent of its inhabitants were Spanish-surnamed. This ranked the county as seventh in the state of Texas in terms of percent Spanish-surnamed. The town of Crystal City, however, has been far more heavily Mexican-American than the rest of Zavala County. The most common estimates place the percentage of its 9,000 residents who are Mexicanos at around eighty-five percent. To find Mexican-Americans in such high numbers in a community the size of Crystal City is not at all common in South Texas.

But it was more than this concentration that was unusual about the town: it was the way the town was ruled, given its heavy percentage of chicanos, which made Crystal City such a powder keg. There were a few other moderate-sized communities in South Texas—Laredo and Eagle Pass being two—where such a high concentration of Mexican-Americans could be found. But these communities, both situated on the border, were older communities with well established Mexican-American families who had always played an important part in governmental affairs. Crystal City, however, was another kind of town. It was a twentieth century town, where Anglos had always dominated and where the Anglos had never been tempered by the need to compromise with the Mexican-American. The town was not founded by Spanish explorers or by later Mexican settlers. It was created by the break-up of the Cross-S ranch

in the first decade of the century. The decision to break up the ranch and the selling and the buying of plots of land were all carried out by Anglos. The town's founding fathers and civic leaders were thus exclusively Anglo.

As is most common with twentieth century South Texas towns, Mexicans were brought in and recruited by the Anglos to work the fields, perform menial labor, and provide the economic base off which the Anglos could make their money. The Mexicans were not supposed to be real citizens of the community. They were recruited to perform the tasks the Anglos told them to do, and if they didn't like it they could always "go back to Mexico." The Anglos themselves were aware of these differences between "their" Mexicans and those of the older, established towns along the border. As one Anglo said to me, "They look different, these Mexicans." Tending to be more Indian than Spanish, tending to be newcomers to the northern side of the Rio Grande, and often having come to Texas by less than legal means, these Mexicans made for much easier control than the old established families along the border. Desperately in search of work of any kind and hoping not to be deported, these Mexicans were not in a position to think of themselves as or to act like citizens of Crystal City.

The degree to which Crystal City was an Anglo-run community with such a heavily Mexican population made the town more nearly unique than general to South Texas. But this situation in itself was not explosive so long as the Mexicans did not think of themselves as people able to challenge the Anglos over issues, run for office, and in general partake in the running of a democratic society. With the levelling off of the economic boom to Crystal City and the whole Winter Garden area during the depression, however, the town's population began to stabilize. Mexicans from the south side of the Rio Grande no longer poured into the city in search of work. As employment opportunities slackened, more and more Mexicans began to take the initiative and head north for employment during the summer as a means of finding more work and of overcoming the seasonal nature of the work in Crystal City. By the 1950s it is estimated that close to one half of the Mexican-American community's population were migrant workers for at least part of the summer. Although many left the migrant trail to settle in other parts of the country, most considered the town their home and always returned in the autumn. But as migrants they began to encounter different experiences and different ways of being treated from those they encountered in South Texas. Being isolated during much of the year and earning wages elsewhere made them less susceptible to Anglo values upon their return. They were somewhat set apart in the community, more difficult for the Anglos to attempt to acculturate or to control.

Those Chicanos who remained in Crystal City all the year were at the same time improving themselves. More and better Mexican schools were established, and the Mexican-American population, both on its own and through the help of Anglos, gradually began to improve its position relative to that of the Anglo. Although there was not even a school for Mexicans until 1925, and through the 1930s there were almost no graduates from high school, by the late 1950s more than half of those graduating from high school were Mexican-Americans. And this occurred while the ratio of Anglos to Chicanos remained basically the same.

Related to the upgrading of the Mexican-American community in Crystal City, and with hindsight perhaps the most important economic development in the town, was the establishment after the Second World War of a large California Packers plant, later to be renamed Del Monte. This plant, which by its very magnitude centralized much of the vegetable growing in the area, was California-owned and was used to dealing with workers throughout the nation. In being owned from outside the area, the plant was subject to some very un-South Texas ideas. The most radical of these was the plant's decision to allow unionization, as all their other plants were unionized. By 1956 a small Teamsters union was established at the plant and was recognized without any friction by the company. The decision by Del Monte to move into Crystal City and establish a large plant, although it was welcomed by many in the city's agricultural-business establishment, ultimately weakened these local Anglos' ability to control the situation. Having a large-scale plant employing hundreds of

workers and then allowing the workers the opportunity to unionize set Crystal City off even further from other South Texas communities.

Even with these three potentially explosive ingredients—an overwhelming majority of Mexican-Americans in the process of improving themselves relative to the Anglo, an Anglo-run community, and a Teamsters union—the situation in the community remained ,close to the same for nearly a decade. No doubt many Anglos realized that complete Anglo dominance could not continue forever, but taking the initiative to alter the status quo was difficult for farsighted Anglos to do. L. L. Williams, the city manager for three decades, was one of these who recognized that the situation would eventually change, and he set about in several ways to bring a few Mexicans into the government, if only to protect the Anglos from a more massive engulfment. By the early 1960s a small but growing Mexican-American middle class had developed and was being consulted on many matters. But it was still quite small, and owing to the history of the community, it was still quite fragile. Neither the Anglos nor the great majority of Mexican-Americans themselves looked to this group for leadership.

The spark that set off the explosion in Crystal City was in fact an Anglo. Andrew Dickens, a retired oil-field worker, moved to Crystal City in 1961 and thereby proceeded to set up a doughnut shop. This in itself was hardly a radical step, but it turned out that Dickens' shop was located on property the city wanted. Dickens considered himself to have been "taken" on his property lease by the city, and when he tried to get help in fighting the arrangement, he found that both the city government and the county government were in agreement. He could get nowhere. Outraged, he vowed to the mayor and the county judge that he would work to turn the place over to the Mexicans in order to beat the "machine."

As a start Andrew Dickens contacted the union at the Del Monte plant and talked to its business agent, Juan Cornejo. These two, together with several others from the union, talked over the idea of organizing against the city government. They then journeyed to San Antonio to talk with the President and Business Manager of Teamsters Local 657 of San Antonio, Ray Shafer. Until that time Shafer had not been interested in putting his union on the line in Crystal City, but when the possibility of success appeared, Shafer was interested and told the group to begin by launching a poll tax drive.

With the help of outside organizational expertise, consisting particularly of Carlos Moore and Henry Munoz of the Teamsters, and including bookkeeping which allowed some of the Mexicans to pay their $1.75 in installments, the poll tax drive turned out to be extraordinarily successful. At the end of January, a whopping 1,139 Mexican-Americans had paid their poll taxes while only 542 Anglos had. This contrasted starkly with the previous year's figure of 792 Mexican-American and 538 Anglo poll taxes. Thus it was not just that the Teamsters had been unusually successful in their drive; this had occurred at the very time Anglo poll taxes had remained stationary. A quirk of fate allowed the Chicanos to increase their registration greatly without any "backlash" in Anglo restraints, and this alone may have been enough to make the difference between victory and defeat for the Mexican-Americans. The able city manager, L. L. Williams, died in the fall of 1962 and was replaced by James Dill. Dill was not familiar with the situation in Crystal City as L. L. Williams had run it. Previously it had been the practice to watch very closely poll tax payments as they were coming in. The town's Anglos were quite aware that they were in a minority, and a group of the town's businessmen and agricultural leaders had set up a contingency fund to be used to buy Anglo poll taxes if the Mexicans began buying too many. As was related to me, more than once the mayor of the city and other city personnel asked the new city manager how the poll tax payments were coming, and he assured them that he would check and that things were under control. James Dill did not check. The result was the disaster of several hundred Anglos not paying their poll taxes at the very time Mexicans had dramatically increased their number of eligible voters.

When the results of the poll tax drive were made known, Shafer of the Teamsters became even more interested, as he and everyone else working on the drive now sensed victory. Shafer drove down to Crystal City and called the first of several strategy meetings. But the choosing of candidates to run became more difficult than they had expected. A number of people declined to run, some through fear for their jobs and some through fear for their families. At the same time apparently the middle-class Mexican-Americans in the community would have nothing to do with the movement. The organizers were thus forced to comprise a slate of those few candidates who were willing to run. The five candidates, called *Los Cinco*, were Juan Cornejo, the business agent for the Teamsters at the Del Monte plant; Manuel Maldonado, a clerk in the local Economart store; Antonio Cardenas, a truck driver; Reynaldo Mendoza, operator of a small photography shop; and Mario Hernandez, a real estate salesman. None was well-known in the community; none had graduated from high school. None was in any of the Mexican, much less the Anglo, middle class organizations.

Along with the selection of candidates, the strategists faced another major problem—how to play down the influence of the teamsters in the election. By 1963 the Teamsters were in serious trouble with the United States Government, and the mere mention of their name evoked horror to most of the Anglo community. Being a labor union was bad enough, but being the Teamsters was even worse. Ray Shafer and two of his most trusted lieutenants, Carlos Moore and Henry Munoz, devised a two-fold plan to try to deflect the focus in the election from the Teamsters. Although earlier they had tried to conceal the identity of Teamster organizers, Anglos had eventually discovered them. Something more geared to active campaigning was needed. First, a local campaign committee was organized, called the "Citizens Committee for Better Government." This local organization thus channelled most of the outside help. Secondly, the Teamsters approached the Political Association of Spanish-speaking People (PASO), which was a new, militant political organization that had originated from the Viva Kennedy Clubs during the 1960 presidential campaign. PASO had been having serious troubles following its disastrous attempt to wield influence in

Texas, and a number of its leaders believed that in order to establish a more solid base, the organization needed to concentrate its activities at the local level. Crystal City fit in with this strategy brilliantly. By commissioning the help of PASO, the Teamsters were able both to get valuable help and to deflect some of the attention from their own involvement. Albert Fuentes, the state executive secretary of PASO, and Martin Garcia, a district director who was employed by the Teamsters, became the main PASO contribution to the campaign.

With the naming of the candidates and the establishment of the local campaign organization, the campaign had broken out into the open. Although worried by the developments taking place in their town, the Anglos still had reasons to be confident. Not only was the weight of tradition completely on their side, but owing to the quality of the Mexican candidates, the middle-class Mexican-Americans were staying rather firmly in line.

After *Los Cinco* had filed, several of the community's most prominent Anglos approached the local Mexican Evangelical Baptist Minister, Arnold Lopez. Explaining to him that the five candidates running were unqualified and not representative of the "better Mexican element" in the town, they convinced the minister that he ought to run for office. Whether these men's motives were to be able to vote for a responsible Mexican-American who was also concerned for the welfare of his community, or whether they rather wanted to split the Mexican vote, is not clear. None of the Anglos who came to the Reverend, however, were close to the mayor and his administration. But when the minister began launching attacks upon the five candidates, charging that they were being managed and run from outside and that they were unqualified, it became clear that his support might come more from Anglos in the community than from Mexicans. At this point the same Anglos who had talked Reverend Lopez into running came to him again and urged him to withdraw because he was splitting the anti-Teamster vote. In refusing to withdraw at this point, he added an uncertainty to the Anglo problems of retaining control in the community. And this problem was heightened by the entrance of another independent candidate, Dr. Henry Daly, who also refused to withdraw from the race.

These independents emphasized problems the Anglo establishment faced in trying to retain control of the community. The old leadership had never been seriously challenged, although a number of Anglos themselves felt that newer, more innovative leaders were needed. Like most small communities in America, its younger citizens often left the community to seek better opportunities elsewhere, thus perpetuating the old rule. Because of the form of government—a weak mayor and council with a strong city manager—the offices of mayor and councilmen were not very appealing and went unpaid. The current mayor had been in office since the Twenties, not so much because he wanted to continue to be mayor but because no one else in the Anglo community seemed interested in taking his place.

Little had happened in the town government in the decade before 1963. Only two developments had occurred which seem to have had an impact on the town's government. The first was the veterans land scandal, which was a statewide scandal involving several people high in the Shivers administration. A program intended to help veterans obtain land had instead been used by interested land speculators to buy land that the state thought was going to veterans. It had also been used to get the state to buy land for veterans from the realtors at grossly inflated land values. In Crystal City the scandal turned out to be a rather blatant case of Anglo land speculators using Mexican veterans to obtain more land or money for themselves by "buying off" the veterans' right to the land. More than one Mexican in the community mentioned that this scandal was the first time the Mexicans in the community had followed local government or had realized that the local leaders were engaging in activities which other Anglos considered to be illegal. The immediate results of the scandal were rather small, however. It was rather something for the Mexican community to remember at a later date.

The second development in the community over the decade preceeding the revolution was the city government's decision to apply for and use urban renewal funds for a renovation of the city. The town had long been one of the poorest in the state, with almost no streets in the Mexican sections paved and with less than half the town having sewage connections. In 1950 the average Mexican-American twenty-five years of age or older had received slightly over one and one half years of education, and their average family income was considerably less than $2,000 a year. The decision to apply for urban renewal and to float bonds was not prompted so much by these statistics, however, as by city statistics showing that the city was not dying but was growing more rapidly than at any other time since before the depression. The decision to adopt an urban renewal program was made in 1957-1958, but the program was proceeding at a snail's pace and was having only limited impact on the community by 1963. Nevertheless the reaction of many in the Mexican community to urban renewal was one of hostility toward the condemning of their homes and the relocations that might be forced on them. Most important of all, the city government was now making itself more conspicuous to the people, Mexican-Americans as well as Anglos, migrants as well as permanent residents.

Viewed from this perspective, both urban renewal and the land scandal were liabilities to Anglo rule because they dispelled apathy toward local government. And under any minority government such as existed in Crystal City, apathy is an essential element of stability, whether that apathy is caused by basic agreement with the way the government is handling itself or whether it is caused by a feeling of hopelessness regarding change.

The old Anglo elite in Crystal City quickly had to realize in 1963 that the traditional apathy toward local government was being shattered. Their reaction, which had been remarkably lenient throughout the poll tax drive, now stiffened. Here were outside agitators, Teamster agents and militant chicanos from San Antonio, coming into their community to stir up the Mexican-Americans, organize them, and forge them into a powerful challenge to the decades of Anglo rule. A series of incidents followed, testing the very foundation of a democratic order. First there was trouble in filing for the elective posts. When the five Mexi-

canos went to file for office, the city clerk had "run out of forms." *Los Cinco* surmounted this problem by typing their own forms, which were accepted. The most serious incident occurred at the Del Monte plant during March, with less than a month to go before the election. Several employees were dismissed "for wearing campaign tags." How this incident was handled provided another instance of the crucial role the Teamsters played. Normally in South Texas such firings would have been final, and the men would have been without jobs. Had these workers in Crystal City lost their jobs now, in the middle of the campaign, the morale of the workers would have plummeted and fear would have become central for all those involved in the campaign. But the Teamsters, now more than ever willing to put their prestige on the line, interceded with the company and warned the management that the workers would have to be reinstated. This victory for economic security in the face of political activity bolstered the campaign activities of *Los Cinco* and the morale of all their supporters.

While the harassment was proceeding, and perhaps partly because of it, the campaign began to take on a tone that was most unusual for a city election: the issue of discrimination was raised. Mexicans began charging that they had been discriminated against on city improvements, such as the paving of streets and sewage connections. They noted that no Mexicans had ever been members of the city policy force and charged that local justice was such that Latins were punished more severely than Anglos for the same offenses. Rumors spread that the city's swimming pool, which apparently had been segregated until recently, had been disinfected each time after the Latins used it. These charges put the Anglo community on the defensive, and they began denying that there was racial discrimination now, although many admitted that there had been in the past. But the Anglos did not stop here. They charged that outside agitators were coming into the community to stir up the Mexicans, and they argued for local control of the community.

Both the general charges of the Anglos and of the Mexican-Americans were essentially correct. The charges against the Anglos of discriminating against Latins on street pavement and sewage, however, would have been more correct had the Mexicans charged that there was discrimination against the poor rather than against Mexican-Americans. Crystal City's decisions concerning these matters was based upon the normal American practice in local government of determining whether or not one was rich enough to afford to pay for it. Of course in actual practice this meant that paved streets and sewage connections were located overwhelmingly in the Anglo areas of town, but it upset the Anglos greatly that the Mexicans should have charged discrimination based on race when in fact concerning these city functions it was discrimination based only on poverty.

As to the Anglo charges that outside agitators were coming into the community to mastermind the Latin campaign, this was patently true. Teamster and PASO expertise was being used throughout the campaign, and was crucial from the beginning. The five candidates had had no experience in running campaigns, and they were watched and coached carefully on what to say and what not to say at rallies. This understandably infuriated the Anglo community and was an embarrassment to better-off Mexicans.

Two further issues developed out of the campaign itself concerning questions of discrimination. During the campaign the local Lions Club announced that it would be supporting an all-Anglo Boy Scout troop. Whereas this normally would have proceeded with scarcely a stir, it was seized upon by organizers and used as proof of Anglo discrimination. A further incident occurred late in the campaign. Martin Garcia, the PASO-Teamster organizer, was asked to leave from a restaurant after having ordered a beer, and he immediately charged racial discrimination. In fact the incident was somewhat manufactured: the management did not serve beer without food, and when informed of this, Garcia asked for a piece of bread with his beer. At this the management asked him to leave. The management did of course normally serve Mexicans, but it was also most reluctant to serve the kind of Mexican that Garcia was. Realizing the value of such an incident, Garcia in effect created it. Both these incidents emphasized the difficulties the Anglo

community faced in confronting the Mexican campaign. If the campaign was to be run at all along democratic lines, without relying largely on intimidation, it meant that at the very time Mexicans were getting belligerent, Anglos had to be very careful not to engage in discrimination against them.

Discrimination, then, became the major issue of the campaign, as one would have expected with an all-Latin slate running in a community overwhelmingly Mexican-American yet governed by Anglos. But by 1963 the Anglos no longer ruled by blatant discrimination against all Mexican-Americans. Indeed there was already one Mexican, Salvador Galvan, on the city council, and another councilman, Ed Ritchie, was part Mexican. The schools, which had been segregated at the elementary level for many years, were no longer segregated on criterion of race. Thus the issue of racial discrimination was in several respects quite different from the more clear-cut, obvious discrimination existing in the South between Negroes and whites. In Crystal City discrimination revolved more around questions of class and of culture than of race. Anglos were quite willing to admit that social discrimination against Mexicans did exist. But the great majority of Mexicans were not concerned with whether discrimination was based on "subtle" distinctions of class, culture, and social factors rather than upon race. They knew they had been discriminated against, and that was enough.

As the campaign approached its last few days, both Anglos and Mexicans increasingly realized that los Mexicanos were becoming more and more involved: *Los Cinco* rallies were now drawing hundreds of supporters. In response Anglo women organized a telephone committee to get all 542 Anglos to cast ballots, and the Anglo leadership engaged in more harassing tactics.

They called upon the Texas Rangers to come into Crystal City to maintain order. For over a century the Ranger concept of maintaining order had been quite different from the Mexican-American's idea of what this should entail. Bringing in the Rangers might have panicked the Chicano community into being afraid to turn out for rallies and vote. But again in a brilliant tactical move the Teamster strategists decided to circulate the fallacious rumor that they themselves had requested the Rangers in order to insure that there would be order in the community for the rest of the campaign. This rumor was not as implausible as it might now seem, because talk had been circulating throughout the town that there might be wholesale violence against the Mexican activists. Although Captain Allee of the Rangers was extremely upset over the outside agitators in Crystal City, this fact was kept fairly well-hidden until after the election, both by Allee himself and by the Mexican activists whom he visited.

One final harassment occurred when the city government refused to allow poll-watchers during the election. There had, of course, never been any before, and the city saw no reason for them now. When Carlos Moore, who specialized in Texas election law, showed the city authorities that part of the election code which specified the right of candidates to have poll-watchers, the city relented rather than face legal action.

The campaign from the beginning had been a series of Anglo mistakes, caused first by overconfidence and later by inability to decide upon a coherent strategy to counteract the Mexican activists. And the campaign had been a series of victories for los Chicanos. Morale in their community was running high and confidence in their right and ability to challenge the city fathers was increasing by the day. The initiative had been so taken by the activists that middle-class Mexicans were beginning to feel pressured. Several even put up signs supporting *Los Cinco,* but the great majority of those better off continued to side with the Anglos against the "rabble" trying to run for office. In fact Mexican and Anglo businessmen were so closely aligned that the week before the election the Mexican Chamber of Commerce joined the Chamber of Commerce in sponsoring the following advertisement:

We believe that city government should be local, representative government.

We believe in continuing the excellent racial relationships we have attained over the years and are against tactics designed to create racial issues.

We believe in voting for men who through their education, knowledge, business experience and good judgment are best qualified to handle the city's affairs.

Although the advertisement did not specifically endorse the incumbents, it was obvious to all that if one's criteria for voting were going to be a candidate's education and business experience, there would be no contest at all.

The amazing aspect of the Crystal City election, and that which made it such a radicalizing election, was that the Mexicans of the city were not listening to their own "leaders." The historical weakness of the local middle-class Mexicans and the independence of the city's migrant workers were clearly being felt. Enthusiasm for *Los Cinco* and respect for their courage in challenging the Anglo leadership was increasing. By election eve the final campaign rally for *Los Cinco* drew somewhere from 1,500 to 3,000 enthusiastic supporters. Again outside support was prominent as leading San Antonio liberals such as State Representatives Jake Johnson, Rudy Esquivel, John Alaniz, and PASO organizer Albert Fuentes spoke to the crowd, increasing both their confidence and enthusiasm. A letter from Albert Pena, head of PASO and a county commissioner in San Antonio, was circulated which stated that *Los Cinco* were "the only true 'Mexicanos' in the race for the City Council." This remark caused tremendous resentment in the Anglo community. Anglos, who were already upset that their opposing candidates were all Latin, charged that Pena's letter was further proof that it was the Latins, not the Anglos, who were discriminating.

Election day was long and tense, but with no real incidents. Trying different tactics, Anglo agricultural leaders suddenly doubled wages for that day to $2.00 an hour for those working in the fields. Certainly the possibility of making $2.00 an hour presented a painful choice to families who had little money to spare. Del Monte also announced suddenly that it was going into overtime production on election day. In both instances because of careful organization and outside assistance, this did not prevent the Mexicans from voting. With Del Monte, the Teamster organizers pointed out that even on overtime the company had to allow the workers the opportunity to leave their jobs temporarily to vote. Not to do so would have been a violation of the contract and an invitation to legal action or a strike, as the Teamster organizers made clear to the management. Because the Teamsters were willing to use their muscle, the management complied. To handle the wage increases in the fields, the organizers made sure that all drivers were to return with their workers by the early afternoon, vote them, and then return them to the fields. By setting the time early enough in the afternoon, the organizers would have time to send someone else out to bring in the workers should the original driver be lured into staying. As it happened, however, all the drivers returned from the fields with plenty of time to spare. Election day was in fact an impressive show of organizational strength by the Teamster-PASO coalition. From poll lists to see who had voted, drivers to bring people to the polls, cards with the candidates' names, and even a marked string to help illiterates know which of the seven candidates to scratch out, the Latins were so well prepared for election day that as many people voted in the city council election as had voted in the entire county in the Nixon-Kennedy presidential race three years before.

The Anglos spent the day uneasily eyeing the long voting lines. The Rangers patrolled throughout the city, but did little more than make themselves visible. Late that night the results were made known, and they electrified the town and South Texas. Soon they received national and international publicity. Los Cinco had swept to victory in a close count, defeating all five incumbents. The results were as follows:

Manuel Maldonado	864
Juan Cornejo	818
Mario Hernandez	799
Antonio Cardenas	799
Reynaldo Mendoza	795
Ed Ritchie	754
W. P. Brennan	717
Bruce Holsomback	716

J. C. Bookout	694
S. G. Galvan	664
Dr. Henry Daly	164
Rev. Arnold Lopez	146

Unfortunately for those who had worked so hard to bring about the electoral victory, governing the community turned out to be far more difficult than winning the election. The nature of the victory—the inexperience of the candidates, the dependence upon outside help, and the vulnerability of the Mexican community in a town which had always been dominated by Anglos—came back to haunt all those who had worked for the success.

The day after the election, Manuel Maldonado, the top vote-getter on the ticket and the man ironically most respected by the Anglos, lost his job at the Economart store. Anglo pressure had been strong enough that his employer reluctantly caved in. Another member of *Los Cinco*, Antonio Cardenas, found that his wages were halved from $77 to $35 a week. Within a few days a third member of *Los Cinco*, Mario Hernandez, had turned against the other four and began echoing the charges the Anglos were leveling at the council-elect. Ranger presence not only continued in the town after the election, but it became obvious to all that the Rangers were most upset with the election results. Captain Allee remarked that he was only trying to keep outside agitators from coming into the community, but of course outside agitators were essential to the whole movement.

This vulnerability of the Mexican community also had its impact on the selection of mayor for the town. By tradition the candidate named mayor was to be the one with the highest number of votes. This would have been Manuel Maldonado. But after Maldonado was fired, the next highest man, Juan Cornejo, actively sought the post. Aided by his connections with the Teamsters and the job security that this afforded, Cornejo managed to persuade the rest of the council to elect him mayor. This came at a time when journalists from all over Texas, Mexico, and the nation were becoming increasingly interested in what was happening in Crystal City. From being a dutiful worker at the Del Monte cannery, Cornejo was thrust into international publicity with what turned out to be disastrous results. The sky now seemed the limit to him. But the city charter was constructed so that the city manager, not the mayor, ran the city. Although the Teamster-PASO coalition managed to find an excellent, independent Mexican-American engineer named George Ozuna to become the new city manager, he was to run into trouble from Cornejo. Cornejo could never understand why he, having been elected mayor, should not be running the city. In the struggle to follow, it became increasingly apparent how much the whole institutional procedure for governance was premised upon middle-class and business-oriented Anglo ideas.

In the face of overwhelming publicity and wholesale Anglo resignations from the city government in the hopes that the new government would topple, George Ozuna thought that his most important task was to keep the city government running and to prove to the Anglos and to the world that the Mexican-Americans could govern Crystal City efficiently and justly. Cornejo, however, looked upon his assumption of leadership and upon the Anglo resignations as an opportunity to put his friends into office. His concept of government was more that of a traditional boss politician, or *patron,* who was interested in establishing a machine of the sort that other areas of South Texas had known. ... In the end George Ozuna and Juan Cornejo remained deadlocked because of certain procedural regulations in the city charter. Not only did the city charter provide that the councilmen should receive no salary, under the assumption of course that only sufficiently wealthy people would be councilmen; it also prohibited council members from being in debt to the city on any of their bills. Fired from jobs, unable to find work, and increasingly in debt, the council members had to face this crisis as best they could. The two who couldn't make it and were expelled from the council by the courts were part of Cornejo's three to two majority in favor of firing Ozuna. Thus the government stayed deadlocked with both Cornejo and Ozuna remaining in office. This struggle between Ozuna and Cornejo and the

two different concepts of government they represented went on until the end in 1965. This feud greatly weakened the strength and prestige of the new government and gradually reduced the image of Cornejo, who after the victorious election had been viewed as a hero and savior. ...

The unity under which the whole electoral campaign had flourished so amazingly now crumbled under Anglo threats, inducements, and the wave of publicity that changed the lives of all the men involved. The city government was swept from one difficulty to another. And somehow lost in the personal squabbles and rivalries were the numerous improvements the city government had made in such areas as paving, lights, sewage, police policy, and job opportunities.

While this battle within the Chicano camp was raging, the Anglos were increasing their own activity. What overconfidence and inactivity they had displayed earlier during the campaign were quickly overcome. When an investigation of the election failed to turn up grounds for calling another election, the Anglos devised the strategy of forcing a recall vote. However, Texas law required that in order to have a recall election a majority of those who voted in the election must request that a new election be held. The Anglos could not hope to get this many people to sign for a recall. Instead they devised a plan which was nothing short of brilliant in its ability to weight the procedures of governance in their favor. Calling their petition not a recall petition but a "charter revision," so that only 10 percent of the voters would have to sign, the revision proposed to increase the number of seats on the council from five to seven. All five councilmen would be forced to run again with the added stipulation that the election was to be held on October 1st, before all the Mexicans working in the fields up north would return. Although the district judge agreed completely that the petition was a "charter revision" rather than a recall petition, legal appeals managed to postpone a decision until the October deadline passed and the question became moot.

Although stymied in this attempt to use institutional procedures to throw out the government, the Anglos also set up a new organization to prepare for the next elections. Realizing that they could no longer rule as they had before the revolutionary election, they assiduously began courting the favor of the "better Mexican element." They were aided in this strategy by the new government's inexperience in ruling and inability to keep together a winning coalition. For example, shortly after the election representatives from the Mexican Chamber of Commerce approached the Cornejo administration in a conciliatory manner. When they were rejected by the new government, which quite understandably resented these businessmen's support of the old Anglo administration, the middle-class Mexicans had little alternative but to combine with the Anglo leadership. Together they formed a powerful coalition. This in itself would probably not have been enough to bring down the new government had it remained united, but once the militants' organization began to crumble, the Anglo-Latin business team assumed a commanding position. By nominating a slate of three Mexicans and two Anglos, and by promising to bring stability and local control back to Crystal City after the two years of bickering and shattered hopes, the new coalition was victorious. Mayor Cornejo and his battered and divided forces were crushed by a united, confident coalition of Anglos and middle-class Mexican-Americans while the Teamsters and PASO stayed out. Shortly afterwards George Ozuna was asked to resign. In losing, however, Cornejo received more votes in 1965 than he had in 1963. A turnout even greater in 1965 than in 1963 signified that although Cornejo had lost, Chicanos had solidified their role as participants and that the *ancien regime* could not be restored.

The lessons of this first Crystal City revolution lie in the nature of the revolt. From the beginning the revolution was dependent upon outside support and assistance. Because of the lack of opportunities and consequent inexperience in the local Mexican population, the Teamsters and PASO shouldered the questions of organization and of strategy, at the same time devoting little time to the question of what kind of government the new government should be and what goals it should strive for once it was in power. When faced with choosing candidates to run, the organizers were forced to choose from the very narrow field of those willing to run. Both the Teamsters and PASO hoped they were getting candidates they would be able to work with and continue to advise, if not also control. But because of their very success, new factors came into play—questions of what type of government the city should have, and questions concerning the need to keep receiving advice and consent from these outside organizations. Much of the failure must rest on the shoulders of Juan Cornejo. . . . But to blame a man of such limited experience for failure to carry through under conditions of tremendous difficulty and extreme pressure, having to use institutions designed much more for Anglo businessmen than for a semi-literate worker, is somewhat misleading. The Crystal City story of 1963 was a story of failure more because of the very inexperience and lack of opportunity which had produced these very leaders. The lesson to be learned would seem to be that in the end force of change and of revolution is contingent upon the local people who must do the leading and the following. And here the vicious circle of inequality and inexperience cuts in, for the ability of the local people is conditioned by the type of rule they have known. For the Chicano political movement in the future, more effort would need to be spent building up local, indigenous organization and leadership. For outside expertise to slight this factor would invite disaster. The uniqueness of the Crystal City organizational base of Teamsters supported by migrants was enough to win an election, but it was not enough to govern. If it was the uniqueness of Crystal City that allowed for the revolution in 1963, it was its very similarity with the rest of South Texas—similarities regarding poverty, inexperience, and vulnerability—that brought about its downfall.

John Shockley

Crystal City: La Raza Unida And The Second Revolt

After the Chicano takeover of Crystal City in 1963, throughout South Texas the town became a symbol of hope and pride to Chicanos and of fear to Anglos. Although the town's political revolution ultimately ended in defeat, Crystal City was to continue to be a pace-setter for Chicano politics. A second political revolt, occurring in the spring of 1970, was destined to have a far greater impact upon the community and upon politics in South Texas than did the first. Clearer goals, a different organizational base with a different strategy for mobilizing the Chicano community, and a vastly different kind of leadership all seemed to make this revolution far more exportable to the rest of South Texas.

The first revolution, it should be noted, did have as its goals the elimination of discrimination and the securing of Mexican-American representation in the community. But between 1963 and 1969 throughout the Southwest a great deal of thinking about the purposes of a Chicano movement had taken place, spurred on in part by the rising militancy of the Black movement. Integration became less of a goal than the recovery and protection of a Chicano identity. A rebirth in history led to an increased awareness of the Chicano's prior claim to the Southwest, which in turn led to an increased militancy and to a greater confidence in confrontations with "the gringo." In the process of seeking to become the "masters of their own destiny," new organizations were founded with new leadership and new goals. The most visible of these new organizations in South Texas was the Mexican-American Youth Organization (MAYO), which was founded in 1967. Composed of young militants, often quite well-educated, MAYO adopted as goals a program to fulfill "the destiny of La Raza." These goals consisted of forming third parties separate from either the Democrats or the Republicans, gaining control of the educational systems in Chicano communities, and ending Anglo economic domination by the development of their own businesses and cooperatives. Chicano experience and intellectual thought had thus developed a great deal in the six years between 1963 and 1969, and this had its impact on Crystal City.

74

The second revolt in Crystal City differed from the first in that it was organized around specific examples of discrimination in the school system. Instead of being based as in 1963 upon the anomaly of the Teamsters Union, the second revolution had its organizational base in school children and their families. By mobilizing the family, the new revolution utilized one of the central points of Chicano culture.

The second revolt further differed in that leadership was not based upon outside organizational expertise and inexperienced local representatives. The new revolution was led by José Angel Gutierrez, a young man far more ideological, far more confident, and far more competent than his predecessor, Juan Cornejo. As a native of Crystal City, Gutierrez had gone on to receive a master's degree in political science and had developed his political training and expertise as president of MAYO.

In noting these changes within the Chicano movement, it is still necessary to examine the nature of the rule in the community which La Raza was fighting.

Reacting to the developments in Chicano thought and action throughout the 1960s, Anglos not only in Crystal City but throughout the Southwest became more defensive and began to assert their interest in integration, albeit Anglo-style. With a community of the composition of Crystal City, the Anglos had always been faced with basically only three ways of ruling: outright intimidation, cooptation of certain Mexicans, and the creation and maintenance of apathy. Their rule from the beginning had been a mixture of all three, with a gradual increase in the need for cooptation as the Mexican community began to improve its lot. This was, I should add, not necessarily done either deliberately or viciously. It was quite natural for the Anglo community to begin to extend ties to those Mexicans who were becoming increasingly like Anglos in attitudes and life-styles. But the revolt in 1963 upset the Anglo routine and forced the process to become far more deliberate. From the time of the all-Latin sweep of the city council elections in 1963, the Anglos realized that they could no longer rule in the same manner as previously. Common, ordinary Mexican-Ameri-

can "rabble" were now used to voting and to participating in the government. With a fundamental and permanent change in the voting rolls and in Mexican political behavior, the Anglos realized as never before that they simply had to have Mexican support in order to win. What emerged was a coalition with the "better Mexican element" which allowed these Mexicans to shoulder as much of the visible concerns of the town government as possible. This coalition became all the more necessary as traditional means of intimidation became less effective, both because of changes in federal and state laws and enforcement, and because the Mexican community was becoming better able to counter this intimidation.

From the successful defeat of Cornejo in 1965 until the second Chicano revolt, a majority of the city council was always Mexican-American. The town's Anglo leadership always made sure that a majority of its council candidates were Mexican-Americans. But as time passed the elaborate organization the Anglos had developed with middle-class Mexicans in opposition to Cornejo gradually began to wither. This happened both because of Anglo overconfidence and through the increasing disenchantment Mexicans began to feel with the policies of the local government and the manner in which the Anglos still treated them. Realizing how much the Anglos needed them, many Mexicanos who had originally felt that a coalition was needed to get rid of Cornejo now began to feel used. They began to doubt the sincerity of Anglo claims of integration and coalition government, particularly via the issue of discrimination in the schools.

Throughout the history of the community, progress had taken place in the schooling for Mexicans. Anglos offered this as proof of their sincerity and benevolence and as proof that any Mexican who really wanted to work could get ahead. In the early days there was no school at all for Mexicans. After 1925 a series of small Mexican schools were set up around the community. Those Mexicans who continued beyond elementary schools were then able to enter integrated schools. After the famous Supreme Court decision in 1954, the Anglo elementary school was integrated with a few Mexicans and the tiny handful of Negro children in the community. But continuing up until 1960 the only integrated school in the community was the Anglo elementary. The other elementary schools were totally Chicano. In 1960 a protest over the policy of continued de facto segregation led to a breakup of the system, although Anglos still tended to be separated from Mexicans in individual classrooms. This protest, which involved around 500 Mexicans under the leadership of the Mexican Evangelical Baptist Minister, Arnold Lopez, and a mail carrier, Gerald Saldana, surprised the Anglo community. The board and administrators at first indicated intransigence, but once it became clear that Mexicans were protesting and that legal action seemed imminent, school authorities quickly gave in. Having accomplished its goal, the first mass action by the Crystal City Chicano community quickly disbanded.

At the same time as *Los Cinco* Mexicanos were running for the city council in 1963, two Chicanos also ran for places on the city school board. Jesus Maldonado and Lorenzo Olivares came within a few votes of ousting the two Anglo incumbents four days after the city council election. In this campaign, however, discrimination in the schools was not a primary issue. It was more a question of gaining representation for the Latins, who had never had a member on the school board in the history of the city. The fact that the school district also encompassed some rural areas of the county, made up almost completely of Anglos, is probably the main reason the Latin candidates lost the school board election in 1963 at the same time they were winning election to the city council. The closeness of the vote, together with the shock of having elected an all-Latin city council seemed to influence the all-Anglo school board. Within the year one member resigned his post and overtures were made to one of the defeated candidates to see if he was interested in being appointed. He told them that he could never accept appointment rather than election to the board because he would forever feel indebted to them. The Anglo board did finally find a Latin willing to be appointed, however, and from that time on first one and then two Mexicans were always on the seven-man board. This maneuvering seemed successful because through the rest of the decade never

again did a Latin slate run against the incumbent board, even as city council seats were hotly contested.

While this successful cooptation was occurring on the school board, the school faculty was gradually increasing its contingent of Mexican-American teachers. From a faculty around 10 percent Chicano in 1960, by the fall of 1968 over one fourth of the faculty were Mexican-Americans. The dropout rate for Chicano children also declined. Although for the 1951 entering class of first-graders only nine percent graduated from high school, of the entering class in 1958 17 percent graduated. So there was improvement, but to many Mexicans the rate of progress seemed slow indeed. A dropout rate of over 80 percent was by national or state standards phenomenal, and even as the faculty composition changed gradually, all principals remained Anglo. The faculty ratio itself also remained enormously unreflective of the composition of the student body, because as the dropout rate gradually declined, the student body became increasingly Chicano. By the fall of 1968 nearly 87 percent of the student body was Chicano.

The spark which set off the second revolt was the election of cheerleaders at the high school in the spring of 1969. For most of the history of the community cheerleaders had been elected by the student body. As more and more Chicanos began to enter high school, however, the system was changed so that a select committee of the faculty would choose who they thought were the best cheerleaders. Because the Anglos could afford to send their daughters to cheerleader training schools, judgment on the basis of competence almost always meant that Anglos were selected. An unofficial system was devised so that three Anglos and one Mexican girl were always chosen. In the spring of 1969 the normal, routine practice again occurred. This time, however, two of the Anglo cheerleaders had graduated leaving vacancies and a Mexican girl, Diana Palacios, was considered by the student body to be as good as any of the Anglos trying out. The Mexicans, however, already had their "quota" in Diana Perez, so the faculty judges again chose two Anglos to fill the vacancies. The system of discrimination in the selection was thus exposed to the student body in an unusually clear manner. Since the protest was over the retention of the status quo, however, this also indicated that along with the basic developments in Mexican-American thought in the 1960s, Chicanos were becoming increasingly rigorous in their definition of what constituted discrimination.

After the new cheerleaders were announced, a group of Chicano students protested to the high school principal. He considered the matter a bunch of "phooey." The students then went over his head to the school superintendent, John Billings, at the same time increasing their demands to other issues involving discrimination. Billings discussed the matter with the students and agreed to adopt an explicit quota system for cheerleader selection: three Anglos and three Chicanos. The other demands, concerning the election of twirlers, high school favorites, and the establishment of bi-lingual and bi-cultural education, were met either with more quota systems or with a commitment to "check" what other communities in the area were doing.

The reaction of the Chicano students to their meeting with Billings was mixed, but most of them were pleased with what had occurred. Open segregation with separate but equal treatment seemed about the best they could hope for. Although throughout this period of agitation there had been talk of a walkout, none occurred, and Billings considered that he had been successful in avoiding a walkout. Dampening the students' desire for a walkout as well, however, was the realization that since school was almost over they would have little leverage and might all be flunked. The Anglo reaction to Billings' concessions was generally one of concern and disapproval, and a group of Anglo students went to see him. The old method of cheerleader selection seemed fair to them, and they feared that by pandering to the hot-headed students Billings might be opening a pandora's box. That June in fact the school board nullified Billings' concessions to the students and also passed a resolution dealing sternly with student unrest. With school closed and with many students and their families on the migrant trail, nothing was done to protest the board's reversal of the superintendent's policy.

But this action seems to have strengthened the hands of radical students by exposing the weakness of the school superintendent and by making the board appear completely insensitive to Chicano students. Word spread among the students that the board had cancelled the agreements, and plans for a school boycott were again discussed.

That same month José Angel Gutierrez and his wife returned to Crystal City from San Antonio, at the close of his tenure as president of MAYO. They returned hoping to put into practice the principles of the militant youth organization and immediately set about re-establishing connections and recruiting a staff to coordinate the effort, not only in Crystal City but in the neighboring counties of the Winter Garden area. His timing was important. In the spring elections of that year, before the school agitation, the all-Chicano slate had made its poorest showing since its 1963 victory. To increasing numbers of Chicanos new leadership and new issues seemed necessary if they were to beat the Anglo-backed coalition.

But for Gutierrez becoming the leader in the Chicano community was neither obvious nor immediate. His ideas and those of his staff were examined and their leadership was tested in numerous discussions and meeting places around the community. Fundamental to their strategy was a Saul-Alinsky-type interest in direct confrontation, and through this they hoped to expose, humiliate, and "eliminate the gringo" as the Chicano community united.

Although the school system continued to be the issue to mobilize the community, that fall a new example of school discrimination presented itself. The Crystal City High School Ex-Students Association decided to have their own queen and court at the annual homecoming football game. In previous years they had always considered the football queen to be their queen as well, but to increase interest in the organization, the Ex-Students decided to have their own election. Again hoping to further interest among Ex-Students, and with possibly other motives as well, the organization established a rule that for a girl to be eligible to run in their election, one of her parents had to have graduated from the Crystal City high school. Chicano students, already restive over the unresolved issues of the spring, seized upon this issue as a clear-cut example of Anglo discrimination, and the ruling was quickly labelled a "grandfather clause." As the discussion of the history of Mexican-American education in Crystal City should have made clear, very few of the Chicano students were daughters of parents who had graduated from high school. In fact of the twenty-six eligible candidates, only five were Mexican-Americans. When Superintendent Billings gave the Ex-Student Association permission to have their coronation at the homecoming game, school board complicity in the discrimination seemed clear.

In early November Mexican-American students and parents presented to the board a list of grievances, headed by the demand that the Ex-Students not present their queen at a school-sponsored event because of the association's restrictive clause. At the packed board meeting Gutierrez, now a consultant to the students, threatened that if the crowning of the queen did take place, students would disrupt it. Under the pressure of disruption by an increasingly organized Chicano community, the school board reluctantly voted to deny the Ex-Students Association the right to the field. This granting of the students' most explosive demand did not take momentum out of their protest. Because the board had so clearly reversed itself only under Chicano pressure, it was made to look weak. Having won one of their demands, student attention now focused on those which had been objects of contention since the preceeding spring. The board had postponed a decision on the other demands until their December meeting, hoping no doubt that the protest movement would cool off over the ensuing month. Anticipating that the board would turn them down on their long list of demands, however, students began preparing for a boycott. Enthusiasm and determination among the students grew during this period, helped by numerous rallies and the reaction of the Anglo community. By developing a siege mentality, uniting in the face of such a hostile threat, the Anglo community seemed to support all the radical students' claims of discrimination. Although many of the Anglos thought the Ex-Students Association had made a colossal tactical blunder, even more thought the

board had "sold out" and knuckled under to the pressure, and scathing attacks were made upon those Anglos who were thought guilty of being soft. The minister for the most influential church in the Anglo community, the Reverend Kenneth Newcomer of the First United Methodist Church, had worked tirelessly in his two years in the community to develop a spirit of reconciliation in his totally Anglo congregation. Now, however, he was to see his congregation slowly but surely pull back from any form of compromise in the face of such an obvious radical threat. By reacting in such a manner, the Anglos were helping to polarize the community in exactly the manner the radical Chicanos wanted: "gringo" versus Chicano.

When the school board met in December, the board announced that it felt the charges of discrimination as set forth in the remaining demands were false, and that the board would therefore grant none of the demands. At this the students presented a new list of grievances, even longer than the first, and told the board it would have to face the consequences of refusing to act.

The next morning the school strike began. By the end of the first day over five hundred students were picketing and a number of parents had gathered nearby to protect their children and help keep them orderly. The boycott became larger and more effective with each passing day, and journalists and television commentators poured into the community. Parents were standing solidly behind their children. For both parents and children the concern was to prevent the children from suffering the indignities the parents had endured. In this manner the confrontation was strongly buttressed by a united family structure.

The school board realized that it would have to do something. The boycott was too effective to be ignored. Representatives from the Texas Education Agency in Austin were invited down and the board proposed to set up a meeting with parents of the striking students. The board refused, however, to talk to the striking students. To have sat down at a negotiating table with a bunch of teenagers, much less Mexican rabble, was too much for the school board to stomach. This angered the students, who felt that they should be the ones to discuss the matter with the board. They also realized that their parents would be more vulnerable to the board because of lack of education and fear for their jobs. Parents stood fast with their children and refused to attend the meeting, and conditions remained at an impasse. A churchman's committee was formed from Catholic, Methodist, and Baptist clergymen and laymen in the community to try to bring about dialogue between the two groups. In the end it was unsuccessful because of polarization within the group and the resentment of the school board and administrators towards the purpose of the group. With tensions mounting and the community divided, attempts by local people to negotiate became doomed.

Having chosen what to the Chicanos were clear-cut examples of discrimination in the schools, the radicals also increasingly succeeded in immobilizing many of the middle-class Mexicans who were in the city government. The moderates' sympathy with many if not all, of the students' demands left them paralyzed, unable and unwilling to help the intransigent Anglos. As a consequence the Chicano community was more united than probably at any time in the history of the community.

As the week passed, the boycott spread even to elementary school children and publicity grew. By the last day before the Christmas holidays, from half to two-thirds of the entire school enrollment were absent from classes, but still no negotiations were taking place. Bolstering the publicity and the morale of the strikers, educators from around the state converged on the community to teach the striking school children during the Christmas holidays. Through the offices of Senator Ralph Yarborough, arrangements were made to fly three of the boycotting students to Washington. There they met with Yarborough and with officials in the civil rights divisions of the Departments of Justice and Health, Education, and Welfare. The Justice Department eventually became involved through its community relations service and two mediators were sent down at the invitation of both the board and the students. Through several days of tense and bitter negotiations, the Justice Department mediators eventually hammered out an agreement acceptable to the students and the board. Continuing support and involvement by the students and their families in the boycott led the school board to capitulate on practically all the demands. But also involved were the increasing publicity about the walkout, state and federal presence (if not pressure), and talk that Chicano supporters from the area were going to converge on Crystal City to add strength to *la causa.* With the resolution of the conflict, the most successful Chicano walkout in the history of Mexican-Americans in the Southwest had ended. No disciplinary procedures were taken against the striking students and they did not receive unexcused absences with resulting grade penalties. The board agreed to pursue the establishment of bi-lingual and bi-cultural programs in the school system, agreed to try to find new means of testing preschool youngsters, and consented to cheerleaders and nearly all school favorites being elected by the student body. Dress codes and the censoring of the student paper were to be reviewed. The board even consented to the establishment of an assembly period on September 16th, the Mexican national holiday. Except for a few points, such as the election of twirlers, the students had scored a stunning victory.

As with the victory over the Ex-Students Association in the preceeding months, however, this success did not cause momentum to subside. The greater clarity and ideological nature of Chicano goals were again revealed when toward the end of the boycott, the Chicano community began a selective economic boycott. The targets were a Chicano school board member unwilling to support the strike and an Anglo business which had tried to pressure the students by firing two of his employees involved in the strike. Although the boycott did not last, this reversal of economic intimidation further threatened the security of the Anglo business community and also threatened Mexican-American businessmen who were not willing to help in the strike.

School policies, economic domination, and soon political offices were all involved in this broad movement to unite and bring self-determination to the Chicano community. Building upon their successes, the strike organizers continued to proceed after another MAYO goal, the formation of La Raza Unida party. School board and city council candidates not only filed in Crystal City, but in the neighboring counties of Dimmit and La Salle, where organizing efforts were also taking place. With school policies now so much in the forefront of political concern, mere Mexican representation on the board became totally inadequate. Control of the school system and redirection toward Chicano needs became the goal, and Gutierrez headed a slate running for the three positions up on the seven-man board. But a sweep of the five-man city council was no longer possible. Changing the political set-up so as to discourage a repeat of the 1963 disaster, the Anglo and middle-class Mexican coalition had successfully adopted a charter change to provide for overlapping positions on the council, alternating three seats up one year with two the next. For the spring elections in 1970, only two of the five council seats were up for election. As it turned out, La Raza Unida party was extremely lucky to have even two candidates running. Discouraging poor candidates, the city charter included a requirement that any candidate for the council must be a property owner. Shortly before the commencement of absentee voting, the city attorney and city manager disqualified Pablo Puente, one of the two Raza Unida candidates, because he did not own property. With help from the Mexican-American Legal Defense Fund the question was immediately taken to court. As the Anglo city fathers had no doubt expected, the Fourth Court of Civil Appeals ruled that the question of putting Puente's name on the ballot was moot because balloting had already started. Appealing the case to the federal courts, attorney Jesse Gamez of the Legal Defense Fund claimed that such a decision by the Court opened the door to fraud. Any community, he argued, could wait until just before the start of absentee balloting to deny a candidate a place on the ballot for any of a number of clearly unconstitutional practices and could do so successfully because the question would immediately become moot. With Puente agreeing to forfeit the absentee ballots, the Federal Judge ordered Puente's name placed on the ballot barely in time for the election.

The anti-La Raza Unida coalition, although demoralized by the school strike, fought vigorously, if not always completely legally. For the council the two incumbents, one Anglo and one Mexican-American, chose to run for re-election. For the school board, significantly, all three incumbents chose not to run again. Their position in being opposed to the Chicano demands and yet capitulating had left them in a peculiarly vulnerable position from both sides. Nominated to take their places by the anti-strike coalition were two Mexican-Americans and one part-Mexican, part-Anglo. This in itself was a further move toward accommodation of Mexican-Americans by the Anglo community, but again as in 1965 the Anglos had decided to run a slate with a preponderance of Mexican-Americans only after an explosive issue had mushroomed in the community. The reaction of the local paper throughout the election campaign was also indicative of greater accommodation. Whereas in 1963, 1965, 1967, 1969 the *Sentinel* editor had run front-page editorials warning of community disaster should non-business, unqualified candidates win, in the 1970 election the *Sentinel* had only a short, perfunctory editorial the last issue before the election. Because the owner, an Anglo, had long been identified with the ruling Anglo group, it was apparently felt that to have run editorials again would have been counter-productive. Increasingly in the community, far more so than in 1965, it was felt that Mexicans themselves would have to tackle the militants. More than ever before, Anglos had to work behind the scenes and through Mexicans who were sympathetic to their cause.

The town's industrial establishment, however, did place large unsigned advertisements in the local paper, in English and Spanish, saying that to improve the economic welfare of the town industry was vitally needed. This was something which nearly all residents could agree upon, but the ad went on to say that

> Industry officials seek a community with harmonious relations and a stable government. They avoid areas where there is agitation by militant groups which could hinder their progress. The working people of Crystal City hurt themselves when they vote for candidates for the school board and city council who are associated with militant groups that are unfriendly to industry.

The implications contained in this advertisement referred not only to new industry but to current industry in the town. In 1963 after Los Cinco Mexicanos won office, one of the packing sheds in the city moved to a nearby town. Word was being spread by Anglos that the huge Del Monte corporation might close down if the city tried to make it pay any taxes. In fact this seemed unlikely to happen. Although Del Monte's profit figures were kept secret, their Crystal City plant reputedly had a higher margin of profit than any of their other plants in the country.

In the face of such activity by businessmen, one might have expected the Teamsters Union to have been in the forefront again in support of the candidates against the city's business establishment. But in contrast to 1963 the Teamsters Union at the Del Monte plant was completely inactive. Feeling within the plant and in the Chicano community at large was increasingly that the Teamsters were trying to use and to control the Chicanos rather than to help them. Although this feeling stemmed from the firing of Mayor Cornejo as business agent for the union in 1964, it was increased by the Teamsters' reluctance to stand up for Chicanos when their jobs and rights were repeatedly being violated. By 1970 the union had moved full circle into being dependent upon management, not workers, for support and encouragement in the face of efforts to de-certify it and form a local Chicano union.

Being thus based almost completely upon the local Chicano community made the second revolution both more remarkable and more far-reaching. In not having the resources of the union to call upon, the similarity of Crystal City to other communities in the area was emphasized more than the town's uniqueness. The issues of the campaign thus emerged as the school strike, the Raza Unida movement, and the character and ideas of José Angel Gutierrez, who increasingly became the most visible of all the candidates. But in opposing Gutierrez, his adversaries could not use the main arguments levied against the 1963 revolution. As a native boy well-known in the community, Gutierrez could not be called an outside agitator or labelled a puppet of anyone. Charges that he was inexperienced could hardly be made after the masterfully executed strike. Charges that he was uneducated and unqualified could not easily be made against his eighteen years of education and two degrees. Instead the opposition centered their attack around the claim that Gutierrez and the ideas of La Raza Unida were "un-American" and dangerously radical. . . .

To counter some of the charges during his campaign, Gutierrez showed at his rallies such things as autographed photographs from Ted Kennedy and George McGovern, and his invitation to the Nixon-Agnew inauguration. But his major issues were those that related to the school strike, the MAYO goals of self-determination, and all that the community had experienced in the last year.

In terms of campaign organizations and get-out-the-vote drives, both sides were extremely well prepared. As an indication of voter interest, the turnout was considerably higher than in the 1968 Presidential election. Gutierrez and his running mates, Mike Perez and Arturo Gonzáles, won with around fifty-five percent of the vote. Three days later Ventura Gonzáles and Pablo Puente, his name now on the ballot, were elected to the city council with margins of slightly over sixty percent. In nearby Carrizo Springs and Cotulla the results of La Raza Unida work also produced victories. These were perhaps more remarkable because neither town had ever gone through the political mobilization and trauma which Crystal City had known from 1963 to 1965 and during the school strike. Such victories in nearby towns confirmed the belief that the second revolt was based upon strategies far more exportable to other South Texas communities, but the degree of success in these other communities is not yet clear. At the electoral level, at any rate, La Raza Unida had been stunningly successful.

Although their electoral success was unquestioned and their intellectual competence and expertise were in marked contrast to the first election of Mexicans in 1963, there were again serious difficulties to be faced in governing. In the first place, only a minority of the total number of seats on the city council and school board were up for election. On both boards, however, a critical swing vote was provided which allowed La Raza Unida candidates to gain control of the governing bodies. In three years on the school board, Eddie

Trevino had gradually evolved into a quiet, one-man opposition to the board's policies. Although he was originally appointed by the Anglos on the board, he welcomed the victory of the La Raza Unida. Francisco Benavides, who had been an independent voice on the city council, also swung over into support for La Raza Unida. Although he had originally been asked to run in 1969 by an influential Anglo politician, he had never been closely associated with the dominant Anglo ruling group. These two men gave La Raza Unida a 3-2 majority on the city council and a 4-3 majority on the school board. Although these developments could be considered as strokes of luck, they were clearly more than that. In the aftermath of the strike there was considerable social pressure being brought to bear by members of La Raza. Benavides, as the owner of a grocery store, could not have been unaware of the consequences which might follow from his refusing to join forces with La Raza Unida.

The loss of Trevino and Benavides to the opposition, in marked contrast to what happened in 1963 when one member of *Los Cinco* became a renegade, demonstrated the fundamental problems Anglos faced in trying to co-opt Mexican-Americans into their leadership. If Anglos picked Mexicans that were absolutely trustworthy, they could also be sure that such Mexicans would carry little weight in the Chicano community. If they picked men who were independent and respected in the Chicano community, then Anglos would not be able to rely on them in critical situations.

La Raza Unida thus surmounted its first hurdle, gaining a workable majority on both councils. But the lame-duck council and the school board had both done their best to tie the hands of the incoming officials. The city council had quickly voted to grant the Del Monte Corporation a seven-year reprieve on being annexed into the city so that they could continue to pay no taxes. And the school board shortly before the election had hired under three-year contract a new school superintendent, John Briggs. To try to void each of these actions, the newly-elected officials had to become embroiled in legal controversies. In working to bring changes into the community, the new council and school board increasingly had to resort to legal

pressure. Simultaneously they had legal pressure brought to bear against them by the losing Anglos.

The extent to which the legal system was crucial to determining the degree of change in the community was no more clearly illustrated than in the contest to take control of the county in November, 1970. In January of 1970, both for ideological and for practical reasons, La Raza Unida was organized as a third political party. If their candidates had chosen to run as Democrats, as the Cornejo slate had done in their losing attempt to gain control of the county in 1964, they would have had to pay expensive filing fees and would have had to run in May, when many of the migrant workers had already gone north. By running as a third party in the November elections, La Raza Unida hoped to avoid both these problems. But the Texas election code is unclear at best, and misleading or contradictory at worst, on what procedures a third party must use to get on the ballot in a specific county. When county officials refused to place the names of La Raza Unida candidates on the ballot, the party filed suit. After an enormous amount of legal maneuvering and appeals, the party still could not get on the ballot. The only action left was for the party to conduct a write-in campaign. Owing to the nature of the procedures for write-in votes under Texas law, such a campaign was doomed. Stickers could not be used; names had to be written in. In a community where many, if not most, of the Chicano community were functional illiterates, getting them to write all their candidates' names correctly and in the proper place was an insuperable task. All the candidates lost although in several cases the write-in candidates captured more than 40 percent of the vote. Doing this well may have been a symbolic victory for La Raza Unida, but the incumbent county commissioners and county judge, all Anglo, were re-elected. Because terms were for four years, La Raza Unida could not hope to gain control of the county for at least another four years. Thus in spite of all the activity, mobilization, and involvement in the Chicano community, with highly able and qualified leadership, all county commissioners and the county judge remained Anglo in a county which was three-quarters Chicano. County policy would continue as before. In terms of tax rates, police policy, and welfare policies, the county might have been important in upgrading Chicano life. Instead it stayed steadfastly opposed to the Chicano activists, just as it did in 1963. Without control of the county, one of La Raza Unida's most difficult but most important goals would remain impossible: that of land redistribution. At present almost all the land in the county belongs to Anglo farmers, ranchers, or absentee landlords. Several important Texas politicians, such as John Connally, are important absentee owners in the county. Only through high taxation could the Chicano community hope to get any of this land, or at least get money for improved services.

Significant changes, however, have occurred in Crystal City. In matters affecting the schools in particular, the system has continued to feel the effect of the successful strike. The faculty has changed considerably since the strike, and after resignations and the ending of some of the lame-duck board's contracts, it is likely to change even more. For the first time close to half the faculty is now Chicano. And many of the new teachers, both Anglo and Mexican, are quite different from their predecessors in outlook. Because the Crystal City school district is establishing itself as a beachhead for Chicano power, or as Gutierrez says, for "extending education to the Chicano," the teachers accepting appointment tend to be more or less sympathetic to the aims of La Raza Unida. Bi-lingual education has been started in the early grades, courses in Mexican-American history are being taught, a free breakfast program for children has been initiated and the free lunch program has been greatly expanded. The district is more aware of and more willing to accept federal aid. A Title IV grant has been accepted for the purpose of facilitating integration and increasing faculty sensitivity to problems Chicano children face in the school system. The school district has refused to allow army recruiters onto school premises or to permit any employee from serving as registrar for the Selective Service System. Further emphasizing their anti-military policy, the school board has hired a draft consultant who has had training with the American Friends Service Committee. In support of the César Chávez lettuce strike, the school board has refused to allow

non-farm workers union lettuce to be served in the cafeteria.

Although these policy changes are important, the school district remains severely limited in its financial resources. The problem has been compounded because Anglos in the community have begun to withhold their school taxes. Coming at a time when the board is trying to institute new policies, this has placed further limits on what the board can do. For example, textbooks not recommended by the state adoption committee must be paid for by the local district. In trying to counteract the traditional Anglo story of Texas history told in textbooks, and in trying to bring new books for Spanish and for bi-cultural courses, the board has found itself without the money for any extensive book buying. Although over one hundred Chicano dropouts have returned to school on their own following the change in administration, the board still has not been able to inaugurate a program designed to bring into the schools the estimated 10 percent of Chicanos who are legally of school age but who are not in school. Again owing to limited financial resources, building facilities remain overcrowded and inadequate. Any new building program would require the use of bonds, yet it is quite possible that given the nature of the school board, bond companies would be reluctant to buy the bonds should the local district approve their sales. Recent investigations by the Texas Education Agency found numerous deficiencies in the implementation of the migrant program. They further criticized several aspects of the school system in general, such as the absence of the teaching of patriotism in the schools. Because of the board's reluctance to use standardized tests on its children, alleging that they are discriminatory in favor of middle-class Anglo precepts, the school district has run into continued pressure from federal and state authorities. With the board employing so many new ideas and new personel, many disruptions of normal school activities have occurred, particularly concerning where and when classes would be meeting. At present, the goal of many Anglos is to get the Texas Education Agency to revoke accreditation to the district. This move would have a shattering effect upon the schools, among other things denying them federal and state funds. From this turmoil and example of mis-management, Anglos with sympathetic Mexicans might be able to oust the incumbent board members. But denying accreditation to the school system is most unlikely, partly because it is such a drastic step. The future rather seems to be one of continued innovation, severely circumscribed by the limited resources of the district, and by both the regulations and the rewards of state and federal resources.

In the city government important changes have also taken place. With the hiring of Bill Richey, a former VISTA worker and close friend of Gutierrez, as city manager in the early summer of 1970, the city had an educated, efficient administrator and a tireless worker for La Raza Uñida. Richey's Anglo background made him an anomaly in Crystal City and yet made charges of "reverse racism" against La Raza Unida less credible. Since taking office he has improved the quality of the city's staff and police force and has hired and trained Chicanos to the extent that now Chicanos are holding positions they have never held in the city bureaucracy before. But the city itself has also been hampered in much that it is attempting to change. Their ability to annex the large Del Monte plant on the edge of town is still being settled in the courts, and in attempting to change policy in the huge urban renewal project they have also run into legal difficulties. The massive urban renewal program has poured millions of dollars into Crystal City. Throughout its existence since 1958 it has been run by Sam Anderson, a former relator. Although Anderson has been an able director willing to use the numerous funds from the federal agency, he is resented by the Chicano militants for his close ties to the Anglo business world and his reluctance to hire Chicano contractors. Also resented is the awareness that along with the progress, urban renewal has uprooted people and forced a number of families to move into other slums. How much this is the fault of the director and how much the fault of the program itself is more difficult to determine. As a step towards ousting Anderson as director, the new city council tried to appoint two new commissioners to the urban renewal board. The mayor, who was a holdover from before the spring election, refused to appoint the new members even though it was the wish of the majority of the council. In trying to oust the mayor so that their appointments would be valid, the Raza Unida majority was reprimanded by the federal authorities in San Antonio, who cut off all urban renewal funds. However the crisis is revolved, it is another example of the constraints put upon the activists seeking to change policy as well as personel.

In the area of attracting industry, the city administration was also trying to pursue a new policy. Richey claimed that the Crystal City Industrial Foundation and other business groups were interested in attracting only certain kinds of industries, those wanting cheap and non-union labor such as textiles. He has tried to get government contracts, especially through provisions of the Small Business Administration which allow for minority group businesses to get contracts even if their bids are not competitive. Citing the large amount of federal military spending in San Antonio, Richey hoped to attract some of these jobs to Crystal City. Attracting industry and jobs has remained a critical problem for the city and is compounded by the lack of opportunities for migrant workers in the north. Because of continued mechanization in the fields, the future for the migrant worker is dim. Hoping to stem the departure of the jobless from Crystal City to the urban ghettos, Richey has noted, "We've got to get industry or repeat the saga of the Blacks migrating to the cities." The success of this effort to attract jobs to Crystal City will take longer to determine, as economic development will take longer to bring about than educational reform or political change. But in terms of the future of the community, this will be the most important factor in determining the success of the revolution. As in most of rural America, young people of Crystal City, both Anglo and Chicano, have been leaving the community in search of better opportunities elsewhere. The decline in population for the county between 1960 and 1970 emphasized this problem. Certainly the new administration has been aware of the problem and has been trying to handle it in ways the Anglo elite either was not aware of or was not willing to try. But ultimate success will depend upon far more than the community's willingness to try new approaches. It will depend on industrial attitudes and on what kinds of federal programs are available. At this level between 1963 and 1970, however, important national developments have aided the reformers, particularly the tremendous increase in aid to education and the war on poverty. National foundations and churches have also become much more aware of problems of poverty and discrimination and have been willing to help out in Crystal City, in both public and confidential ways. These changes have made the leadership far less vulnerable to local economic intimidation than was the leadership in 1963, but these national organizations have at times also been quite concerned about the militancy of the leadership.

From this review of the school, city, and county governments, it should be clear that any assessment of the success of La Raza Unida Party in Crystal City, or its applicability to the rest of South Texas and the Southwest, must be qualified. In comparison with the first Chicano takeover in 1963, the current regime shows tremendous differences. Their goals are clearer and more unified. Their leadership is more confident and experienced. The community now has more resources available to it because of changes in federal policy and national awareness. But tremendous tasks still face the new regime. After a year in office the Chicano community is still dependent to a great extent upon José Angel Gutierrez and the outside people he has brought into the community. Second-level leadership in the Chicano community remains weak, although it is improving in experience. The egalitarian spirit of the revolution and the common struggle in the Chicano community have as by-products introduced women and children into the leadership councils of the movement. Tapping both these resources has already strengthened the leadership. Federal programs and national foundations have been helpful, but they have carried with them serious constraints in being designed much more for incremental change than radical innovation. Owing to these and to further institutional constraints which are placed upon protest organizations, La Raza Unida has been thwarted in important ways even as it has also won astounding victories. It should also be remembered that in Crystal City there are peculiarly auspicious circumstances for revolt: the history of settlement, the Chicano-Anglo population ratio, the heavy concentration of migrant workers, and the large Del Monte canning factory with its historically important but currently defunct Teamsters Union. With these points in mind, it would be both naive and adventuristic to say that the experiences of Crystal City can be duplicated elsewhere. In communities such as the older border towns, where Mexican-Americans have always had an important role in government even as their substantive policies have been oppressive, it is difficult to see how the Crystal City strategy can work without important changes. In communities where a majority of the population is Anglo, not only must the strategy be modified in important ways, but the impact of the rhetoric of Crystal City militants may be damaging to those Chicanos who must work in coalitions.

Finally, even though the goals of La Raza Unida are far more carefully constructed than were those of Los Cinco Mexicanos, the regime will eventually be faced either through success or through failure with deciding upon what the whole policy of self-determination for the Chicano community really means. Just how to relate to Anglo cultural domination, whether and how to blend with it or to fight it or to isolate themselves from it, are questions and are solutions which remain unresolved. How much should the Chicano movement be one of separate cultural nationalism, and how much should it be one which will eventually prepare Chicanos for integration with Anglos as equals? These questions are not unique to Chicanos of Crystal City, of course. They involve fundamental questions facing all cultural minorities and all oppressed peoples. In fact they involve all h man beings, who must in the end decide as individuals what their identity should be.

But the example of Crystal City on its own indicates two points which may be applicable to more of American society: the veneer of democracy, with explosive concerns suppressed beneath this veneer, and the extent to which integration has not only failed but has been used, for good or for evil, to mean cultural domination by one group over another.

In facing all these problems and difficulties, however, the Chicano community can call upon the very resources which were opened up by their struggle in Crystal City: the confidence, the pride, and the feeling of community. Their successes have brought a feeling of control over their own destiny that is simply not measured in terms of dollars spent, legal suits filed, or theoretical problems which must be resolved. The stereotype of a fatalistic Juan Tortilla, a loyal servant happiest when he is stooped in the fields picking spinach, has been shattered for both Anglos and Chicanos. As the Chicano community goes about trying to overcome the enormous problems they must face, this faith in themselves may be their most valuable possession. It will mean that the choice will be theirs to a greater extent than it ever has been before.

David M. Fishlow

*David M. Fishlow is a young newspaper editor in McAllen,
Texas, committed to social and economic equality. This
impassioned account of what Mr. Fishlow believes to be
police brutality is an example of the moral indignation, and
a new type of hard-hitting journalism coming from the more
radical newspaperman.*
Copyright held and reprinted by permission of the TEXAS
OBSERVER.

Pancho Flores Is Dead

Pancho Flores is dead. He was standing on a
sidewalk in Pharr, Tex., with his hands in his pockets, on Saturday night, Feb. 7. Half a dozen witnesses say he was shot by a policeman.

"Full Scale Rioting Sweeps Pharr Streets"
screamed the *Valley Morning Star* the next morning. "Massed Police Quell Youth Riot at Pharr"
said the *McAllen Monitor.* Even the more reliable
Corpus Christi Caller-Times had a double-
column, front page story headed "2 Policemen
Hurt in Clash at Pharr."

No policeman had been shot in the events that
occurred on Saturday night, but when it was all
over, Alfonso (Pancho) Loredo Flores, a 20-year-
old construction worker from Pharr, was dead.
Thirty-one people had been arrested and released

on bail. And Pharr, the Hub City of the Valley, was
a frightening place to live.

Since the "riot," the people have been waiting.
Eight hundred of them marched silently in Pon-
cho's funeral. The streets are quieter at night than
before, especially in the *cantina* district along
North Cage (U.S. Highway 281). Rumors scamper
around town like malevolent rats, stopping to
gnaw first at one soul, then at another.

It started out as a normal, hot day. Saturday
morning is a busy time in most places, with business bustling and traffic heavy on the main streets.
Pharr, where Hwy. 281 crosses U.S. Hwy. 83 before proceeding on to Mexico, is typical. But on
the north side of town, under the water tower, is
the Pharr police station. It used to be a dirty-look-

ing brown, with a poorly painted fist pointing to the "Entrance." Now that it has a fresh coat of white paint, it looks less like the *calabozo* from an Antonio Aguilar movie, but it is still a squat, graceless building.

On Saturday morning, there was a picket line out front. A couple of dozen people, mostly teenagers and young people, with a scattering of children and middle aged working people, strolled up and down carrying signs saying *"Más justicia y menos garrotazos"* ("More justice and fewer beatings"); *"No necesitamos policías salvajes"* ("We don't need savage policemen"); and *"Fuera con Sandoval y Ramírez"* (Get rid of Sandoval and Ramirez").

The picket line had been planned by a group of local people working with community organizer Efraín Fernández. The issue—police brutality—is an old-fashioned one, but one which permeates every kind of public activity here in Pharr. In this town, you don't muck around with the government or the police, and when you do, there is bound to be trouble.

Chicano families have long complained about beatings in the Pharr police station, and in recent weeks the complaints have been more frequent. Guadalupe Salinas, 24, is a slender warehouse worker who got picked up at a service station a couple of weeks ago, was hauled into the police station and came out with blood all over his shirt, cuts, bruises and a black eye. He told whoever would listen that he had been beaten by Sgt. Mateo Sandoval, a smooth-talking ex-Harlingen cop whose sworn testimony in federal court has been known to differ substantially from versions offered by other witnesses I believe to be reliable.

A week before Salinas made his charges, 44-year-old Manuel Mata of Pharr said his two broken ribs were the results of a beating by Sandoval.

Daniel Vasquez is a disreputable-looking Pharr man in his early thirties and with some serious emotional problems. He often walks around town with a briefcase and a necktie—neither very common around here—and announces himself as president of existing and non-existent organizations. Vasquez has complained on several occasions that he was beaten by Pharr police, and the attorneys who investigated the complaints believe that his charges are true.

Others, too, have complained of beatings and brutal treatment in the Pharr jail. Noé Rocha, 23, told a reporter from the Spanish-language paper *¡Ya Mero!* he once was sprayed with some kind of gas by the police, and after he was thrown in a cell the only water available to wash the stuff off was from the toilet.

Police Chief Alfredo Ramírez is a tall, white-haired sharpie who likes to appear in court in a bright green suit and red cowboy boots. He, like every other city employee in Pharr, is utterly dependent for his job on R. S. Bowe, the balding, 60-year-old mayor and, as the front man for the little political machine that rules here, the undisputed czar of this community".

Saturday's picket line followed several meetings among the Mexican-American community. Though the protest was ostensibly directed against Sandoval and Ramírez, the issue goes far deeper. Basically, there is no representation for the poor people who constitute the vast majority of Pharr's 15,000 residents. The city commission is a rubber stamp for Bowe; I have been unable to find in the city records a single negative vote on any issue whatsoever in the minutes of all meetings held since 1966.

Special meetings are almost as common as the regularly scheduled ones, and notice of commission meetings is sometimes forgotten. The only jobs in town or in the area are in the fields, and the agricultural interests pull most of the strings. The Bentsens and others own huge tracks of land in the area, and the gas and oil wells bring in money for the owners, but little gets to the people. Until a month ago, the head of the welfare department was an unsuccessful candidate for sheriff who spoke not a word of Spanish and had no training in social work.

For several years there has been a parade ordinance on the books which defines "one or more persons" or "one or more vehicles" moving down the street as a "parade," subject to the regulation of the Mayor, who has the option of issuing a permit if he approves.

Once Federal Judge Reynaldo Garza asked Chief Ramírez, "If two women from the League of Women Voters walked up and down in front of City Hall with signs saying 'Register to Vote,' would you arrest them?"

"I would," said the chief.

"Well," said Judge Garza, "we public officials may not like picketing, but people have a right to do it." He then proceeded to instruct the good chief in some basic principles of Constitutional government:

"If they want to walk up and down outside the federal building with signs saying 'Judge Garza is Unfair,' I may not like it, but there isn't a thing I can do about it." Not exactly an earth-shaking statement from a federal judge, but Mayor Bowe, Chief Ramírez, and their lawyer, looked stunned.

By Saturday, though, they evidently had decided that they, unlike Judge Garza, *did* have something they could do about it.

The picketing had been relatively uneventful all day. Though Efraín Fernández and 14-year-old Daniel Magallán had been arrested in December for picketing city hall, this time the police made no arrests.

All afternoon, they' lounged in the doorway, slack-jawed and grinning, bellies bursting the buttons of their too-tight blue uniforms. Nobody in Pharr speaks English except on official occasions, and the cops made jokes in Spanish, laughed at each other's gross humor, and made cracks at the young girls on the picket line.

Chief Ramírez, in sporty-looking "civvies," paraded around with a camera hanging from his neck as he, Sergeant Sandoval, and other officers photographed the pickets. The chief left several times during the day, oozing his big, gold-colored Monte Carlo in and out of the dusty police parking lot as the pickets parted to let him through.

Mayor Bowe, the most elusive public official south of Austin, as usual, was nowhere to be seen. Though he is a full time mayor ($400 per month plus "expenses") he keeps no regular office hours, and is frequently hard to find.

As it grew later, a large crowd, perhaps two or three hundred people, gathered across the street and on the sidewalk east and west of the police station. Perhaps two thirds of the spectators were teenagers and children, who laughed and hooted at each other's jibes. By evening the picket line consisted of about a dozen adults and a dozen children. Mrs. Virginia Ramírez, a middle-aged lady, convinced one of her friends that they, too, should picket because *"sería más respectable tener unas*

señoras ahí. No es cosa de puros chavalos." (It will look more respectable to have some ladies over there. This isn't just a thing for the kids.")

The kids were singing some jingles they had made up for the occasion, none of them particularly respectful to the police, but certainly not obscene. One, in Spanish, was to the tune of "I've Been Working on the Railroad":

> *Que hermosos son los marranos;*
> *Que hermosos son . . . oink, oink.*
> (How beautiful are the pigs,
> How beautiful they are . . . oink, oink.)

Another was in English, and sung to the tune of "Who's Afraid of the Big Bad Wolf?"
Sandoval's a big fat pig, a big fat pig, a big
    fat pig;
He likes to beat the people up, the people
    up, the people up;
We have to stop the beatings now, the
    beatings now, the beatings now,
and so on.

Then Daniel Vásquez, whom everybody in town knows as an amiable crank, began making up little ditties, and the crowd loved them. *"¿Qué te pasó en la cárcel?"* he sang, and then answered his own question: *"Me caí, me caí, es todo."* ("What happened to you in the police station? I just fell down, just fell down, that's all.") The hooting and hollering grew louder, and the police started looking edgier, but there was no physical abuse of anybody, no rock-throwing; just noise.

About 7:30, Chief Ramírez came out of the station and approached Fernández. Since the conversation was official, it was in English:

"Mr. Fer-nan-deez, your people are being abusive. This is not longer a peaceful picket," Ramírez said. The picket line moved around him and Efraín as they talked. Efraín was furious, but determined to keep hold of himself.

"They're just yelling," he told Ramírez through clenched teeth. "That's how they feel, and they're just yelling." And then he added: "If you leave them alone, nothing will happen. Just leave them alone and nothing will happen. They're just yelling . . ."

Ramírez turned on his heel, and went back inside. Soon sirens could be heard and a couple of white Pharr fire engines from the station across the tracks pulled into position behind the police station. (The firehouse in Pharr is on the "right" side of the tracks; the police station and jail, of course, are on the "wrong" side.)

A police car pulled into the middle of the street, and from an unseen loudspeaker, like the voice out of the whirlwind, came the anticipated announcement:

"This is no longer an authorized picket," or something to that effect. "You are hereby ordered to disperse. If you fail to disperse, further action will be taken." Maybe a third of the people present—those who speak English and were old enough to know what "disperse" means—understood, but the crowd whistled and hooted its answer. The police car pulled away. Tension grew. As the door of the police station opened and closed, I could see a group of men talking to the police. They were the same bunch that had been drinking beer on the back porch of the nearby Texas Bar during the afternoon. Sergeant Sandoval came around the building as the fire engines moved up to take positions on either side of the police station, facing the street.

"Have they been warned?" he asked. Somebody answered "Yup." The pickets kept moving, but it was obvious what was going to happen. One picket went to lock a portable tape recorder in the trunk of his car.

Suddenly the high pressure nozzles were opened, and firehoses drenched pickets and spectators alike. All became chaos.

The kids in the crowd unloosed a barrage of rocks and bricks picked up in the vacant lots near the police station. The crowd surged back and forth, and the pickets ran from behind the parked car where they had taken refuge from the water and rocks. But *El Loco* Daniel stopped running, turned around, and started to throw a brick at the police car behind which the pickets had "hit the deck."

In the midst of the water and rocks, with hundreds of screaming kids to choose from, Ramírez ran out of the police station and jumped Daniel. He was joined by two or three cops, and they hustled the terrified, struggling Daniel into the jail.

Witnesses later said they literally threw him into a cell.

Most of the crowd moved west, toward the main highway. Suddenly the shooting started. We could see rifle barrels sticking up from behind the police car parked near the door.

"*Son tiros de salva!* It's blanks!" somebody yelled. The crowd flowed back and forth, with most of it ending up on 281, swirling up and down the sidewalks in the midst of the *cantina* district.

Ramírez, probably on the O.K. of the invisible Bowe, called for reinforcements, and he got them from everywhere, it seemed, except San Juan, the next town east. Soon Pharr was a crazy battleground with only one side armed. Texas Rangers, DPS officers in gray uniforms, local police from McAllen in riot helmets, Hidalgo County sheriff's deputies and others driving around, running through the streets with night sticks and guns, and clearing the *cantinas* and stores.

Bullets were being thrown around like confetti, and whoever had yelled they were blanks was a wishful thinker. As firing and tear gas filled the streets, the Saturday night crowd became reluctant to leave the bars. Soon tear gas was being fired into some of the establishments. An M. Rivas supermarket was cleared when it became filled with the choking fumes.

"Pepe" Saldaña and another man each had several shots fired into their pickups. Night sticks got plenty of use. But hardly any windows were broken; no policemen were shot; none of the people were armed.

And one of the cops shot Alfonso Loredo Flores. Witnesses are unanimous in saying Flores was a bystander. A newspaper photo of him lying in a pool of blood in front of Stan Ramos' barber shop, show his hands still in his pockets.

Now the people are waiting, and they are not overly optimistic about "justice" being done. Just two months ago, a Cameron County sheriff's deputy shot a 14-year-old kid, Victor Nava, in the back of the head. It was self-defense, the deputy said; he thought Victor was coming at him with a knife, which later turned out to be a stick about a foot long and maybe half an inch in diameter. Other kids testified Victor was shot as he ran away. The grand jury returned no indictment. The FBI is investigating. Sheriff Boynton Fleming said it was a fine example for other lawmen.

Now, another kid is dead. He was 20 years old. He had a wife and a daughter aged three months. He had just found a construction job in hurricane-ravished Corpus Christi and was commuting on weekends. He was in Pharr on Saturday night. He went to see what all the commotion was on North Cage. He was shot.

They took him to McAllen General Hospital, and from there to Harlingen, and they told the papers he had been hit with "flying missiles." He died Sunday night. The doctors dug the fragments of a lead slug out of his head. They were sent to a ballistics lab, but supposedly they are too battered to show the gun from which they were fired.

By early morning, 31 people had been arrested and taken to Edinburg for arraignment before Justice of the Peace Jim Wilson.

By the time the Monday papers came out, public officials all over the valley were covering their tracks. Just as the hole in Flores's head was supposed to have been caused "by a thrown brick," now dents in one of the fire engines "appeared to have been bullet marks, indicating lawmen weren't the only ones armed."

Chief Ramírez read invisible Mayor Bowe's statement for the TV cameras. The mayor was conducting his own investigation, and he therefore felt it was "inappropriate" for him or any of the police to comment about the events of Saturday night.

The papers were almost unanimous in saying the rock barrage started the whole thing. Eyewitnesses, including this writer, say that is nonsense.

Soon the wheels of federal justice began to turn, but mostly they were just spinning. Richard Avena, field director of the U.S. Civil Rights Commission's southwestern regional office, arrived Sunday night. Manuel Velasco of the Justice Department arrived Monday morning with his wife, and promptly announced that he was not here to investigate the Flores killing or the causes of the so-called riot, but rather to do followup work on the Nava case from Brownsville. He told assembled relatives of the victim and witnesses that the FBI was investigating, and then he went off to talk

to some of his "good friends and buddies from law school," including Judge Jim Wilson and Pharr city attorney Ramiro Martinez.

Yet on Monday afternoon, the FBI told Avena they could not investigate until they got a formal request from the Flores family. On Sunday, Mayor Bowe said *he* was going to ask the Hoover boys to "make a complete investigation of the facts leading up to the riot, as well as the riot."

César Chávez was in town Monday for a speech at Pan American College and an evening rally for farm workers. What was supposed to be a razzle-dazzle rally was turned into a mournful memorial for Flores.

Chávez was cheered as he called for a boycott of Pharr's businessmen until Ramírez and Sandoval are removed and the police department is brought under control. *"Son los comerciantes que tienen el poder aqui."* (It is the businessmen who hold the power here,") he said, and he reiterated what he had said earlier at a press conference: "All the people wanted was a hearing by city officials. (Fernández had tried for two weeks before the picket to meet with Bowe). Brutality is widespread on the part of the police and one life lost is too much. Such things have to be resolved peacefully, or somebody tries to resolve them the other way. Mexican-American policemen can be as brutal as Anglos."

That, of course, was the crux of the problem. Bowe is mayor by the grace of the real powers in Pharr: a handful of businessmen and growers who hold all the strings. Ramírez and the other cops are all chicanos and utterly dependent on the little Pharr machine for their jobs. In Pharr it is not just the Anglos against the *Raza*, but also the economically powerful against the unprotected.

On Tuesday, some of the businessmen had a meeting with the city commissioners. Father Roberto Flores of the Texas Conference of Churches, one of the three priests who had tried to mediate between youths and police Saturday night, attorney David Hall, who represents the Flores family, and attorney Ben Canales of Austin had been invited to the meeting by the man who owns the little taxi company. The three went to see what kind of communication could be set up between dissidents and the "establishment"; they got thrown out of the meeting.

Judge J. R. Alamia, whose 92nd District Court handles most local criminal matters, called the grand jury together, and charged them with making an investigation. "The scope of your investigation," the judge said, "should be such that no doubt will be left in the minds of anyone but that it was fair, impartial, complete, and conclusive so that it will impress upon people the fact that confidence and reliance can still be placed in our courts and our institutions."

That is going to be hard to do in Pharr. D. A. Oscar McInnis has already asked the D.P.S. to investigate. That, to the *chicanos,* means the Rangers are being called on to investigate the Rangers, and they remember how the big federal Ranger trial of three years ago got all kinds of publicity, but that no judge has even bothered to issue a decision. They also remember how reluctant McInnis himself was to prosecute State Sen. Jim Bates for pistol whipping a Mexican truck driver in 1969, though Bates was later convicted. They remember how Bates was fined a measley hundred bucks.

They are also worried that the grand jury, scheduled to convene Feb. 18, will end up indicting people for rioting instead of taking care of the Flores shooting.

San Antonio City Cmsr. Albert Peña came down quietly on Sunday, Feb. 14, to make a private investigation.

By Wednesday, Feb. 10, the day of the funeral, Pharr was still tense, though an inspection of the business district and the area around the police station would have revealed little evidence of a "full-scale riot" three days previously. The only broken window in view was in the front of the police station, obviously from one of the many rocks thrown after the water was turned on.

Business was back to normal, except that the police had ordered no beer sold after 6 P.M. on the day of the funeral, and the street in front of the police station was once again blocked off Wednesday night.

About 30 monitors were named from among the MAYOS and other young people in Pharr, and they supervised the funeral procession; eight hundred people walking four abreast behind the slow moving black hearse in total silence except for the tramping of feet.

The column moved from De Leon's Funeral Home to St. Margaret's Church for the mass, and from there to the cemetery. There was a collection for the widow, and you could tell the congregation was a poor one: the baskets jangled rather than rustled.

It was not a very elegant funeral by urban standards. Some of the pallbearers wore jackets which did not quite match their pants, and they scorned the fancy collapsible wheeled cart, preferring to carry the casket. The ladies, some of whom I had seen Saturday in the picket line, were more elegantly dressed, but they walked with the same tireless patience I had noted then. They have walked in too many parades and processions to expect much change from that one.

Lupe Salinas was there, wearing a black turtleneck and sunglasses. I had not seen him since he came to complain about Sergeant Sandoval; the bruises and black eye were gone. He, like most of the young people, was subdued, solemn and tired-looking. The only bright clothing around was worn by a TV cameraman from Weslaco, who chose a yellow shirt and white bell-bottoms for the funeral. Most of the women wore *mantillas.*

That night the staff of *¡Ya Mero!* worked late to get the paper out. It was on sale in Mexican grocery stores all over the valley on Friday, stores kept calling for more papers. *"La Raza pierde otro hermano. Alfonso L. Flores muere de bala en la cabeza,"* was the banner. ("La Raza loses another brother. Alfonso L. Flores dies from bullet in the head.")

Then on Thursday some elderly people, former melon strikers from 1967, drove the 40 miles from Rio Grande City to find out what had happened. They said Sheriff René Solís, convicted of election fraud and sentenced to 30 days and a $2,000 fine, was still the sheriff. Why wasn't he in jail? What do you tell people? We explained that his lawyer, Jim Bates, had appealed, and that it might take years before Solís went to jail, if he went at all.

Friday, nearly 200 people crowded into the weekly Colonias del Valle meeting to talk about what will happen now. Will the FBI arrest the cop who killed Pancho, they want to know? People glance at the Flores family as a speaker explains what a grand jury is. Maybe he will be arrested after the 18th. Maybe not? *¿Quién sabe?*

Someone says he read in the Reynosa paper President Nixon had taken a personal interest in the case, which would be solved soon. He is told the story is a fantasy; the Justice Department lawyer came on Monday and was gone by Tuesday.

You drive down Highway 83, past the Cactus Drive-in, familiar as the place where the crassest of skin-flicks are regularly projected across a giant outdoor screen, as drivers just miss crashing into each other while they rubberneck to catch a glimpse of technicolor flesh. You see they're still playing Saturday's feature: "A Bullet for Sandoval." Somebody tells you Sandoval and Ramírez have moved their families out of Pharr in fear of some kind of retaliation, though there are no rumors that anybody is planning anything. You know some of the community organizers are staying in San Juan to avoid the Pharr police. Efraín Fernández says he hopes if they come to arrest him they don't do it in front of his little girl.

You drive past the high school and remember reading of time when there was enough freedom for Fred Hofheinz to hold a great outdoor debate with the late R. C. Hoiles, owner of the Freedom chain of newspapers, which oppose public education as socialist. Twenty years later, the first *chicano* student body president, and an active

MAYO, Armando Castro, is removed from office for circulating a petition asking for the freedom to circulate petitions. You remember the new president is named Joey Stockton. You can be sure he's no MAYO.

Two of the Flores brothers tell you they flew down from Chicago as soon as they heard the news, but Pancho never regained consciousness. Now they have to get back or lose their jobs. Do they have to stay for the trial? The lawyer tells them there will be no trial for months, probably. They look surprised; say nothing.

You remember talking to Sheriff Claudio Castañeda's badge-wearing secretary the Friday before the riot as you wait to interview the sheriff. She is a *chicana* named Mrs. Larson. She gives you a lecture about how the union is bad, because all the other Mexicans except her and her labor-contractor father are lazy. Her sister married a *chicano,* and boy, was she sorry. All he does is drink beer and lie around. If you raise wages, the people just drink more and that makes more work for the sheriff. You wonder how many of the deputies carrying guns on Saturday night felt the same way.

You remember your mother teaching you the policeman is your friend. She wasn't running a game on you either. She meant it.

And you wait. And the people wait, to see if anything will happen. Probably not, and you start crossing the street every time you see a cop.

What else is there to do?

Clark Knowlton

Clark S. Knowlton participated as an expert witness in hearings conducted before the then titled Inter-Agency Committee on Mexican Affairs on June 9, 1967 at El Paso, Texas. Professor Knowlton testified on problems concerning land tenure in New Mexico. His testimony points out for the student the many ramifications of that long-simmering problem. Probably the Federal Government's belated concern for Mexican American grievances, as expressed by this conference, was an attempt to soothe Chicano discontent in the Southwest. Nevertheless the report of that committee, The Mexican American: A New Focus on Opportunity *(1967), serves as a valuable source for students interested in the Chicano movement in general, and the specific problems of land rights, and compensation. By permission of the Inter-Agency Committee on Mexican Affairs, and the author.*

Recommendations For The Solution Of Land Tenure Problems Among The Spanish American

Mr. Chairman, honorable guests, Ladies and Gentlemen. Before making recommendations for the solution of land tenure problems among the Spanish American people of northern New Mexico and southern Colorado, I would like to make the following observations. The land question among the Spanish Americans is no longer a simple economic, political, or social problem subject to discussion, legislation, or economic analysis. It has become a fundamental moral issue upon

94

which all their hopes, aspirations, bitterness, resentments, and longings are focused. It is also a moral measuring rod by which they have measured the moral concepts of Anglo American political, economic, and judicial systems and found them wanting. The Spanish Americans as a people are profoundly convinced that they were conquered in war, forced to become American citizens against their will at the time, and robbed of their land and water rights by the Anglo Americans aided by some Spanish American accomplices. This massive theft was, they believe, aided and abetted by state and national politicians, judges, government employees, Anglo-American merchants, ranchers, and businessmen.

As a result the Spanish Americans are completely skeptical of the moral claims of American democracy. They have little faith in any American political party. They have no trust in the American judicial system. They have little confidence in any private or public state or national department or agency. As a people, they are more deeply alienated from the values and concepts of the predominant Anglo American society of the United States than almost any other ethnic or racial group in the country. The Spanish Americans have the psychology of a conquered, dispossessed, and impoverished people who believe that they have suffered serious injustices at the hands of the dominant Anglo American society.

Until they, as a people, experience the physical return of all or a good part of the land taken from them or receive what they define as an adequate compensation, the deeply rooted burning emotions of resentment and of having suffered historical injustice will continue to exist. The poisonous abscesses of alienation, rejection of Anglo American society, and poverty can not be eliminated. It is of utmost importance that these abscesses should be lanced. If they are not, the accelerating slide of the Spanish Americans toward rural violence cannot be halted.

Furthermore, the Departments of Interior and of Agriculture have a direct responsibility for heavy land loss among the subsistence Spanish American farmers located along the major river systems of New Mexico. The development of almost every major irrigation and flood control district in the state such as the Rio Grande Conservancy District and the Elephant Butte and Caballo Dams drove thousands of Spanish Americans from their lands through their inability to pay the financial charges imposed upon their small farms. The policies of both departments are such that the majority of their programs benefit the larger commercial heavily subsidized Anglo American farmer and not the small more subsistence Spanish American rural village farmer.

One authority estimates that the Spanish Americans conservatively lost between 1854 and 1930, a minimum of over 2,000,000 acres of privately owned lands, 1,700,000 acres of communal or *ejido* lands, and 1,800,000 acres of land taken by the Federal Government without remuneration. This massive and still continuing land loss destroyed the entire economic basis of the Spanish American rural villages. It has played a major role in the formation of a large distressed area marked by high indices of poverty and social disorganization.

I would like to suggest that a high level Government Committee be organized by the appropriate departments to study the land question in depth in New Mexico, southern Colorado, West Texas, and other neighboring areas. The committee should begin its study with Spanish and Mexican land owning customs and practices established in New Mexico, the impact of American conquest upon the Spanish Americans, and the causes of continued land loss from that date until the present. The committee should be empowered to hold hearings in the Spanish American areas, to examine records, and to subpoena witnesses. The staff of the committee should contain Spanish American and Anglo employees familiar with the language, culture, and history of the Spanish American people. The committee should be directed to recommend ways of settling the land issue.

The formation of such a committee would undoubtedly arouse great concern and anxiety among Anglo American landholders in the Spanish American areas as well as in the offices of local state governments. Land values would be affected, and existing land titles might come into question. Nevertheless, these problems are not as ominious nor as serious as the rapid increase of unrest and bitterness among the Spanish Americans alienated from the Anglo American society. The leaders of some Spanish American groups are seriously considering violence as a means of bringing the land issue to the attention of the American people and to force the Federal Government to act.

As most of the land lost by the villages was grazing and timber lands taken from the *ejido* or communal village lands, the returned land should be added to the communal lands that remain. The villages receiving land should be required to set up a bonded governing board composed of resident village inhabitants selected by the resident village population. Provisions should be made in the deed for the management of the land, the payment of land tax, the settlement of disputes over land use, regulation of grazing and timber cutting to prevent erosion, and perhaps provisions for royalties if minerals are discovered. It is of paramount importance for the welfare of the Spanish American areas that title to the land should be vested in the village as a land owning entity and not in individuals or the land will ultimately be lost again.

Spanish American resentment and hostility are steadily increasing toward the management of the Kit Carson National Forest in northern New Mexico. This resentment is reaching the explosive point where the lives of Forest Personnel may be in danger. Spanish American bitterness has originated over three points. One: The majority of the inhabitants of the mountainous Spanish American villages located in and around the National Forests are convinced that much of the forest lands were taken by the government without compensation or purchased from large timber and cattle companies that had first stolen the land from the Spanish Americans. Two: The Spanish Americans are convinced that the management of the National Forests are trying to force the Spanish Americans out of the villages in and around the forests. Three: A sharp wave of hostility swept the Spanish American villages when they learned that forest personnel were used to guide police and national guard patrols searching for Spanish Americans involved in recent events in Tierra Amarilla.

I would recommend that a study be made of all the land acquired by the National Forests to find out if the Spanish Americans are right about land being taken from them to create the National Forest in northern New Mexico. The Spanish American villages around the National Forests are almost completely dependent upon forest lands, the villagers should be given priority in forest use in northern New Mexico. Furthermore, the Forest Service should develop an extension division to assist the local Spanish American people to improve their livestock herds, to develop privately owned and village owned woodworking and handicraft industries utilizing forest resources, and to develop village owned recreational facilities of the Swiss village type. Techniques learned in northern New Mexico could be applied to the economic and cultural development of mountainous forested lands over the world.

Where the land can not be returned to the Spanish American villages without serious injustice to numerous small Anglo American farmers or suburban dwellers, then the villages should receive adequate compensation. Some of the money provided ought to go to the heirs of the men who lost the land, but most of it should be reserved as development capital and utilized to improve, the economic, social, and cultural conditions of the Spanish American rural village population.

The heirs of private Spanish American landholders who were deprived of their lands have the right to receive compensation for these lands. This will require proof of heirship and registration of heirs. Let me say again, that unrest and dangerous resentments in northern New Mexico and southern Colorado can not be reduced until the Federal Government makes a serious and concerted effort, as it has with some Indian tribes to resolve the land issue to the satisfaction of the majority of the Spanish Americans.

Land without water is useless in a semi-arid environment. Water adjudication procedures now going on among the Spanish American rural population are arousing anxiety and hostility. The State of New Mexico is trying to pinpoint individual ownership of water rights. The state officials are applying Anglo American concepts of water use that are quite different from the traditional Spanish American practices. In the villages, water is traditionally owned by the village and allocated by the village or ditch water master selected by the water users. I would recommend that water rights be vested in the villages and regulated and utilized according to village tradition and practice.

The irrigation systems of the Spanish American villages are antiquated and hand made. Large amounts of water are lost every year, and the crops frequently wither away. It would be very easy to develop a program in which the appropriate federal agency could provide technical skills and the use of machinery to be matched by labor and raw materials provided by the village people. A secure water supply would definitely enhance the productivity of Spanish American farms.

Many undoubtedly will argue that the state governments of New Mexico, Colorado, and surrounding states should assume the responsibility of improving conditions in the Spanish American segments of their states. Perhaps they should. However, these state governments have been in existence a long time. During this period, the majority of their agencies and departments have seldom shown any interest or concern in the welfare of the Spanish American people. Time has run out. Neither the Spanish Americans nor the United States can await the awakening of state governments to their responsibilities. The situation now is too threatening and dangerous for long delays for a discussion to take place over whether the state or federal governments should assume responsibility.

The social fabric of the majority of the Spanish American rural villages has unraveled under the impact of poverty, out-migration, land loss, apathy, and social disorganization. Community organizers sponsored by VISTA and O.E.O. programs are just beginning to knit the fabric together in a few villages. I would like to recommend that state and federal agencies should send trained community organizers into the villages to assist the villages to overcome apathy and factionalism, to develop village wide organizations, and to train a local village leadership.

As the communal tradition is far stronger in the villages than the idea of individualism, the appropriate government agencies should encourage and assist the villages to develop producer and consumer cooperatives. Because of low volume and almost complete ignorance of market trends and of Anglo American business values, Spanish American farmers are now at the mercy of local merchants and jobbers. Credit unions would be an invaluable need for village population that is seldom able to secure credit at local banks.

The state agricultural extension programs should receive funds and encouragement to conduct research on methods of improving agricultural productivity on the small Spanish American landholdings. Irrigation facilities should be modernized. Agricultural machinery suitable for poor small farmers might well be developed by the U.S. Department of Agriculture or perhaps the Interior. Here the experiences of the Japanese could perhaps be studied with considerable profit. As much of the produce consumed in Albuquerque and Santa Fe must be imported from out of state, there is room for the development of truck, poultry, and perhaps even of frozen foods and processing plants in the Spanish American areas.

In the rural Spanish American villages a once lavish handicraft tradition is dying. It is hard now to realize that at one time the rural Spanish American villagers possessed a handicraft tradition as rich and varied as that of the Southwestern Indians. While the Federal and State Governments and private agencies have encouraged and aided the Indian artisans and artists through the establishment of special arts and craft schools, nothing has been done for the Spanish Americans. I would therefore recommend that a foundation or the appropriate state and federal departments set up a handicraft board to train Spanish American artists and artisans, set standards, assist them to secure raw materials, and help to provide a market for their products. Unemployment and underemployment are chronic in northern New Mexico and southern Colorado. While few Spanish Americans could ever hope to provide for their families from hand work, they could certainly supplement a scarce income in the long cold winter months through furniture making, metal working, jewelry, pottery, woodworking, and weaving. The Handicraft boards of India and Siam perhaps could be analyzed for ideas that could be applied to the Spanish American village.

The Spanish American areas are marked by deplorably poor roads. Many of the villages are almost completely isolated during winter months. Federal and State Funds could be provided to develop a network of roads linking the villages with each other and with the major highways that almost completely bypass the Spanish American areas. The roads would also assist in the establishment of industry, the transportation of village products, and inhance the ability of village people to find employment in nearby urban centers. The Spanish American areas are in the same condition as Appalachia and perhaps the Ozarks as far as isolation and lack of roads go.

I would now like to discuss some of the reasons why past present state and federal programs have not been able to materially assist the Spanish Americans to escape from poverty. Lessons derived from the failures of other programs can assist us to improve programs of the future.

The files of state and federal agencies are filled with studies of the socio-economic conditions and problems of the Spanish Americans. Few additional studies are needed. The basic needs and problems of the Spanish Americans have been identified for over twenty-five years. Unfortunately the majority of programs based upon these studies litter the Southwest as dead and dying hulks. They failed primarily in spite of the excellent intentions of their originators because they must learn when to use Spanish and when not to in communicating with the rural people. The Anglo-American employee who learns enough Spanish to communicate with the rural people can break down barriers, make friends, and win an acceptance of ideas and programs.

And still another problem that complicates planning and program development among the Spanish Americans is the decay of the traditional rural village social systems such as the patron system and the extended patriarchal family. Outmigration has carried away the younger adults. The majority of villages are afflicted with anomie and social disorganization. Among the village population there are very few individuals who have a working knowledge of American culture and society. Marked by apathy, land loss, poverty, malnutrition the village populations tend to be factionalized and exploited by local political leaders who control public employment in the region.

Partially anglicized families are found in all but the more isolated rural villages. These families are able to relate quite well to Anglo American professionals. The average Anglo who meets them tends to assume that because of their facility with English, their familiarity with Anglo American habits of thought, their possession of a higher material standard of living than the mass of village people that they are village leaders. Many of the partially anglicized are often able because of this assumption to exploit both the Anglo Americans and the village population.

Precisely because these people are somewhat anglicized, deprecate Spanish, and tend to look down upon the local people, they tend to be rejected by the Spanish American masses. The real leaders are often intelligent men and women who because of poverty, a lack of education, and an ignorance of the English language and of American customs lack the ability to provide adequate leadership even though they have considerable prestige in their own village circles. One of the most serious problems of the entire region is the lack of good Spanish American leadership.

Any comprehensive program developed for New Mexico, Colorado, and nearby sections should have a leadership discovery and training component as a major part of the program. The village leaders to be effective must be men and women who speak both Spanish and English, who are firmly grounded in local Spanish American values and yet who comprehend Anglo values and procedures. There are very few of them, but the welfare of the Spanish American people depend upon their coming.

The Spanish Americans are a very proud people. Extremely reluctant, even under conditions of extreme poverty, to receive charity they respond very readily to programs that they believe will improve the economic or social conditions of the village. It should here be underlined that they accept more readily programs for group welfare than for individual welfare. Programs designed for the Spanish Americans in view of these factors, wherever possible, should involve the Spanish Americans in contributions of donated labor and raw materials.

One of the most successful programs in northern New Mexico was a state financed and sponsored program to improve the simple archaic inefficient irrigation systems of a group of Spanish American villages along the upper Pecos River. The state provided technical services and equipment. The Spanish Americans enthusiastically donated raw materials and labor. Every dollar provided by the state was matched by five dollars contributed by the Spanish Americans. Unfortunately poorly informed Anglo American politicians brought the program to a halt before more than a small handful of villages had benefited.

The harsh refusal of the dominant Anglo American population and the Anglo dominated state legislatures to permit the expenditures of state funds for programs to assist the Spanish Americans is quite ironic in view of the fact that the Anglo-American population is far more subsidized by state and federal governments than the Spanish Americans. This statement is supported by an examination of the evidence. The network of superhighways constructed by state and federal funds somehow always bypass the Spanish American areas suffocated by an inadequate transportation system. Lavish airports seldom utilized by the Spanish Americans mark the Anglo American cities. The poor small subsistence Spanish American farmer seldom sees the enormous subsidies received by the commercial Anglo American farmer. The Federal Government has financed expensive flood control and irrigation projects that drove the Spanish American off of his land for the economic benefit of Anglo American city dwellers and farmers. Considerable funds are spent in the natural forests for the Anglo American hunter, fisher, and camper to the neglect of the grazing facilities needed by the small Spanish American village livestock owner. And finally it is exceedingly curious that virtually all of the defense and military installations in New Mexico are located in the Anglo-American areas.

In closing I would like to state that the Spanish Americans can not escape from poverty living on small subsistence farms. However, if the villages can obtain the grazing and timber lands taken from their *ejidos,* grazing and forest activities can increase their income. If handicrafts and woodworking industries are encouraged, another source of income is added. If the villages are assisted to cater to the recreational needs of the larger society on a year round basis then additional revenue is provided. It is not at all impossible that industries suitable to the natural environment of the region could not be induced to enter the region. By the development of various sources of income, a viable way of life can be created for the Spanish American people of the area.

The alternatives are too drastic to consider. A laissez faire policy will mean that northern New Mexico and southern Colorado will continue to be one of the most serious regions of poverty in the United States. Extremely high rates of hunger, poverty, social disorganization, welfare and unemployment will continue. Out-migration will continue to send out of the region hundreds of poorly educated unskilled semi-acculturated workers to add to the social problems of our larger cities. It is far easier to struggle with the problems of rural New Mexico and southern Colorado than it is with the problems of the large slums and ghettoes of the Southwest, the Pacific Coast, and the Rocky Mountains.

And finally, I would like to stress with all the power of my command that time is running out. The land issue has reached a crisis point. If it is not resolved soon Spanish American desperation will increasingly find an outlet in violence.

Jorge Lara - Braud

Jorge Lara-Braud (Director of Hispanic-American Institute, Austin, Texas) heads an ecumenical organization that collects and develops materials that will aid Spanish-speaking communities in the United States. The Institute receives support from eight Protestant denominations in Texas and is deeply committed to the Chicano movement. The call for bilingualism by Dr. Lara-Braud is the official position paper adopted by this varied coalition. By permission of the author, and THE HISPANIC-AMERICAN INSTITUTE.

Bilingualism For Texas: Education For Fraternity

OUR COSMOPOLITAN ENVIRONMENT

The Southwest is the most cosmopolitan region of this nation. No other area of the United States encompasses a wider diversity of races, religions, and national origins, or a greater variety of cultural development of the people who belong to them. California, Colorado, Arizona, New Mexico, and Texas contain together some of the largest groups of American Indians, virtually all U.S. Indians of hispanicized heritage and of Mexican origin, four-fifths of those whose Spanish surnames are this nation's uninterrupted link of four centuries

to the legacy of Spain and Mexico, the largest groups of Orientals in the continental United States (two-thirds of the Japanese, two-thirds of the Filipinos, and over half of the Chinese), a third of the country's Asian Indians, Koreans, Polynesians, Indonesians, and Hawaiians, and some three million of the nation's blacks. As Professor Fred H. Schmidt states, "In the truest sense of the word, the region is cosmopolitan—its people belong to all of the world, and the ties of many with other parts of the world are still recent and unsevered, for here are found one-third of the nation's registered aliens."

100

Of course, what makes any cosmopolitanism functional rather than purely statistical is the survival of the language of each cultural group represented in the regional "cosmos" in coexistence with the lingua franca of the nation to which the region belongs. In this respect, nothing contributes more to keeping the Southwest cosmopolitan than the persistent confluence of Spanish and English. Figures from a pre-Census survey of the Spanish-American population of the United States in November of 1969 reveal there were in this country 9,200,000 persons of "Spanish descent," not including inmates of institutions and members of the armed forces. Spanish was reported as the mother tongue of 6,700,000, despite the fact that 72.6 percent were U.S. born. More revealing even is that 4,600,000 reported Spanish as their current language, that is to say, their primary language in the home (even though more than 80 percent are U.S. citizens and a larger percentage is quite likely able to use English for social, educational and occupational purposes with varying degrees of proficiency).

More than half of the 9,200,000 "Spanish-Americans" of the November 1969 pre-Census survey, were Mexican-Americans living in the Southwest. Nearly two million reside in Texas. Roughly one out of every five Texans is a Mexican-American. There are no recent published Census statistics to determine what percentage of Mexican-Americans in the Southwest (including Texas) would report Spanish first as the mother tongue and then as the home language. Based on inference from the pre-Census survey and other studies, and on extensive empirical observation, we estimate 85 percent and 70 percent would report Spanish as the mother tongue and home language respectively. Let it be remembered we are dealing with a group overwhelmingly non-alien. Some 90 percent are U.S. citizens, whose ability to communicate in English ranges from faltering to glittering.

The persistence of Spanish in the Southwest may be fascinating or perplexing to non-Spanish speakers. Perhaps nothing clouds the understanding of this phenomenon more than the parallels drawn between Mexican-Americans and other so called "language minorities." All other language minorities ceased to be replenished with the end of heavy immigration from the country of origin. More often than not immigrants left that distant country with no expectation or desire of ever resuming vital cultural ties with it. The ethnic enclave—with its concomitant survival of a foreign language—was seen, particularly from the second generation onwards, as a transitional stage in the process of assimilation within the unilingual national mainstream. The nation had quite early defined its pattern of cultural unity primarily in terms of the language, religion, folkways, and institutions of the dominant English-speaking Protestant founders and their descendents. There was no perversity in discouraging diversity. The youth and relative insecurity of the new republic virtually demanded a "melting pot" policy. This posed no insurmountable problem for those who could melt. It did create difficulties for others, ranging from annoying to intolerable, depending on how distant their difference was from the primordial founding community. That meant many would be regarded as less then American, and subject to permanent or protracted rejection, no matter how eagerly some sought to expiate for their unintentional deviancy.

THE GRANDEUR AND MISERY OF DIFFERENCE

Against this background, the parallel between Mexican-Americans and other language minorities turns out to be no parallel at all. Rather, the contrast stands out. By the time the Southwest became U.S. territory following the military conquests of 1836 and 1846 Spanish had been the language of population centers for the previous three centuries. The region, though sparsely settled, was pervasively Mexican, a rich blend of Spanish and Indian culture. The "Anglo" conquest was traumatic. The native Spanish-speaking inhabitants, theoretically protected from cultural or economic depredation by local gentlemen's agreement and international treaty provisions, within two generations had been reduced to hewers of wood and drawers of water. Their language, religion, skin-color-and above all their status as a conquered people—made them ineligible even for an invitation to the melting pot. They were by no means totally cut off. To be sure, social institutions left them little or no room to participate. But compassionate individuals in the dominant group, especially members of churches, mitigated their plight through numberless acts of friendship and redress. Others, less compassionate, found or created ways to capitalize on the enormous reservoir of cheap labor they constituted. It would be impossible to explain the existence of mining, railroad, cattle, sheep, and agricultural empires of the Southwest apart from the massive use of Mexican-American labor, often in conditions of virtual peonage.

Meanwhile, throughout the second half of the 19th century and the first third of the 20th, Mexico was intermittently convulsed by bloody social disorders. Mexicans headed north by the hundreds of thousands to the U.S. Southwest and by the thousands to the industrial cities of the Midwest. There, they were to swell the ranks of friends and relatives engaged in menial work. Bedraggled refugees could hardly enhance the image of a people long reduced to wretchedness. The massive infusion of steady arrivals did, however, immeasurably contribute to further Mexicanize the environment and to revitalize Spanish as the ongoing mother tongue of Mexican-Americans. A curious accomodation was made by the dominant Anglos, more instinctive than intentional. Since neither the Mexicanhood of the Mexican-Americans nor their language appeared to be on the wane, but quite the opposite, the unwelcome replenishment of their "foreignness" could be deflected to folkloric attraction. Accordingly, a spirited promotion of Mexican food, Mexican art, Mexican music, Mexican crafts, Mexican festivals got underway. This was happening precisely at the time when Mexican-Americans were frequently denied admission to public establishments, when they had been driven to avoid as denigrating the self-designation Mexican in favor of Latin-American or Spanish-American, and when speaking Spanish in school halls and playgrounds was an offense punished with suspension, fines, after-school detention, or even corporal punishment. Incidentally, alarmed at the escalation of anti-Mexicanhood in Texas, and the refusal of Mexico to send her nationals to

replace in the fields men now in uniform, the State Legislature was driven to enact formal legislation in May of 1943 recognizing the people of Mexican extraction as Caucasian, and entitling them to "whites only" public services.

Ironically, it took a war, the Second World War, to create conditions more favorable to intercultural fraternity. Mexican-Americans earned the admiration of fellow Americans for their disproportionate record of casualties and heroism. No other ethnic or racial group earned a larger proportion of Congressional medals. The G.I. Bill provided heretofore denied educational opportunities for college careers. Many Mexican-Americans moved on to well-paid jobs formerly the exclusive preserve of Anglos. Vigorous associations came into being for the redress of cultural and civil rights. Many of the blatant barriers against Mexican-American participation in public life, particularly in social institutions, came down under Anglo initiative or Mexican-American attack, or both. There lingered, however, even among Mexican-Americans (especially "success" types of the immediate post World War II period) a definite discomfort about the continuing persistence of Spanish. A century of sustained anti-Mexicanhood had taken its toll in many ways, one being the suspicion that no Mexican-American could attain the *sine qua non* of true U.S. citizenship, mastery of English, until he ceased to speak Spanish.

In the meantime, Mexico and the United States, close allies in World War II, emerged out of the conflict enjoying an unprecedented degree of friendship. Both made great economic strides in the ensuing decades. Immigration from Mexico, even though subject to no quota, slowed down considerably. However, the international border, never quite so much a boundary as a gateway for two-way traffic, registered booming crossing figures in both directions. In the year 1967–1968, the U.S. Office of Immigration reported 135 million crossings from Mexico to the U.S. It is estimated by this writer no less than 100 million were made from the U.S. to Mexico. Added to these astounding figures, the vibrant quest of Mexican-Americans for their long suppressed identity, the renaissance of Spanish among them and in institutions of higher learning, and the shrinking of the world into a multilingual global village—all make for a drastic questioning of the unilingual tradition of education in a bilingual, multicultural Southwest.

BILINGUAL EDUCATION: MISCONCEPTIONS, DEFINITION, APPLICATION

The foregoing historical review throws light, we hope, on the human realities underlying the confluence of Spanish and English in southwestern United States. When we deal with language we deal with life at its core. It is the means by which an individual decodes the meaning of his existence in the world and encodes his experiences for creative dialogue with others. Memory, affection, aspiration, reflection, anxiety, discovery, religion and a myriad of other personal experiences are mediated through language. There is no other path to self-awareness and self-disclosure. It is no coincidence that in the Bible nothingness and chaos are turned into creation and order by the Word and words. Man's dominion over the earth begins as a function of language, the naming of created things. The holiness of language is not a concept of cultural chauvinism. Rather, it is a fundamental notion of the Judeo-Christian tradition.

This brings us to *the* issue before us. Where two languages coexist, no matter how socially distant may be the respective communities which speak them, a unique human chemistry has been catalyzed. Neither community has remained untouched by the other. Certain commonalities of history, environment, style and perception have resulted. Some appropriate them at the superficial level of folklore, others at the more basic level of biculturalism. The former, quite probably unilingual, have a low ceiling of tolerance for difference. The latter, quite probably bilingual, possess a high appreciation for diversity. Prejudice, not inevitably but frequently, flourishes among the first. Fraternity, not automatically but naturally, thrives among the second. The magnanimity of Mexican-Americans in forgetting and forgiving present and past indignities is not due to any inherent nobility. Rather, it has to do with their enlarged ability as bilinguals to decode much of the motivational world of the dominant group. Conversely, Anglos who have earned the affection of Mexican-Americans have been able literally to "communicate" beyond the limitations of one language and one culture. Both experience less discomfort with the culturally different at home and abroad than their unilingual counterparts.

Bilingualism, nevertheless, is still hindered among us by at least four quite prevalent misconceptions: 1) English cannot be mastered as long as the individual retains another language as the mother tongue. 2) Using two languages as mediums of instruction cause academic retardation and even psychological confusion. 3) The low educational achievement among Mexican-Americans is directly attributable to their retention of Spanish; 4) retention of a foreign language impedes the Americanization of those who speak it.

We might better deal with these misconceptions if we first define bilingual education. It is "instruction in two languages and the use of those two languages as mediums of instruction for any part of or all of the school curriculum. Study of the history and culture associated with a student's mother tongue is considered an integral part of bilingual education" education.

Let us now deal with the first two misconceptions. They are closely related. Mastery of English while retaining Spanish as the mother or home language has been accomplished by countless bilinguals in the Southwest, particularly if instruction in both languages began at an early age. The main reason why this fact is not readily apparent is that until 1963 it was a phenomenon confined to individuals. It was not an officially approved educational policy anywhere in the U.S.A. (except for schools in New Mexico throughout the second half of the 19th century following language educational provisions of the 1848 Treaty of Guadalupe Hidalgo). The heavy influx of Cubans into the Miami area led the Dade County Schools in 1963 to undertake a completely bilingual program in grades one, two, and three of the Coral Way School, with plans to move up one grade each year. There were equal numbers of English and Spanish-speaking children. Approximately half of the instruction was to be given in Spanish by Cuban teachers, and half in English by American teachers. Now on its seventh year, the program has proven an astounding success. Children speak the second language with little or no trace of an accent, while being fully proficient in both across the gamut of all subject matter taught.

In 1964 a quite similar program was begun in the United Consolidated School District of Webb County, outside Laredo. As in Coral Way, half the children were English speakers and half Spanish-speakers. The teaching in English and Spanish in all elementary school subjects has been done by bilingual teachers who are native speakers of Spanish and fluent also in English. The results equal those of Coral Way, not alone in academic achievement, but also in intercultural fraternity. A recent evaluation of learning of mathematics in this program is additionally revealing. The achievement is greater for both Anglo and Mexican-American children when the subject is taught bilingually rather than in English alone.

Convincing results from programs such as these and from others equally successful, though different in implementation, and in some instances with English and a language other then Spanish as mediums of instruction, greatly contributed to make possible enabling federal and state bilingual education acts. On January 2, 1968 the Bilingual Education Act, with bipartisan sponsorship led by Senator Ralph Yarborough, passed by the United States Congress On May 22, 1969 the 61st Legislature of the State of Texas passed *unanimously* a similar bill. These legislative landmarks underscored bilingualism as a sound educational concept and committed the nation and the state to enlarge its dimensions.

Interestingly enough both bills dispell the misconception of possible retardation and confusion as a result of the use of two languages as mediums of instruction. The two pieces of legislation imply that non-English speakers will more readily attain mastery of the national tongue if they are first taught in the language of the home. Confirmation of this insight comes from a group of international experts gathered in Paris under UNESCO auspices in 1951 to study the uses of vernacular languages in education. Here is their consensus: "It is axiomatic that the best medium of teaching a child is his mother tongue. Psychologically it is the system of meaningful signs that in his mind work automatically for expression and understanding. Sociologically, it is a means of identification among the members of the community to which he belongs. Educationally, he learns more quickly through it than through an unfamiliar linguistic medium."

The experience of some Indians in Latin America at one time speaking only their tribal language proves very instructive in this regard. Those who were taught Spanish and Portuguese without first mastering the basic skills of reading and writing in their native tongues went on to record apalling statistics of social maladjustment. In contrast, those who were fortunate enough to have their native tongues reduced to writing by lingustic anthropologists (notably missionaries known as the Wycliff Translators), and then taught to read in a script corresponding to the sounds inherited from their ancestors, had little or no problem learning the national tongue. Their psychological and social adjustments were remarkably favorable. The crucial difference in experience is not hard to explain. When people are denied the continued use of their language, they are also denied their personhood, their history, their memories. One cannot adequately decipher the meaning of his reality through the mute subtitles of someone else's tongue. The foreign tongue ceases to be foreign only when it is filtered through the familiar sounds and signs of one's own.

Here is the logical point to deal with the misconception that the low educational achievement of Mexican-Americans is attributable to their retention of Spanish. There is no denying that the group has the lowest index of school years completed in the entire nation. Their dropout rate of 80 percent with respect to high school completion is the highest in the country. Earlier in this paper we reviewed the history of animosity to their linguistic and cultural difference—particularly the concerted effort to eradicate Spanish as a functional language in the Southwest. Would not the evidence suggest that their massive educational destitution is directly attributable to the school's failure to capitalize on their bilinguality? Could it not be that the educational process has been so conceived and implemented as to unwittingly penalize the Mexican-American in direct proportion to his attempt to remain bilingual? Could it not be in fact that much of his social maladjustment rather reflects the maladjustment of a society so misguided as to regard a functional second language as a liability instead of an asset, while in the course of such folly inflicting untold psychic, social and economic damage? The irony is that all along the teaching of Spanish as a *foreign* language was encouraged in high school and colleges when it was too little and too late for either Mexican-Americans or other Americans. This absurdity was forcefully pointed out to the Special Subcommittee on Bilingual Education of the United States Senate in 1967 by Bruce Gaarder, Chief of Modern Foreign Language Section of the U.S. Office of Education: "It is as if one said it is all right to learn a foreign language if you start so late that you really cannot master it. It is all right for headwaiters, professional performers, and the rich to know foreign languages, but any child in school who already knows one is suspect." By the way, on that occasion Dr. Gaarder also observed that the greatest unfulfilled need for Foreign Service personnel and Fulbright - Hays lecturers and technical specialists sent abroad was for those able to speak French or Spanish."

The last major misconception is that which assumes retention of a foreign language impedes the Americanization of those who speak it. The misconception, to begin with, implies a sadly provincial view of patriotism as unilingual conformity. The nation may have at one time discouraged diversity for the sake of consolidating its youthful existence, but even then the plurality of its origins was regarded as the genius of its universality. The melting pot has been proven more myth than reality. The country is richer for its failure. More visionary patriots have favored such imagery as a "mosaic of minorities" or the "symphony of mankind" to denote the blend of peoples and languages from all over the world which undergird the American Dream. No country in history has ever attained a more farflung influence on the face of the earth through the presence of its citizens and institutions. In the light of the country's multicultural genesis, multiethnic population, and multinational commitments, loyalty to it may well require a repudiation of its long held contradiction

of unilinguality. A more cosmopolitan view of the national experience to date suggests that bilingualism is a minimum requirement for true Americanhood. Texas is fortunate to provide a natural laboratory to put these notions to the test. Our neighborhood with Mexico and Latin America makes the need to test ourselves successfully a matter of hemispheric responsibility. Let us not forget that by the time this year's first-graders are in their middle thirties, English will have become a minority language in the hemisphere. Native speakers of Spanish and Portuguese together will number roughly twice as many as those will be native speakers of English. Spanish surnamed U.S. citizens will then number approximately twenty million, of whom about four million will be Texans.

If the evidence produced, the statistics quoted, and the arguments marshalled thus far are in any way credible, we can no longer waste time arguing whether bilingualism is a sound educational concept for *all* children in this state, whether their mother tongue is English, Spanish, Czech or German. Of course, the need for such education is greatest among children for whom English is not native. There, the backlog of educational dereliction requires urgent and massive corrective measures.

Psychologists agree that more than half of the growth of intelligence in an individual's lifetime occurs prior to the age when children normally begin school. We are, then, talking about an ambitious undertaking which goes much farther than our traditional school time tables. Ideally bilingual education should begin no later than the third birthday of a child and extend as much as possible beyond the end of the present sixth grade. We are also talking about monumental tasks of specialized teacher training, development of new teaching tools, expansion of in-service programs, and considerable expenditure of additional resources. The Texas Bilingual Educational Act appropriated no fresh monies for its implementation. It assumed the use of federal appropriations. Nevertheless, the Texas Education Agency has created the Division of International and Bilingual Education under the able direction of Dr. Severo Gómez as Assistant Commissioner of Education. The Bilingual Education Act of January 2, 1968 authorized fifteen million dollars *for all the nation* for the fiscal year ending June 30, 1968. Actually no appropriation was made until the year ending June 30, 1969. Even then, of the authorized thirty million dollars, only ten was appropriated nationally, of which Texas received only two. For the present fiscal year of 1970–71, our state will share only four million of the total national appropriation. These amounts are obviously inadequate. In 1969–70 only 10,003 Texas students could benefit from the national Bilingual Education Act appropriation. For the year 1970–71, the beneficiaries nearly doubled to 20,000. Even then, they continued to be almost exclusively Mexican-American, out of a total potential Mexican-American elementary and secondary school constituency of some 600,000! The challenge of supplementing the national ap-propriation is even more staggering if bilingual education is to be made available to the total Texas primary and secondary school population numbering in 1970 some three million. Since we have couched the concept of bilingualism in the context of fraternity, it is not unfitting to remember the Biblical word, "For where your treasure is there will your heart be also."

This writer happens to be one of those fortunate bilinguals educated by Church institutions. Across his twenty-three years of intimate knowledge of Texas, he has learned that its resourcefulness, often expressed in ingenious practices of prejudice, is even more ingenious in its practice of fraternity— and that it is willing to pay the price of any challenge if it is convinced of its worth. Let us hope it will no longer be dubious about the rich dividends of bilingualism as education for fraternity.

Jesus Luna

Jesus Luna (who presently holds a Ford Foundation Grant in Mexico City, Mexico) came from a migrant worker's family to earn a B.A. from Pan American University and a M.A. from East Texas State University. "Luna's Abe Lincoln Story," chronicles Mr. Luna's early life "on the road of hope" and gives some insight into the New Chicano consciousness. The goal of the Mexican American is not simply faceless assimilation, but rather they now demand cultural acceptance, and their rightful place as "equals" in a society of equals.
By permission of the author.

Luna's Abe Lincoln Story

For many years the word Chicano had a derogatory meaning, but today the term has acquired a new meaning and the new *breed* of Mexican Americans uses this term to designate themselves as a proud minority group. In the context I do not consider myself a Mexican or a Mexican-American, but a Chicano. My parents Gustavo and Antonia Luna were born in Texas, but my grandparents were born in Mexico; thus I am of Mexican descent but I am an American. Being an American is what constitutes one of the problems that the second largest minority group in America is faced with today. My ethnic group, which consists of over six million Chicanos, has not received the benefits that were guaranteed to us in 1848 under the Treaty of Guadalupe Hidalgo that ended the Mexican War. Since 1848 the Anglos in Texas, southern California, New Mexico, and Arizona have looked at the Chicanos condescendingly and have never treated them as their equals. Today, in the 1970s, the decade of the Chicanos, the White Anglo Saxon Protestant (WASP) establishment recognizing the growth of self identity among Chicanos, has suddenly become aware of and wary of a new feeling among Chicano groups in the United States—especially where Chicano concentration is high. As usual the Anglos are still trying their piece-meal tactics to appease the "ignorant dirty greasers" and many of the *tio tacos* band with the White Establishment to sell their own brown brothers' votes. However, it is my hope that in the 1970s the new breed of Chicanos that went to college in the 60s will not buy the Anglo's loaf of bread but instead sell a new program to their people and keep the interest of the Chicanos in mind.

The following is an account of my life as a migrant child. To those who have argued that the Chicanos were happy, I reply with a resounding *NO*. I was never a happy child; in fact I never felt that I was a child since I had to work from an early age. My recollections of the migrant life are sometimes vague and brief, other experiences are touching, and a few have left their mark on me and have scarred me for life.

I, Jesus Luna, and my family were migrant workers in the 1950s. But our migrations finally came to a halt after I persuaded my parents to stop migrating for the sake of their children so that we could attend school. Since my father was and is a sensible person he agreed and the dreaded cycle ended. Today I am a Ph.D. student at North Texas State University.

There are eleven children in my family, six brothers and five sisters. Most of my family live in Edinburg and the majority of them still live close to my parents on 28th Street in Edinburg, Texas. I guess this in a way illustrates the closeness of the family in the Chicano way of life. My two older brothers, who never finished high school, work as foremen in a meat dehydrating plant outside of Edinburg. Both of them live on 28th Street. My four older sisters are married. The eldest lives in Elsa about five miles away from Edinburg; two others live on 28th Street, however, they and their husbands still migrate to California to pick grapes. Another sister also lives in Edinburg about five blocks away from home. Of the rest of the family; two of my younger brothers are sophomores in college; the youngest is in the seventh grade; and my other younger sister is a sophomore in high school. One thing that should be noted is that before I finished school none of my brothers or sisters had finished school. Today, however, I believe all my younger brothers and sister will finish high school and obtain a college degree. This is the present condition of the Luna family. My father still works as a farmer but owns his home, and my mother is perhaps the best housewife in the world.

The present status of the Luna family varies radically from the Luna's of the 1950s. In 1950 my father, Gustavo, bought a little one room shack behind his mother-in-law's house, here my parents and eight children lived. Dad's economic situation at the time was very bad and since he worked as a farm laborer he was only paid 60 or 70 cents an hour, hardly enough to feed eight kids much less clothe them and provide for medical attention. My two older brothers helped out however, by going out and picking carrots or oranges, or doing almost any job that would bring in a few cents to supplement the family income. Our family was too large for its income and it must have been extremely difficult for my father, who lived close to his in-laws, to see us go without many of the things we needed.

Faced with a difficult economic situation Dad decided to migrate. Our poor economic condition left my father no alternative but to follow the cotton harvest and employ his children as cotton pickers to increase the family income. Now we had always picked cotton in the Valley but after the cotton harvest was over in the summer of 1950 we migrated north. Dad had an old 1946 red pickup, a Ford, I think, and he persuaded several families to migrate with us that first year. Trying to get the people together was a little difficult, and in the evening after work Dad would go and talk to several families like the Melchors, the Granados, and the Aguilar's explaining to them the benefits of going on migration, how the trip would take place, where we would go from Edinburg, how far it was, the nature of the harvest at our destination point, and the conditions of the homes we were going to.

When he finally persuaded them to go everything was set for the day of departure. This was a big day for everyone. The kids would be running around the trucks, joyful because they were going on a trip, the adults would be well dressed and the few belongings were packed into the pickups and cars. Usually Dad's pickup and later on his truck would be the lead automobile. It reminds me today of Wagon Train, and I'll never forget my father giving instructions and wearing his light brown Stetson. Just before we left those relatives or friends remaining behind would gather around the caravan to wish us well. After the cars were checked, tires, oil, water, etc., the migration began and everyone waved goodbye and well-wished one another. We left the X Valley with a prayer asking God to grant us a safe journey. (It was in search of a better economic standard that we migrated. The search of the dollar was the reason that a man with a large family migrated during the cotton harvest.) For us kids it meant two or three months away from school and we enjoyed it until we were out in the cotton fields.

On a labor migration many factors came into play which are not usually experienced by most people. As a child, for example, at the age of six or seven I felt like a young adult because I was part of a group that provided for our family. I know that I did not contribute much but nevertheless I contributed my share. There was really no childhood that I can point to because it was circumvented by work. Often during the migrations many of the families which consisted of seven or eight children had to live in a two or three room house. As a result many of the children either had to sleep with their parents or in the same room, or crowd together in another room. Many a time we had to sleep with our uncles who also traveled with us. These two uncles, Morito and Jose Maria, were Mom's brothers and she washed for them and fed them; in return they paid her fifteen or twenty dollars a week for laundry and meals.

As migrants once or twice we had to live in houses of one or two rooms with dirt floors and in most of the places there were no bathrooms or running water, outhouses were the way of life—sometimes outhouses with two holes. Poor housing, inadequate sanitation, and poor drinking water were among the major problems that we faced as migrants. The adults did not seem to mind very much if they drank water from a flowing stream or a well, but many migrant babies became ill with the water given to them. Another bigger problem was the contempt shown towards us by the Anglos in many of the towns where we stopped. In Robstown, Kenedy, Palacios, Floydada, and many other towns the Anglo community looked at us

with disgust. Many migrants suffered the misfortune of having to pay rent for the sheds where they were staying, or being asked to leave immediately after the harvest. In general the conditions that migrants lived through were terrible.

Picking cotton was no fun job. I can distinctly remember my experiences as a young migratory worker. We used to start the cotton harvest in the Lower Rio Grande Valley and after the season ended in the Valley we would start our trek from Edinburg to Robstown and on up the state of Texas until the final stop in west Texas around Lubbock or Petersburg. On this journey along the "road of hope" one would always witness broken down cars, other migrants sleeping in trucks or city parks, and countless other migrants, usually Chicanos, seeking *Patrones* or bosses to work for.

My first experience in picking cotton was in the lower Rio Grande Valley. I thought that my family was making a lot of money because we were getting paid two or two dollars and fifty cents for every hundred pounds we picked. Since we were a large family we earned roughly from thirty-five to forty-five dollars a day. As a kid I thought this was a lot of money and did not question anything. The only catch involved in picking cotton was that you had to be a darn good cotton picker to pick 300 pounds of clean cotton from sun-up to sundown.

After the cotton season ended in the Valley we would move to Robstown. I hated the town and especially the farm where we usually picked, and every year we went to the same place. This is one thing that should be noted: My father had a contact in Robstown, his brother-in-law, Fabian Vasquez. We always went to pick for his boss because Uncle Fabian would get permission from his boss to allow us to live in some of his houses (actually sheds) while we harvested his cotton crop. My father considered the contact man to be very important. Before we were ready to move after completing one harvest, he would write to one of his previous bosses or *Patrones* farther north in Palacios or Port Lavaca to see if the cotton was ready. If we did not have a *Patron* to write to then the only solution was to go to the town square of a particular town and look for a job. The town square or city park was a sight to witness. Usually the park would be filled with small caravans of trucks, pickups and cars. The rancher who needed hands to harvest his crop would come to the park. Here he could take his pick from the several groups. His decision on whom to hire was based on how much of a crop he had. For example, a caravan of forty or fifty adults would not go with him if he did not have enough houses or sheds and if he only had twenty-five acres of cotton to be harvested. If a group liked the farmer's proposition then the head of the caravan plus several other adults, usually the heads of the other families, would go and look over the crop and the houses. Back in the park the kids would wander around and talk with some of the other groups there. Some of them we knew and others were from the surrounding towns in the valley.

Getting back to Robstown, I hated the place because of its drinking water. Some of the houses here were halfway decent but some of the people who came with us to pick cotton had to stay in sheds where the farm machinery was stored because of a shortage of houses. My antagonism towards the place was based mostly on the taste of the water which was very, very salty. The only way I could drink it was if it was very cold. Sometimes Dad or someone else would drive into town and get distilled water for the babies and it was from this water that I drank most of the time while we were there. I hated myself for drinking this water since it was supposed to be for the babies, but I had resolved that I was not going to suffer.

From Robstown we usually went to El Campo or Palacios. As I mentioned it seems that every year we ended up in the same place and the same old houses because once we had picked for a "patron" Dad would write to him in advance and he would notify my father when to bring the group up. This way Dad could discover the best time to arrive and assure that we would have a job and "housing." Of course housing for migrants entitled one to four walls, a floor—sometimes a wooden floor—if we were lucky, a roof and the usual outhouse with its nest of yellow jackets. The reason Dad usually went back to the same farmer was that housing for the group that traveled with us was provided. Housing although poor was a major problem. Sometimes, some of the farmers for

whom we had picked the previous year did not wait for Dad to write and hired another group. In one such instance in El Campo we had to spend several days sleeping under the stars while Dad tried to find a *Patron* who would provide work and housing for us. During these three or four days my mother cooked in a "kitchen" which Dad constructed by tying a tarp to a tree and driving stakes into the ground. I almost want to cry now when I think about these experiences that we went through. El Campo I did not like because of the mosquitoes which would not let one sleep at night. Also this town is near the Gulf of Mexico and we spent many a day playing poker because the rain did not allow us to perform our daily labor. Sometimes we were out of work for a whole week while the rain continued, yet, we had to survive and were never subsidized by anyone.

From El Campo we usually went to Hillsboro or Waxahachie. The places we picked at in Hillsboro were always hot—that is one of my few recollections of that area other than that in the early 1950s Johnny Cash's song, *I Walk the Line,* became very popular. While we lived in Waxahachie I remember that there were some cool underground springs that flowed near the old house we lived in. I also remember the adults talking about a big city near by and I remember how I pictured Dallas lit up at night, with millions of people in the streets, all of them very happy and buying things. Most of the people that I imagined were *gringos* because I always knew that all *gringos* were rich.

From Waxahachie, West Texas would be the final destination in our "trail of tears." Petersburg or Lubbock or the surrounding towns were the places we picked in West Texas. Dad had another relative in Petersburg who was again his contact man and he would always find out and inform Dad when it was best to come up.

I have some vivid memories of Petersburg. It was here where I saw my first real snow, and the snowman that we used to read about in story books. However, it was in this northern part of Texas where I almost froze to death one cold morning when I insisted that I wanted to go with Dad to pick cotton. I was only six at the time. West Texas also provided many funny experiences: it was in Petersburg where a skunk peed on Pepe, the son of Don Inez Melchor. It was funny to us but Pepe did not appreciate it. However, this was typical of the life of the migrant cotton picker. And whether he was bitten by a snake, peed on by a skunk, or stung by a yellow jacket, he usually had no insurance to take care of him. Most of the time, to save money, we would not go to see a doctor; the only thing to do was to recover and get back to work. No one, except the migrant and his immediate family, gave a damn for the migrant's well-being. Usually when someone in the group was sick home-made remedies were used on him. If these did not work then and only then would one of us go to a doctor. This was the last resort because we could not afford to be under medical attention. In Petersburg an unusual event occurred that relates the importance placed on herbs and superstitition by the migrants.

One evening after a long day in the fields most of the men were gathered around a fire talking and telling ghost stories. One of my uncles, who was married and who migrated with us that particular year had sent his son, Alonzo to get him a pack of cigarettes. It had rained that evening and as Alonzo was coming back he slipped and fell. Since he had always had problems with his bones because of the lack of vitamin D, Alonzo broke his leg when he fell. He was immediately rushed to a hospital. That evening my older brother, Gumaro, just before going to bed went out to urinate and later claimed that he saw (or envisioned) Alonzo who told him, "Cousin, give me your hand, I have hurt myself." My brother knowing that Alonzo was in the hospital walked back in and did not say a word to anyone but was badly frightened.

The next morning his whole body was swollen. No one knew what was wrong and at first Mom would massage him with volcanic oil and give him hot teas made out of lemon leaves and other household remedies, but the swelling would not go away. Finally after two days Dad took Gumaro to two or three doctors in Lubbock and none of them could do anything to cure him. After the third trip to Lubbock an old man in our group said that Gumaro had been badly frightened by someone or something and that he could cure him. My dad agreed and allowed the old man to treat Gumaro for three consecutive nights. The old man would place him on a flat surface, cover him with a white sheet and sweep over the sheet. After the three nights were up the swelling went down and Gumaro was his normal self. Unbelievable but true. I was a witness to this and call it witchcraft or what you may but it worked and this is what a lot of the migrants practice either for "evil eye" or other maladies.

The injustices one suffered in the form of low pay for back breaking labor were minor compared to the degredation one suffered psychologically. The shacks where we lived as migrants were fire traps in the worst of shapes. The Luna family, however, usually obtained the best "home" when we went to a certain area because my Dad, as head of the group and owner of a truck, which he bought in 1952 in Hillsboro. was considered as the *Troquero* or *jefe* (leader). Since Dad carried almost everyone's belongings in his truck free of charge it was only natural that his family get the best residence. The only other compensation Dad received for being head of the group was that when we started to pick for a *patron,* the pickers would get a certain price for the pounds of cotton they picked, while Dad received 25 cents per hundred pounds for weighing the cotton and hauling it to the gin. Our group was an unusually small group and Dad and Don Melchor and the other heads of the families usually would not pick for a farmer unless housing was availabe. Most of the time the houses we stayed in were better than those of most other migrants, but they were still sub-standard. Ants, yellow jackets, cockroaches and often rats were the most common pests present in our make-to-do homes. Complaints to the owners were infrequent and were usually not voiced because of the fear of being asked to leave. Being insecure migrants striving for a livelihood four or five hundred miles from home, our parents usually suffered terrible conditions silently.

I guess the worst kind of abuse suffered by the Chicano migrant was direct embarrassment. Though most of the farmers could not speak Spanish and few of us spoke English, direct embarrassment could and did occur even to those who did not understand the English language. I suffered this embarrassment at the age of nine or ten and it scarred me for life. I will never forget when on the migration trail we stopped in a central Texas town while Dad and the other heads of families went to look at some cotton fields that this particular farmer wanted us to pick. It was in 1953 or 1954, anyway we were parked at the city park, and while Dad and the other men were gone an older member of the group and I went into a restaurant to eat breakfast and to bring back some breakfast and coffee for others. The man with me knew no English so I went along to order. At the restaurant we got a sneer from the waiter and after serving others who got there after we did he finally waited on us. I asked him very politely if we could have some breakfast. His reply was, "Sure you can have some breakfast but you will have to eat it outside." I called him a few choice words and the older man and I left the joint. From this time on I began to ask myself, why do these people hate us? Why do they treat us differently from other men? They want us to work for them—often cater to us during the harvest season—but after the harvest season is over they no longer want us around. They do not want us to talk to their daughters and even their sons adopt a condescending attitude toward us. They are willing to take our money at restaurants, and merchants and supermarkets open their doors to us on pay day yet they treat us with contempt and show no respect toward us as humans. WHY? WHY?

I could never understand this attitude towards the Chicanos as a young boy or a young man. How were they different from me? As far as I was concerned there was no human difference between us. True I had to pick cotton for a living while other farm boys my age drove their dad's tractors. The attitude of the *gringos* bothered me, but I never said much to my parents. I began to mature quicker because working for a living seems to make a person grow a little bit older. In the beginning the life of the migrant seemed to be a lot of fun and I envisioned ourselves as roaming gypsies. Yet as I started growing older and the same routine was followed year after year, the fun of migrating disappeared and disappointment and dissatisfaction set in. I realized that I was getting older, life was passing me by, and we had little other than sore backs to show for our work. I realized at the age of ten or eleven that the only way

to make a living comfortably was to get an education. Yet as migrants we attended schools only when the local authorities forced us to do so. The bosses we worked for never cared whether we went to school or not and never encouraged us to do so. Even when we did go to school while we were away from the Valley, we left very quickly because the work ended or because of the ridicule we suffered. Usually the Anglo kids would make fun of our clothes, our accent, or the beans and tortillas that we took to school for lunch. One time in West Texas I was involved in a fight in school because an Anglo kid made fun of the clothes my sister, Lucia, was wearing. That day we walked home and refused to go back to school. Afterwards we would pick cotton until about 8:30 in the morning, go home, and at 3:30 when school was out we would go back to the fields and pick cotton till dusk. This was the basic migratory pattern of our way of life from about 1950 until 1959. Dad would organize our uncles and the different families that were going to travel with us and every year the same route and routine were followed. During these years my older brothers and sisters married and for a while some of them traveled with us. Also one of my uncles, Jose Maria, married one of the daughters of the Melchor family, and more and more the group became interrelated. During these years Dad not only managed to buy a truck, in 1952, but he also purchased the two lots in Edinburg where my parents now live. This was done following the first season of migration. Afterwards he moved his one room house to its present site and he began to add to it. Sometimes my father would be the carpenter and he did as much of the plumbing as possible. Since 1951 our home has gone through several phases of "remodeling" with Dad splitting some of the work with a hired carpenter. Today our home is a frame home composed of three bedrooms, a bathroom, kitchen, and living room. At Christmas time of 1970 more remodeling was being done to the house by my father. Anyway after our migration in 1958, I noticed that I was beginning to have a more difficult time in school. So when 1959 rolled around I was the oldest child in the family still living at home. I told my mother that if they planned to leave for Robstown that year that they could count me out.

I was not going with them. If they left, I told her, I would stay with one of my aunts and go to school. My mother was furious and shocked at this obvious show of disrespect and only commented, "But you have always managed to pass." After a few minutes of debate with her I persuaded her that I was right and eventually the message was conveyed to my father who never said a word to me. My Dad is a silent type of person who speaks seldom, but since 1959 the Luna family never has migrated.

I had made up my mind that I wanted to go to school and graduate because I wanted to learn and also due to the fact that no one else in our family had really had the opportunity to go to school and to concentrate on getting a high school diploma. My two older brothers were forced to withdraw from school so they could work and help support the family and as far as my sisters were concerned, all they seemed to want was to get married, perhaps because they never did get a fair chance while in school. Too, they were constantly told by Mom to stay home and do the wash or the dishes or take care of the kids.

When we stopped migrating I began to concentrate on my studies. Dad would often take us to work on Saturdays but never did pull me out of school. I guess he began to realize how important education was. As far as his economic condition; it did not really improve. He was still getting paid seventy cents an hour on the Valley farm where he had always worked, and the only supplement to his income was the meager five cents a tree he was paid for hauling trees in his truck. Often he was allowed to be a share cropper but this was not enough to support a family of five plus a wife. However, Mother somehow or other squeezed those forty or fifty dollars Dad brought in per week and made them go a long way. Her favorite expression when we complained about the beans that we had to eat everyday was, "give thanks to God that you have something to eat."

After the migrations ceased our economic status did not improve a great deal, and it was around this time, when I was in the eighth grade, that I began to resent my father at times because he could not give us what middle class kids had. At the time I did not know how lucky I was, but I did know that other kids had better things and that was what I wanted. No, I never could understand that it took money and lots of it to feed seven people, pay bills, pay a mortgage on a house, clothe and send five children to school. Many other people, including myself perhaps, would have looked for an easy way out and would have perhaps gone to the local bars that dot highway 107 in Edinburg—El Matador, El Farol Verde, Robert's Drive Inn—or the countless other bars in Edinburg which would have been perfect places to seek refuge. Dad never did.

The only entertainment he allowed himself was a couple of beers on Saturdays and sometimes on Sundays. On Saturdays he would leave the house around 5:30 in the afternoon and return around 8:30 P.M. a little red in the cheeks, feeling high and friendly, and he would always give my little brother or sister a nickel or a dime or perhaps even a whole quarter. Everyone knew he had been drinking but no one blamed him since this was all the entertainment he obtained after working six days a week at hard labor. My Dad either dug citrus trees, or drove a tractor and for the money he was and is still paid, it is not worth it except to a man that has pride in his family. I call it pride but I really do not know what it is that has kept him going this long.

I guess I never really learned to love and appreciate my father until I moved away from home. As a teenager I resented him in a way for not being the provider that I expected. Later when I began to play in organized sports I resented him even more because he never showed an interest in what I was doing. Whether in sports or academic work my father never really seemed to care about me; yet today I know that he did and when he speaks to others about me he states with pride that I am his son.

When Dad stopped migrating he began to work full time with his old boss, Mr. B. Dad always had a job. He would work for Mr. B. before we left for the cotton harvest and after we came back he returned to his old job. Actually this is another peculiarity which made the Luna family and those that traveled with us different from many other migratory groups. Most of the people that traveled with us had a job to come back to when the cotton harvest was over; this was unlike many other migrants who came home and had no jobs and as a result in the two or three months that they were out of work they would spend their savings. Another peculiar thing about the Luna family and the other families that traveled with us was that all of us owned our homes while many other migrants only rented shacks in Edinburg or outside of Edinburg at a place called *La Hielera* (ice box). During the migration our group was also different in that we seemed to obtain better housing then most migrants and the decision on whether to work for a particular farmer or not was made by all of the heads of families and not by one single individual. Each head of a family had one vote and each individual adult who did not have a family but who traveled with the group had a vote. Usually the man with the largest family was the most influential. Our group was also different in regard to traveling accomodations. Dad never charged anyone to carry him or his few belongings in our truck as other truck owners did. Also my father never did operate like the labor contractors in California, the so-called *coyotes,* who contract people to work in a certain field and take a percentage of their earnings. Indeed it was an unusual group.

Today all of the eleven children of Gustavo and Antonia Luna are still living. Seven of us have married and only three boys and a girl remain at home with my parents. My father still works for Mr. B. and this coming year will mark the twenty-seventh year that he has worked for him. At the present he earns $1.00 per hour. My parents still regard Mr. B. as a nice old man who has helped them in time of need and as one who has loaned them money when they have needed it. They get upset when I tell them that Mr. B. has exploited the Luna's for years because even Dad's father worked for Mr. B. Yet Mom gets furious when I explain to her that the Luna's have made Mr. B. a wealthy man. The system used against my father is that of a landless man who has a family to support and the only thing he knows is farming. Mr. B. takes advantage of this and lends Dad money when he is in need, but all he has to do is call on Dad when he needs a job done and whether the temperature is 35 degrees or 110, Dad will work

for Mr. B. because he feels indebted to him. Even my mother to this day around Christmas time makes tamales to give to Mr. B., otherwise she feels that Mr. B. will not give them a $20 Christmas bonus. I constantly tell them that they have repaid Mr. B. a thousand times over because by paying them low wages Mr. B. has become a rich man. Yet, because they have drunk deeply of the old Chicano spirit that dared not raise its voice, they say nothing and still call Mr. B. a nice old man who has helped them.

This is part of the change that the Luna family has gone through since the migrations stopped in 1959. My father has settled down. Another change has been that the kids have been gaining an education and also Dad and Mom now take an interest in how the children are doing in school and who is running in local politics.

In comparing the Luna family to other migratory workers I would say we were extremely fortunate. Comparing the Luna family today to the rest of the families which migrated with us indicates that the Luna family has done much better than the rest. If we compare the Luna's and the Melchor's who were the two largest families in our group, an interview with Mr. Melchor reveals that none of his sons finished high school. He did state that they continued to migrate to West Texas often by themselves and often with another *jefe* until 1963 and by then most of his children had married. But of his eight children who used to go along with the Luna's, three of his girls married, though óne later got a divorce, and the fourth girl never married and until today she helps around the house. Ramiro, his oldest son got busted for Marijuana and passing hot checks and since he was a naturalized citizen he was deported to Mexico and is currently living in Monterrey. Pepe was about my age is a foreman in a packing shed. Of Don Melchor's two other sons, one is still a migrant and one just got out of the service. Don Melchor himself today works for a lumber yard and is an old man who forgets things easily. Thus in comparing the Melchor's and the Luna's, the Luna's appear to have done very well since 1959.

As far as the other families are concerned, my uncle, José Maria, who married one of the Melchor uncle who used to travel with us never married and is a sick man who only works part time. I never really knew what happened to the Aguilar's and as far as the Granado family, I did know one of their sons who finished school and enrolled in college.

This was the kind of life I went through in the 1950s when we migrated from town to town suffering humiliation in more ways than are mentioned. However, today in 1970, the decade of the Chicanos, times have changed and the new breed of Chicanos like me who are coming out of the colleges and universities will not accept the second class status to which our ancestors were relegated. We are willing to fight if necessary to break down the injustices done to our people. Today the new breed of Chicanos are a proud group who will not stand for stereotypes. We are a group of people who will no longer beg or request changes, instead we will demand them.

I firmly believe that in the 1970s many changes have to be made before this newly emerged group of brown people is pacified. Young Chicanos like myself who did not know any better in the late fifties and early sixties have seen and know a better way of life—a life that can be obtained only if we are offered an equal chance and treated as equals. Today especially in the United States there is much dissent and President Richard Nixon bores his audience with his pleas for unity. Well, I feel that this unity among Americans will come but it will not come; especially here in Texas, until the Anglos realize that there were Mexicans both inside and outside the Alamo. When this realization takes place perhaps a better understanding of the Chicanos and Anglos can take place in Texas. We do not want all of the pie, but we would sure like to know what apple pie tastes like. The Chicanos of the 1940s, '50s, and even early 1960s might have accepted things as they were, but today this new group of beautiful brown-skinned people who are in the universities and in the fields demand a change.

2.

THE URBAN
EXPERIENCE

The Urban Experience

The last section concluded by pointing toward the emergence of a new Chicano dedicated to Bronze Power. Precisely where the movement will go no one knows, but there are weather vanes showing revolutionary winds blow strongest in the urban areas. The migration from rural America to the city has increased each decade, and Chicanos are part of this trend. The city offers excitment, jobs, and very frequently for minority groups, disillusionment. Thus new leaders will emerge from the cities and the urban areas will increasingly become the vanguard of the struggle.

To maintain that poverty in the urban areas will spark protests does not mean that rural Chicanos have a life free of poverty and exploitation. The whole thrust of previous section proves the opposite. Rather, the city presents unique circumstances that allow skillful leaders to foment change. In political terms the urban *barrios* will increase their political strength commensurate with population growth. Either politicians listen to minority votes in the cities or they become ex-politicians. Moreover, newer Chicano leaders realize that many Mexican American problems are not unique, but are a manifestation of the general problems of urban America. Consequently, look for Black and Brown coalitions forming to force change. The key to this "New Politics," as current political scientists call such coalitions, is spreading the word. In the city easier access to communication media exists, and therein lies the method to expand and improve a base of political power. The base is spreading because the Chicano continues to break out of the Southwest and concentrates in other areas of urban America as well. Hence, students need now to understand the urban experience.

The beginning selection by Arthur J. Rubel discusses Chicano attitudes in a small city in South Texas. It should point out two themes to the student. First, a city does not require a population of a million or so to create an urban experience, and secondly, *barrios* in Los Angeles, Albuquerque, or New Lots have more in common as far as economic and cultural conditions than most urban dwellers suppose. Such phenonmena as riots, then, may soon sweep small as well as large cities. The Kerner Commission Report states that poverty created the discontent that led to riots in the Black ghettoes. Consequently, a contemporary article from the thirties in the *Monthly Labor Review,* and Albert Pena's statement corroborates Rubel's findings. They demonstrate also the continuing poverty and the widespread geographic dispersal of the Chicano in the urban areas. The possibility of riots and their backgrounds, is discussed in Ralph Guzmán's report to an American G. I. Forum in Denver, and Richard Griego and G. W. Merkx's discussion of New Mexico.

Rioting has been only one manifestation of urban minority discontent. Another has been the take-over of the inner city by minorities and the confidence this dominance has given them. Elroy Bode writes of the death of an Anglo high school because of a population shift in El Paso, Texas. His picture of the type of Chicano that this shift has produced offers some hint of Chicano politics of the future. Each must make his own predictions, but a reading of James Officer's and Donald Freeman's accounts of politics in South Tucson in the 1960s, where the Chicano has been a majority of the population for some time, and Guzman's sketch of California politics might help. But, the editors leave the student with Rodolfo González' query: "What political role for the Chicano Movement?"

Arthur J. Rubel

*Arthur J. Rubel (Associate Professor of Sociology, Notre Dame University) has written a well conceived account of a Texas barrio—*ACROSS THE TRACKS: MEXICAN AMERICANS IN A TEXAS CITY *(1966). The excerpt reprinted below describes the attitudes and economic life of Chicanos in the* EL PUEBLO MEXICANO *of South Texas. From Arthur Rubel,* ACROSS THE TRACKS: MEXICAN AMERICANS IN A TEXAS CITY *(University of Texas Press, 1966).*

Two Sides Of The Tracks

New Lots is a city bisected by the railway of the Missouri Pacific. In 1921, the town's first year, the north side of the tracks were allocated by municipal ordinance to the residences and business establishments of Mexican-Americans, and to industrial complexes. Mexican-Americans refer to the north side of the tracks as Mexiquito, *el pueblo mexicano, nuestro lado;* even the traffic light north of the tracks is referred to as *la luz mexicana.* The other side of the tracks is spoken of as *el lado americano, el pueblo americano,* and other similar terms. Those who live south of the tracks also distinguish the two sides: "this side" and "the other side," "our side," and "their side," and "Mexican town" are all descriptive terms heard in the city of New Lots.

The north and south sides of the railway are far more than geographical zones useful for purposes of description. Each side of the tracks is a society with its own characteristics; each has a peculiar rhythm. Each side acts on the basis of understandings that were founded on separate traditions. Finally, each side of the tracks reacts to its social universe in terms of a distinctive framework of experience.

The parental generation of New Lots attempts to bring up the children with a sense of right and wrong, one of which is rewarded, the other punished. The right and wrong of one side of the tracks, however, may conflict, and often does, with the sense of propriety of those of the other side.

Until 1946 all of those who lived south of the tracks were subsumed under the term Anglo-Americans, while those residing north of the railway were known as Mexican-Americans. The terms and their equivalents perpetuated the concept that the city was divided into two mutually exclusive zones—this side and the other side, *el pueblo mexicano and el pueblo americano.* (Exceptions to the general nature of the north-side population were provided by about twelve Negro families, who existed as an encapsulated community with its own elementary school and a small church. Furthermore, several Anglo-Americans married to Mexican-American spouses lived surrounded by the Mexican-American community.)

On the south side of the railway the descriptive "Mexican" or "Mexican-American" may often be used pejoratively, but such is not always the case. These terms may simply be used to help describe some presumed or actual general characteristic of the group to which the person referred to belongs; it lends context to the remark. For example, "That Mexican boy who works for me" may simply refer to the only bilingual employee of a business firm. Of course, it may also be meant in a derogatory way, pointing out some characteristic which that employee presumably shares with others of the Mexican-American group, a characteristic not possessed by Anglo-Americans. The critical feature of the utterance, therefore, is not the word "Mexican," but the relative stress which the speaker places on that word. If he stresses the word "Mexican," thus differentiating it from the rest of the statement, it can with a great deal of justice be considered an aspersive remark. On the other hand, if "Mexican" is accorded the same relative stress as the other words, we may rest assured that it is meant as a specifier, not as a depreciative. In any case, the person to whom reference is made will almost surely consider the remark pejorative because of the use of the word "Mexican," however it may be stressed. Such is the manner in which the nuances of language keep alive antagonism and mutual hostilities between the two ethnic groups.

In New Lots, Mexican-Americans almost always attach an explanatory preface to a description of the actions of someone else of the city. This preface places into a larger context the actions of the individual mentioned by intimating that so-and-so performed this action in such a manner *because* that is the way in which the generic Anglo-American does things, or because that is the fashion of the Mexican-American.

A number of other descriptives are used to imply a different way of life as perceived from one side of the tracks about the other. The north side of the railway is spoken of as Mexiquito—Little Mexico—or Mexican-town. *That* side is contrasted with *this* side, and *their* side with *our* side. When an Anglo-American speaks of the Mexican-American segment of the population, he says "they," "them," "the Mexicans," or, more politely, "the Latins." Use of any of those terms encompasses all those residents of New Lots whose background contains some Mexican or Spanish ancestry. The terms are therefore inclusive of a varied group of individuals, for its members are by no means genetically homogeneous, nor possessed of a common citizenship status. A Mexican-American of New Lots may be a tall person of slender stature with blue eyes, blonde hair, and a nose structure either long and slender or snubbed and slender. The term will also subsume those whose pigmentation is dark, whose stature is short and stout, and whose features include brown eyes, straight black hair, a wide nose, and a trace of epicanthic fold over the eye.

A large proportion of the 9,000 Mexican-Americans have either immigrated to the city from the Republic of Mexico in recent years, or are the children of immigrants. Many of the north-siders, however, are individuals from families which have lived for the past two hundred years on the Texas side of the international boundary. Nevertheless the terms used by Anglo-Americans to describe the Mexican-Americans of New Lots refer to citizen and noncitizen alike; to recent immigrant and native-born American; and to those who speak only Spanish, those who are bilingual, and the small number who speak only English. In New Lots the most common denominator of those recognized as Mexican-Americans is the possession of a progenitor of Mexican or Spanish descent.

Today's Anglo-American group of New Lots also represents a variety of distinctive social, religious, and racial backgrounds. The term Anglo-American is umbrellalike and covers a variety of hyphenated Americans: German-Americans; Swedish-Americans; English-, Irish-, and Scotch-Americans; Italian-Americans; and even Japanese-Americans. Persons in these categories are *never* spoken of in terms of their subgrouping, and the subject comes up only during discussions of parental and grandparental backgrounds. By contrast, those with one or more Spanish or Mexican ancestors are *always* designated by Mexican-American, Latin American, or a similar term.

The approximately 6,000 Anglo-Americans in New Lots belong to a number of different religious persuasions. Some are Catholics, but they are relatively few, as the overwhelming majority are Protestants. The churches with the largest memberships are the Baptists and the Methodists, but there are also strong representations of Presbyterians, Christians, Episcopalians, and Seventh-Day Adventists. The Reorganized Church of Latter-Day Saints and a number of Pentecostal groups, supplemented by a small Christian Science institution, complete the roster.

Although the founding stratum of Anglo-American society in New Lots was composed of well-to-do emigrants from small towns of the north-central and north-eastern states of this nation, as well as from Canada, they were joined by a later influx of poor Southerners from East Texas, Louisiana, Mississippi, and Georgia. Each segment contributed its mores to the Anglo-American society of this city. But the alternative ways of behavior of the many strands in the south-side Anglo society tend to be minimized, and the more universal aspects of the "Anglo way of life" are maximized in the face of the numerically more important Mexican-American segment of the town. From the commencement of social life in New Lots the Anglo-American group has striven to protect its mode of living from Mexican-American influences, while assuming at the same time that the Mexican-American way of life should and would be changed.

Today in New Lots, Mexican-Americans speak of the others as *anglos, angloamericanos, bolillos, gavachos,* and *gringos.* When speaking of themselves, the Mexican-Americans speak of the *chicanos* or *la raza;* they also employ two other terms, the *mexicanos* and the *latinos,* or *latinoamericanos.* The last two are utilized only in the presence of a *bolillo* with whom one is not acquainted. *La raza* groups together all those in the world who speak Spanish; it implies both a mystical bond uniting Spanish-speaking people and a separation of them from all others.

The manner in which a Mexican-American attacks a problem, or the way in which an individual chicano conceptualizes a problem, is generalized to indicate that that particular coping behavior or conceptualization is peculiarly chicano. Mexican-Americans are wont to speak of generic attitudes or behaviors uniquely chicano. Quite often the contrast between a presumed Mexican-American solution to a problem and that which an Anglo-American would elect is set forth in the form of a self-turned witticism. For example, Mexican air-conditioning is described as the emptying of a sack of dry ice in the rear seat of an automobile. The self-turned witticism takes other forms as well. At times when the very popular tune "Mexico! No hay dos" blares from the jukebox, a wit exclaims "Gracias a Dios!" (There is but one Mexico! Thank God!)

The numerous stories and the often-quoted witticisms expressive of ambivalence and inconsistency—supposedly inherent traits of the Mexican-American—are tokens of the cultural and social fact that the Mexiquito Mexican-Americans are across the tracks from the Anglo-Americans, and across the frontier from the wellsprings of their traditional culture. Neither fish nor fowl, they are at home with neither of the groups that are significant to them. A young man who is a native-born citizen of the United States, as are his wife and children, posed the poignant problem of identity: "The other day my boy came home from school and asked me, 'Daddy, am I an American citizen?'"

As one walks across the tracks along the main thoroughfare of the city, he leaves one kind of scene and enters another. North of the tracks the whirring sounds of the mechanical belts, which bring the crates of packed vegetables and fruits from packing shed to motor truck and railroad car, are heard throughout the day and often until midnight. Interspersed with this north-side sound is the raucousness of the *ranchero* tunes from the juke boxes of the thirteen *cantinas* of that side of the tracks. These bars along the thoroughfare form the most popular type of commercial enterprise owned by Mexican-Americans, with the exception of food markets. Ten grocery stores front on the Boulevard on the north side, and more than fifty small neighborhood grocery stores are distributed in the residential areas. Although they are conveniently located, their stock is small; most of the smaller groceries cannot sell either fresh meat or milk products, for example, because they lack refrigerating facilities. Consequently, here the forgetful housewife purchases an onion, a single tomato, or a loaf of bread. The major family shopping is done in one of the larger grocery stores, where beans, flour, and rice may be purchased in sacks weighing twenty or fifty pounds. On Friday and Saturday nights the sidewalks in front of the three largest groceries north of the railway are thronged with shoppers; with boxes of groceries and sacks of staples, the families await the truck or station wagon provided by the store to carry them home to the peripheries of the north side, or to the vegetable farms where their cabins are located.

Three of the largest stores fronting on the main street sell work clothing. Prominently displayed in the show windows are high rubber boots, so useful for those who must work in the irrigation canals; denim and gabardine shirts and trousers; and the characteristic wide-brimmed straw hats, which deflect the rays of the sun from the face of the agricultural wage laborer. Two of the large clothing stores on the north side are owned and managed by European Jewish immigrants who escaped from the Polish *pogroms;* the other is the property of a Catholic chicano, who is so devout that he is called Jesusito—Little Jesus.

Four of the shops along the north Boulevard specialize in lending money to Mexican-Americans at usurious interest rates: 50 percent of the principal for short-term, small loans. A number of retail outlets sell used furniture and household ap-

pliances. In fact, more stores sell used articles of clothing and furniture than sell those goods new. Although one of the three drug stores of the north side boasts a licensed pharmacist, all three are heavily stocked with well-advertised patent medicines, which are supplemented by an inventory of brightly packaged *medicinas caseras*—home cures. Mostly balms made from herbs, barks, roots, and oils, these are wrapped in the colorful emblems of Don Pedrito or La Palma, the two wholesale distributors, whose traditional *remedios* are sold throughout South Texas. These remedies are retailed in New Lots at two other shops on the north side as well, both of which also sell Spanish-language periodicals and books. *Policía,* the Spanish equivalent of the Police Gazette, rests between volumes on how to learn English in just a few weeks and a book of instructions in the art of bewitching and beguiling by means of charm and incantation. In addition, traditional remedies are sold in several of the ten grocery stores along the Boulevard.

The remaining frontage on North Boulevard is occupied by a movie house dedicated to the showing of Spanish-language films, by seven restaurants, seven gasoline service stations, three bakeries, a tortilla factory, two photographic studios, a window-glass shop, a shoe repair store, a beauty shop, and a dry-cleaning establishment. All of the restaurants and bars are licensed for the sale of beer, a prodigious amount of which is consumed during the oppressively hot, humid months between April and October.

In Mexiquito, New Lots' north side, is a total of five elementary schools. One is attended exclusively by Negro children; another is a Catholic parochial institution attended by 575 students, of whom 25 are Anglos. The remainder of the grade schools are attended exclusively by Mexican-Americans. It is estimated that the Mexican-American students in the elementary grades total 3,100, but the number of registrants varies markedly according to the migratory work cycle. For example, in the 1957–1958 school year 400 more children were registered in the eighth week of the term than in the first week. During the same year there were 40 more registrants in the tenth week than in the eighth.

Of course, the growth cycle of the fruits, vegetables, and cotton, on which most of Mexiquito's families are dependent for a livelihood, varies from year to year, and school registrations reflect those variations in crop cycles. For example, there were 133 fewer registrants in the eighth week of the 1958–1959 term than in the previous year, and 10 fewer in the tenth week.

In Mexiquito, where most of the students do not continue in school beyond the primary grades, officials estimate a drop-out rate of 75 percent at the sixth-grade level. Because relatively few of those who attain a sixth-grade level ever participate in activities of the senior high school, the administration has originated a special certificate of achievement to be awarded those who discontinue their studies at this time.

There are a number of factors which mitigate against continuance of studies in senior or even junior high school for the bulk of the Mexican-American youngsters. Undoubtedly, the most important single problem is that posed by financial hardship in the families dependent on wage labor in agriculture and other unskilled employment. Furthermore, it is unquestionably true that many of the children are simply not motivated to continue studies past the sixth-grade level, as is true of many others who are not Mexican-Americans. But there are factors which are peculiarly applicable to the bicultural circumstances found in New Lots, factors which discourage students from Mexiquito.

Teachers and administrators of the city school system place an extraordinary emphasis on what might best be thought of as "civic responsibilities" and "personal hygiene," or "citizenship," if you will. This emphasis is apparent in all grades of the school system, but its intensity is exaggerated at the junior- and senior-high-school levels. The New Lots school system is organized to make of its students mirror-images of contemporary Anglo society, a type of society in which one's primary orientations, even if only on the surface, are toward responsibilities to civic and religious groups in which one holds membership. Later sections of this volume will point out that such orientations contrast with the basic values of the Mexican-American society. In many instances it seemed that the personnel of the school system were intent on developing Anglo-Americans out of young Mexican-Americans as a primary goal, and paid far less attention to their academic achievements. For example, an administrator commented as follows about the admission procedures with regard to the transfer of Mexican-American children from the elementary school in Mexiquito to the junior high school located south of the tracks.

We try to get kids' hair cut, get 'em to look like the rest; cut off the *pachuco* style, and the bowl-type haircut. You've been down to Old Mexico where they go around with their shirts unbuttoned all the way down to the navel, and then they tie it around their waist. They think it makes them look sexy. We can't have that here.

Another said:

I don't know what you think about it, but we screen our kids before they are admitted to the school. If a kid wants to stay he has to get a good haircut, cut off the sideburns; we don't allow any mustaches in this school, once the subject has begun to shave.

Despite such hazards a growing number of Mexican-American youngsters enter and graduate from junior and senior high school. Education has assumed major importance as a criterion of achieved social status among young people of Mexiquito. They are quite aware that education, in particular English-language skills, is a prerequisite for attainment of improved occupation and income in the New Lots society. Increased income gained from steady, "clean" employment is the prize won by those who have gained fluency in English.

During the Second World War and the conflict in Korea a number of chicano servicemen received training as clercial workers, mechanics, and technicians. After the wars many returning servicemen took advantage of veterans' benefits to continue their education. Today's work force in Mexiquito, unlike that of former years, contains a significant proportion of laborers engaged in occupations other than "stoop" or "dirty" work. Some chicanos are engaged as physicians, teachers, nurses, pharmacists, and ministers of religion. Many others are salesclerks, and most clerical positions in New Lots—north and south side—are filled by qualified chicano men and women. Furthermore, several retail businessmen today compete successfully with their Anglo counterparts.

These chicanos aspire toward life goals which include social equality with Anglos. Some distinguishing features of this aggregation of mobile Mexican-Americans are its aspirations toward such status symbols as regular income derived from "clean," that is, nonagricultural, employment, English-language skills, high-school and college education, and possession of such other status markers as automobiles, refrigerators, television sets, and barbecue "pits." Among chicanos the status marker which excites the most comment is the type of house in which an individual resides, and the neighborhood in which it is located, that is, whether it is found in *el pueblo mexicano* or *el pueblo americano.*

Within Mexiquito one fails to discover neighborhoods marked by distinctive life styles indicative of social-class differentials. If one strays from the main Boulevard the dust of the unpaved side streets clings to face, hands, and clothing during the hot, humid spring and summer months. In autumn and winter the passage of pedestrian or automobile along these side streets is made difficult, or sometimes impossible by mud and standing water. Homes are generally impoverished and unpainted, with here and there a brightly painted building surrounded by a high wire fence. The residences of the north side range from one-room shacks, consisting of corrugated paper stretched around four posts and covered by a roof of planks, to multi-room structures of wood or plaster, handsomely maintained and painted in bright colors of blue, green, orange, pink, or white. In these, a visitor finds the appurtenances of middle-class life: a bright new refrigerator, a large gas stove and oven, an electric mixer for cooking, an electric washing machine, a suite of well-padded furniture, and, sometimes, a cocktail bar. Homes such as these are scattered throughout Mexiquito's

neighborhoods, where they house teachers, pharmacists, salesclerks, successful businessmen, commercial truckers, and supervisory employees in the packing sheds.

The buildings just described, and the material goods which they contain, are in marked contrast to most of the homes in any Mexiquito neighborhood. Most households north of the tracks clearly show the effect of a prevailing wage of fifty cents an hour; that is, when work is available. Most of the populace of Mexiquito are dependent on seasonal work as agricultural laborers. As a consequence, incomes in Mexiquito tend to be low, seasonal, and undependable.

In this neighborhood, as in South Texas generally, most Mexican-Americans are occupied as agricultural wage laborers. Approximately two thirds of the residents of the north side are employed as field laborers, most of whom are forced by dire necessity to migrate between March and December of every year in search of employment. A study of the earnings of wage laborers residing in South Texas shows that the average daily earnings of a farm worker were as low as $4.02, and that the daily wages earned by seasonal workers while employed in nonagricultural tasks averaged $5.03. These estimates are based on a sample of 594 chicano workers. During late fall and early winter, when agricultural workers reside in this region, the average daily earnings amounted to $4.91. The wage scales which reign here rank among the very lowest in the nation.

Independent calculations made in Mexiquito during the course of the present study fully support the reports by Metzler and Sargent. According to our figures, seasonal workers seldom earn more than $4.50 for a full day's work in the fields around Mexiquito, and even those who are employed as delivery truck drivers, package-boys in grocery stores, and other work of that ilk, earn between $3.50 and $4.00 for a full day's employment. Moreover, those who have been able to secure "clean" nonagricultural, jobs consider themselves peculiarly fortunate because of the regularity of the employment. The low wage scale is not the only serious problem which seasonal workers confront while at home base; as has already been implied, *under*employment in Mexiquito is at least as important! During the period in which they are not migrating in the northern states, chicano agricultural laborers are insured employment only three out of six work days in any single week. The study by Metzler and Sargent found underemployment of laborers to be a problem of utmost gravity throughout the south of Texas.

As a consequence of the underemployment and depressed wage scale, which characterize the Valley economy, almost all residents of Mexiquito who are employed as farm laborers must migrate periodically to other sectors of the nation to augment their income. In 1958 a total of 7,637 migrants left New Lots and a nearby smaller town in search of work during the spring, summer, and fall months of the year. The sum represented approximately 90 percent of the total of interstate migrants, and 60 percent of those who migrated within the boundaries of Texas. In 1956 an incomplete tabulation reported that 4,005 migrants had left the city in search of work elsewhere in the nation. Based on a sample of thirty Mexiquito households, the average earnings per migrant household amount to $2,400 in a prosperous year (1957).

The depressed wage scale which characterizes agricultural employment in Mexiquito affects the wage scale of nonagricultural employees as well. Only those employers of New Lots who are engaged in interstate commerce offer employment which pays laborers one dollar an hour, the minimum federal wage. Most of the work available to the unskilled and semiskilled workers of Mexiquito pays between forty and seventy-five cents per hour. Despite the comparatively low wages, steady, nonagricultural employment in New Lots is at a premium Those who earn as much as $40.00 per week comment that "We're never going to be millionaires but we've come a long ways," while a young family head who earns $27.00 for a sixty-six-hour work week recalls that when he received his first pay check, "I thought I was rich."

There are some Mexican-Americans in Mexiquito who earn well above $30.00 and $40.00 per week, but not many. Among them are one physician, thirty school teachers, approximately twenty successful merchants, some commission-salesmen, and ten municipal employees other than teachers. Those chicanos who do not regularly migrate from Mexiquito regard themselves as a fortunate few, and are so regarded by others. Although their wages are by no means high when compared with wages elsewhere in the nation, their employment is steady and not dependent upon the vagaries of the weather.

Several reasons are advanced by employers for the low wage scale which prevails in the city. Some assert that their trade will not permit an increase in the wages of those whom they employ, and others claim that they do not raise wages of their employees for moral reasons. "Some of those who know the Mexicans best tell us that if we *have* to raise their wages, to do it slowly because their moral fiber can't stand too much money all at one time," according to one Anglo employer.

There are, however, more compelling factors which contribute to the unusually low rate of pay in this city. New Lots' location, just across the international boundary with Mexico, makes it very attractive to illegal immigrants. Inasmuch as the dollar is worth more than twelve times the Mexican peso, wages in dollars seem incredibly high to the "wetback." One young, native-born citizen of the United States described the economic situation succinctly.

The bad thing about New Lots is that people are always wanting to work for less than you are and take your job. Jobs are hard to get; suppose Mr. Smith went up to a boy on the street, one who spoke English, and said to him: "Do you want a job in a store?" "Sure!" he would say. "You bet!" Maybe he wouldn't even ask what the pay was, but if they offered him $18.00 or $20.00 and I'm getting $35.00 he would take it like that!

Then Mr. Smith would come over to me and say: "Well Telésforo, things are slow at the store, and I'm afraid that we're going to have to let you go." That's the trouble with the Mexican people; we need the money so bad, we have to feed our kids, we have to get frijoles into the house. Any job is good; we need the money real bad, and we'll work for anything!

Take that Señora Filomena, she works for any money. One of us—people who were born here in this country—will be working for an Anglo as a maid and getting $8.00 a week, ironing. She'll work from eight in the morning until two in the afternoon. But when someone like Señora Filomena comes around from Mexico she won't even ask what the Anglos will pay her. She'll work from seven until seven and when they hand her $3.00 at the end of the week there's nothing she can say about it. All she wanted was work so that she could get some food in the house. You see, that's the trouble—we don't even have any way to be sure that we have a job. Our people will work for anything, they'll take your job away from you.

Between 1946 and 1957 some, but not all, status-conscious and upwardly mobile young veterans of the Second World War moved across the tracks to the Anglo side. In 1957 a census counted 150 such mobile families. During 1958 four intimate acquaintances of mine made inquiries of realtors about property located on the Anglo side, and so the trend continues. Some of those chicanos now living south of the tracks reside in elaborate two-storied homes, or in more recently constructed ranch-type houses. These tend to cost a sum which amounts to more than $10,000. On the other hand, some who have moved across the tracks now reside in square, weathered, board buildings. In any case, the monetary value of the residence is of far less importance than is the fact that it is located in *"el pueblo americano."*

Some generalizations may be advanced about those chicanos who have elected to move south of the tracks. They are less than fifty years old; the rarely encountered oldsters prove to be widowed parents residing with a married son or daughter. The great majority of those who have moved from the north side are veterans of either the Second World War or the Korean conflict. Those who corss the tracks take advantage of federal veterans' legislation to facilitate the purchase of their house lot, and the construction or remodeling of

their homes. The young men are all bilingual, but some of their wives speak only Spanish. None of these south-side chicanos work as "stoop" laborers in agricultural season labor, and their annual income ranges from $2,400 to $20,000. However, the *sum* of the income is of far less significance than its dependability. All chicanos living across the tracks today are either salaried or self-employed. In many families both husband and wife work; their unvarying income, regardless of its total worth, permits them to engage extensively in credit buying. It is a generally acknowledged fact that one need not possess a handsome income in order to make expensive purchases. Chicanos who move to the Anglo side of town represent an aggregation of upwardly mobile young people with steady incomes.

Those who move south of the tracks and others who seriously contemplate the action share significant objective indicators of social-class status. They have completed elementary or high school, are employed in "clean" occupations, and boast dependable incomes; they also share corollary indices of class position, for example, substantial homes, relatively new automobiles, and such indoor appurtenances as television sets, refrigerators, ovens and stoves, and indoor plumbing.

Not all those who possess these material and cultural goods elect to move to the Anglo side of the tracks. Some decide to erect new homes and bring up their children in one of Mexiquito's neighborhoods, while others leave the city entirely. Whether it is appropriate to move across the tracks and be associated with the *bolillos* is a debate which stirs strong sentiments among chicanos whose acquisition of the aforementioned prerequisites of status mobility makes such a move attractive. Those electing to leave Mexiquito contend that one's obligations are restricted to himself and his family, and that a move to the other side will show Anglos that chicanos are as good as they are. Those who remain in Mexiquito, on the other hand, express the point of view that the more successful chicanos have an obligation to show or demonstrate to the less motivated how to achieve a "better" mode of life. However, from information garnered in private conversations, it appears that those who elect not to leave Mexiquito, although financially capable of doing so, feel less adequate and more timid about moving into *el pueblo americano*. In some cases a wife or coresident mother speaks little or no English, or one of the parents fears that his children's darker pigmentation will invite open hostility from the new neighbors. Hostilities are not, however, unidirectional, for some of the aspiring Mexican-Americans give as their reasons for not moving across the tracks the undesirability of living next door to "white hilly-billies," or to "white trash."

The apprehensions of those chicanos whose aspirations for enhanced social status urge them to leave Mexiquito, but who elect instead to remain, are nurtured by the evident unhappiness and disillusionment of those who preceded them across the tracks. Today, Anglos continue to lump together as "Mexicans" or "Latins," or "Latin Americans," all those with a Spanish or Mexican ancestor, regardless of the side of town on which they reside. The entire *chicanazgo*—laborer and professional alike—is lumped together by Anglos into a subordinate group based on ascribed characteristics. Those chicanos who move across the tracks prove unsuccessful in their attempts to engage Anglo neighbors in fruitful personal relationships. To an objective observer the discouraging response is less a failure by Anglos to validate the newly achieved status of the aspirant than a reflection of the manner by which Anglos organize social life. Among Anglos, friendships derive from consociation in formal corporate groups, such as Lions Club, Rotary, Optimists, Volunteer Fire Department, Chamber of Commerce, Beef Trust, Bible-Study Class, and others too numerous to mention here. By contrast, chicanos incorporate formal groups on foundations of informal associations with acquaintances or *palomillas*. Inability to engage Anglo peers in friendship relations is bitterly galling to upwardly striving chicanos. They interpret the "rebuff" as discriminatory and liken it to the rejection of Negroes by whites. Although there is no doubt that a number of fraternal clubs and church organizations are closed to chicanos, others do cultivate their participation, where as they do not cultivate that of the Negro. When the Mexican-Americans fail to join the organizations open to them, or to participate actively in them,

reluctance is interpreted by the Anglos as unfriendliness, and is considered diagnostic of a lack of civic responsibility. In the final analysis, whatever may be the objective reason why chicanos do not participate with their Anglo neighbors in activities both formal and informal, the chicanos conclude that a ceiling has been placed on their access to higher social status.

As one consequence of the assumed "rebuff," chicanos who reside in Anglo neighborhoods do not cut their ties with Mexiquito; they continue to interact with Mexiquito-based *palomillas* with the same frequency and intensity as before they moved across the tracks. The high frequency of interaction between those on the south side and those who remain in Mexiquito deters crystallization of social-class sentiments in the Mexican-American society. One young couple, who recently moved to the other side of the tracks, offer a representative example of the feelings of insecurity felt and voiced by the mobile young chicanos of New Lots. Both man and wife speak perfect English as well as Spanish and each is a high-school graduate. The young husband manages a retail store, and his wife is employed as a salesclerk elsewhere. The wife is bitterly disappointed with life "over there." "What's the matter with our people?" she asks. "Nobody comes to visit us, and we haven't made any friends over there." The disenchantment of this young couple with life across the tracks is brought forth by other young chicanos as ammunition to support their position that the more affluent and better educated chicanos should remain with "our own people."

The ethnographic evidence reveals the lack of clearly defined social classes among chicanos. Distinctions between ranked categories are at best tenuous and ill-defined, but such concepts are not totally absent from the chicanos' frame of reference. Furthermore, those sentiments seem to be increasing in significance. More explicitly, chicanos on the south side have not developed a sense of solidarity which excludes those who elect to remain in Mexiquito. Mexican-Americans motivated toward upward mobility do not conceive of themselves as filling a unique status vis-à-vis Anglos. One *never* hears south-side chicanos speak of "we," "us," "our," or similar terms to distinguish them from residents of the north side of the tracks.

Two terms, "high Mexicans" and "low Mexicans," were invented by the editor of a neighborhood news sheets to refer to those who move to the south side and to those who remain northsiders, respectively. The former term is being utilized in opprobrium, for a person mentioned in the newsheet as a "high Mexican" is one considered to have "turned his back" on the chicano way of life, though he need not be a person of either affluence or prestige. A "low Mexican," on the other hand, is one who remains a resident of Mexiquito, regardless of income and influence. Neither of the two terms has gained any currency among the chicanos, and their usage appears to be confined to the editor of the newssheet and his family.

Once a very acculturated chicano described as a "bracket" some men whom he planned to invite to an exclusive social function, but I never again heard the term. Similarly, those who perform low-paid "stoop" labor in agriculture are sometimes derogated by the adjective tomateros (literally, those who work with tomatoes). However, in a search for verbal symbols of social distinctions, although it proved possible to elicit the term from informants, I never heard tomateros used in conversation with others, or in discussions that were overheard.

New Lots today reveals two kinds of stratification, one of which is based on ascribed features, the other on achievement. In the first place, Anglos interact with Anglos, chicanos with other chicanos. For example, employees of a retail establishment, Anglo and chicano alike, may banter, bet on the outcome of sports contests, and discuss world affairs in animated fashion. But, at the coffee break or the lunch hour, members of one cultural group separate from fellow employees of the other group, whether or not English is a means of communication commonly shared. Little League baseball games draw enthusiasts throughout the season. The stands are not segregated (nor are any other publicly owned facilities) and chicanos sit right next to Anglo rooters, but an incredible lack of communication between chicanos and Anglos is evident although they may oc-

cupy adjoining seats throughout the season. These are several examples of chicano-Anglo relations, but the list is too extensive to include all observations here. In New Lots one continues to be an Anglo or a Latin, a chicano or an americano. The society is stratified on the basis of ascribed characteristics into two cultural groups, Anglo and chicano.

Within the chicano group are present more subtle stratifications, based mainly on the kind of occupation in which one engages. Those employed as agricultural field laborers do not interact with others not so occupied, nor do members of each of the occupational groups attend public dances in the plaza on the same evening. Observations of behavior in Mexiquito indicate that the schism between agricultural laborers and others is widening, but further status distinctions within the Mexican-American society have been slower to emerge.

An emergent sentiment of class identification by status seekers who share certain symbols, in particular, type of employment and English-language skills, heralds a new phase in the history of group relations in New Lots. Upwardly mobile chicanos aspire to a life goal of equality with Anglos, whose status symbols they have acquired. If aspiring chicanos continue to feel "rebuffed" by dominant Anglos, and if they continue to feel their aspirations are capped by status ceilings, either of two results may be foreseen. Either the socially ambitious will leave the city in an attempt to resolve the perceived status inconsistency or else the qualities of alienation and anxiety, which figure so prominently in their attitudes, will increase in intensity. However, if upwardly mobile chicanos find that ceilings on their status aspirations have been removed, they will channel their energies to achievement of the social status which they seek.

SUMMARY

From its very inception the city of New Lots has been divided into two clearly demarcated neighborhoods. The north side of the railway was assigned to industrial plants and the residences of Spanish-speaking families, while the south side was allocated to English-speaking families. Over the course of the years each side of the tracks became clearly identified as either the Mexican or the Anglo side, *el pueblo mexicano* and *el pueblo americano,* this side and the other side. The lives of those on one side of the tracks were different from those on the other side; each of the neighborhoods preserved its own linguistic, educational, social, and dietary habits.

Today, as one crosses the tracks from one neighborhood to the other, a considerable change is evident from what is reported to have prevailed in the 1920s; yet each side remains distinctive. In part, the differences to be found today are due to the traditional cultures which guide the lives of those who live north and south of the tracks, respectively, but, also, the differences reflect the low income characteristic of Mexiquito families in contrast to the relatively high income of those living in *el pueblo americano.* Furthermore, the level of income is clearly associated with the amount of formal education one has achieved.

In Mexiquito there are five elementary schools, of which three are attended by Mexican-American youngsters, another exclusively by Negroes, and, finally, the fifth, a Catholic parochial school is attended by 575 children from Mexiquito and by 25 others from across the tracks. Beyond the sixth grade the relatively few children from Mexiquito (approximately 25%) who continue their education converge with their Anglo peers on the junior and senior high school, both located south of the tracks. Over the years, and especially since 1946,

increasingly large numbers of Mexican-American children have attended high school. The manifest goals of these highly motivated youngsters are English-language competence and "clean," steady employment, which is its correlate.

Moreover, beginning in 1946 the south-side bars on Mexican-American residents were lifted, and one now encounters approximately 150 such families in what was formerly an exclusively Anglo neighborhood. Characteristically, the adults of these newcomer families are young, are competent in both Spanish and English, possess a high-school or college education, and are engaged in occupations other than agricultural field labor.

Despite the differences in income, level of education, occupation, and bilingual skills, which set apart those chicanos now living south of the tracks from their counterparts in Mexiquito, no sense of solidarity binds together those on one side and excludes chicano residents of the other side. The failure of such a sense of solidarity to develop may be traced to two factors, of which the most important is that many chicanos, who are high-school and college graduates, who are employed in regular clean jobs, and who control English as well as Spanish-language skills, choose *not* to leave Mexiquito for the other side of the tracks. Secondly, those who have so elected to cross from the north to the south side have not yet been assimilated into the Anglo way of life. In New Lots, cultural differences continue to divide Anglo-American from Mexican-American, no matter on which side of the tracks a family resides.

The MONTHLY LABOR REVIEW. *This article is based upon the writings of Paul Taylor. It tells of recruiting and conditions of a Mexican labor colony at Bethlehem, Pennsylvania from 1927 to 1930. This colony can be considered a typical one.*
By permission of THE MONTHLY LABOR REVIEW.

Mexican Labor Colony At Bethlehem, Pa.

The Mexican colony in Bethlehem, Pa., was built up mainly by the transportation from the Southwest of Mexican workers under contract with the Bethlehem Steel Co. In 1923 the settlement reached its peak population of about 1,000. Since then its numbers have rapidly declined, and in 1929 there were probably 350 or 400 in the colony, with those arriving and leaving about balancing each other. A monograph dealing with this colony forms the sixth of the published researches made by Paul S. Taylor on a grant from the Social Science Research Council and issued by the University of California. He made three visits to Bethlehem—the first in the early part of 1928 and the last in the early part of 1930.

Previous to 1923 there were only a few Mexicans in Bethlehem. In the spring of that year, however, there was an industrial revival and the steel company's idle furnaces were again started up. In order to meet the increasing demand for labor, efforts were made to secure Mexicans, with the result that between April 6 and May 30, 1923, there were 912 Mexican men, 29 women and 7 children transported from Texas to Bethlehem. Mexican workers were also sent to other plants of the company.

The recruiting was done through Texas employment agencies, cooperating with the Mexican consulate general in San Antonio. One of the company's Spanish employees was detailed to

132

Texas to aid in procuring and handling the desired labor. A representative of the Bethlehem Steel Co. and the Mexican consul general in San Antonio signed the contract covering the Mexican nationals shipped out of that city, as the latter wished to protect his departing countrymen.

According to the agreement, the cost of transportation was to be deducted from earnings in semimonthly installments of $3.50 each, but those who remained in the employ of the company one year were to receive back all deductions. The transportation of families was paid by the company without reimbursement. Quarters and board were provided in company houses for $1.10 a day. Wages were to be a minimum of 30 cents per hour, for such hours as were permitted by Pennsylvania statute, and were to be the same as those of men of other nationality doing the same work. Mexicans were not to be discharged without just cause, and any who might become public charges for whatever cause were to be returned at company expense to San Antonio. Under the latter provision the company did return some injured Mexicans, not only to San Antonio but to their homes in Michoacan.

The boarding house at Bethlehem was run by a commissary company which used Mexican cooks. Certain families did their own cooking. A Mexican with a small store sold groceries and other commodities which his countrymen desired, and for awhile was protected against bad debts by company deductions from wages.

The coming of the Mexicans was without doubt a shock to the people of Bethlehem and gave rise to exaggerated statements about this newly imported labor. It was rumored that these workers were strike breakers taking the places of natives who were reported to have left the plant demanding higher wages. Some weeks before there had been danger of serious labor disturbances. The company representative, however, regarded these reports as propaganda to keep Mexicans from coming to Bethlehem and denied the existence of a strike. An investigation was made by the Mexican consul at Philadelphia, who found conditions satisfactory to the imported laborers.

In 1929 a minor official of the company said, in reference to the attitude of the other workers toward the newcomers: "The other employees knew there was a shortage of labor, so they accepted the Mexicans.' That the Bethlehem workers were not pleased at the advent of the Mexicans is quite obvious, however, the writer thinks, from a newspaper item published about the time of their arrival. The claim that there was a dearth of labor at this period is corroborated by the Pennsylvania State employment office report under date of March 15, 1923, that "in the iron and steel industry it is impossible to supply the needs for unskilled workers."

In order to avoid the importing of diseased workers to Bethlehem, prospective recruits were required to submit to a physical examination in Texas.

LABOR RELATIONS

Some Mexicans come to Bethlehem in search of work because they hear of the large steel mills in that locality. If they get jobs they stay, if not, they leave. Considerable numbers of them have come to Bethlehem because they had relatives already employed in the town. Frequently, money has been forwarded to Mexico or Texas to enable them to make the long trip. A remarkable instance is that of one of the group shipped from Texas in 1923, who has been followed by 7 brothers and 3 sisters, together with the families of those who were married, making a total of 30 persons.

As soon as the Mexicans reached Bethlehem in 1923 they began to scatter to look for more attractive jobs than the steel company offered. The greatest number on the pay roll of that company in any month of those who were originally brought from Texas in 1923 was 790 in May of that year. By the middle of the summer there were 24 percent less, by November the number was 53 percent under the maximum, and by the close of the same year 71 percent.

In the spring of 1930 only 46 Mexicans who were known to belong to the original group shipped in 1923 remained on the company's rolls.

Estimates of the total number of Mexicans employed in 1930 range from 90 to 150. Including Mexicans born in the United States, the writer considers 125 a conservative figure.

Upon arrival in Bethlehem the original contingents of Mexicans were concentrated in bunkhouses in a labor camp. In a little over a year, however, the scattering of Mexicans to other localities in the East, their return to the Southwest or Mexico, and their dispersion to other domiciles in Bethlehem depopulated the camp. The company then ceased to provide special arrangements for boarding Mexicans. Some of the solos were already boarding with Mexican families; now they are found boarding with Polish, Wendish, Slovak, Spanish, and Mexican families. Some of them live in groups, renting and housekeeping for themselves, each man buying his own food and doing his own cooking. Most of the Mexicans live in town houses, but a number, both of families and solos, still live in company-owned houses at the coke plant.

The greater number of the Mexicans of Bethlehem live scattered about the southern front of the works. They are not segregated in such clearly defined districts as characterize Mexican colonization in the southwestern part of the country. Early in 1929, about 124 Mexican men, women, and children were living in the neighborhood of the coke works, according to an estimate made by two Mexicans. This group included 17 families with 56 children and 34 unattached persons.

There are also a few Mexican workers who are not employed by the steel company, 4 having become machinists and 3 machinists' helpers in Allentown which is close to Bethlehem. In Bethlehem itself there were probably 2 or 3 Mexican men who are not employees of the steel company. There are 7 or 8 Mexican girls working in a cigar factory, while a couple of boys and a few girls are employed in a silk factory. A 5-and-10-cent store has a Mexican clerk, and a hotel steward employs a Mexican boy part time.

Almost all of the Mexican employees of the steel company are laborers. There are, however, a very few skilled mechanics and semiskilled workers among them. According to a statement of a Mexican, there are artisans among the Mexican laborers—carpenters and machinists—but they are not asked to follow their trades. This informant added, however, that these men do not speak English.

On the whole, the comments of numbers of executives on the Mexicans' industrial qualities were favorable. One executive, who had more direct experience with Mexican labor than some of the other reporting officials, made the following statement:

I don't think that the Mexicans are inherently different from other people. They are very easy to handle if they are given just treatment and are greeted with a smile. We rule them, but we are just. We tell them what to do and expect them to do it; but we don't worry them with what not to do. I take a personal interest in each Mexican, and have obtained their confidence. If they are sick or in trouble of any sort, they usually come and tell me. If they are sick, we send them to the hospital.

The Mexicans were reported as not standing the cold as well as other nationalities, but as being especially good for hot work on the open-hearth or blast furnaces. The rapid scattering of the Mexicans shipped to Bethlehem in 1923 to other employment led to the report that these workers were unreliable. Their "steadiness," however, was said to have increased. Possibly this latter observation was due to the departure of the more nomadic employees as much as to the better adaptation of Mexicans to industrial regularity. The following observations of a Mexican are of interest in this connection:

The foremen like the Mexicans. The American people don't like to work; the Mexicans do anything. The family men are steady and like steady work. The single men say, "Let the married fellow work. To hell with the work, we are going to have a good time."

The survey showed that the proportion of families has increased.

In making comments upon their employment the Mexicans noted both favorable and unfavorable conditions. The following observations were made by a group of Mexicans:

There is no discrimination in movies, restaurants, barber shops, but there is in the work. The bosses give protection to their own race. They give the most dangerous work and the lowest-paid jobs to Mexicans. The Mexicans get less. Yes, if they are doing the same work they get equal pay. The Americans do not make distinctions. The Americans are superintendents.

Even before the steel company had recourse to Mexican labor an attempt had been made to scatter nationalities and place a neutral, if possible an American, in charge.

We try to keep them split up pretty well; we think we have a little better control over them then. If we have a Slavish foreman on one shift, we put a Wendish foreman on another. The Slavish foreman would put most of the work on the Wendish, and vice versa.

SOCIAL RELATIONS

Prejudice against Mexicans in Bethlehem because of their color apparently was not strong and only occasional, if it had any existence. No color distinction was reported in the case of the few Mexican children in the schools.

In 1927 a characteristic mutual benefit society was organized but expired. It was succeeded by another which in 1930 claimed a membership of 120. The initiation fee was 50 cents and the monthly dues $1. After a waiting period, sick benefits of $8 a week are paid for 13 weeks and longer if the society votes approval. The death benefit is $100 plus a collection of $1 from each member.

Only a very small percentage of the Mexicans living in Bethlehem or in other parts of the United States have become American citizens, most of them expecting to return to Mexico. However, in Bethlehem they learn English more rapidly and

adopt the characteristic American urban garb more readily than in the rural Southwest. In 1929 four Mexicans had bought homes in Bethlehem. The town also had a Mexican grocery, a barber shop, a pool hall, and a stand for selling Mexican newspapers. A considerable number of the Mexican workers buy company stock.

No criticisms were made in Bethlehem concerning the cleanliness of Mexicans, and the record of Mexican children in school, according to the reports of teachers and school officials, "was at least equal to that of the other children, a large proportion of whom were of European parentage."

Mexicans take little part in politics. Voting is restricted to the few, 18 in number, according to a report made early in 1930, who are naturalized citizens or were born in this country.

Apart from their grievances against foremen of European stock, little friction existed between Mexicans and other nationalities except the Poles. Intermarriages of Mexican men with women of other nationalities were reported as comparatively frequent. None of the Mexican women had intermarried. The Mexicans have some sense of kinship with other Latin Americans living in Bethlehem. Some Mexicans were included among the members of a Spanish club. Spaniards were eligible for membership in the Mexican society, although when the inquiry was made in the early part of 1929 none had applied for admission.

While the northern climate has without doubt been a factor in the departure of many Mexicans from Bethlehem, others have become accustomed to the colder temperatures.

THE FUTURE

Whether or not additional supplies of Mexican labor from the Southwest will be drafted for Bethlehem, the author thinks is a question not to be answered at present. The colony in that town, however, has proven that it is able to maintain itself at a long distance from its source without recurring shipments by the company. With or without such importation it is, according to a subordinate executive, "a nucleus for the future."

Albert Pena

Albert Pena (Politician, San Antonio, Texas) is an excellent example of a successful Mexican American politician who retained his militancy while working within the system. Pena has always spoken for the dispossessed of San Antonio, and in this article he asks for a Marshall Plan for the Mexican American of the Southwest.
By permission of the author.

The Mexican American
And The War On Poverty

First of all, Mr. Shriver, one of the young ladies advised that you looked like Governor Connally. I told her that's where the similarity stopped. I told her also that I would very much like Johnson to take Connally to Washington and send you to Austin.

I want to apologize to you, Mr. Secretary, for not having sent you a transcript. I just made up my mind three days ago to attend. I was reluctant to attend. I couldn't reconcile myself to attending the conference sponsored by the Federal Government concerning Mexican American problems when the Federal Government back home is the worst offender.

I talk specifically about Kelly Field and I am sure this is true of other Federal installations throughout the Southwest and throughout the United States. This is one of the reasons why I thought I would not attend, so you will please forgive me for not having sent you a transcript.

The fact of the matter is that, being last, my speech has already been delivered three or four times, so we'll try to hit some of the highlights, some of the things that I believe we can do to help accelerate the war on poverty.

Perhaps I'm the least qualified to speak on this subject. I'm not a social worker and I have systematically been kept out of all the anti-poverty com-

136

mittees for some reason or other. Basically, I'm a politician, and I accept this conference and I think we all should as a political fact of life. We came here to say something, all of us have, in one way or the other, and we hope that in Washington and in Austin, they are listening because if they're not listening now, we won't be listening next November.

I know that is as subtle as a meat axe but I don't know how to say it any other way.

I want to be completely democratic so I'll address you as ladies and gentlemen and others . . . and if you're half Anglo and half Mexican, neither, but this is one of the things that has always concerned me, the image, the Mexican American image. We're called so many things we don't know what we are. We're called Mexican Americans, Spanish speaking, Spanish Americans, Americans of Mexican descent. I think some nut called us Iberian Americans. So I have come to this conclusion, that I am three things and in this order: first of all, I'm an American because I was born here. Second, I'm a Texan because I was born in Texas, and third, I'm a Mexican without a mustache because no one will let me forget it.

It's very difficult for Anglos to erase from their mind the stereotyped serape draped Mexican sleeping in the shade with an empty Tequila bottle to his side and with the burro over here waiting for him to wake up.

Every time I meet an Anglo for the first time, or most of them, they try to impress me first with the fact that they made a trip to Mexico and that they love Tequila, they like bull fights, they like Mexican food, and some of their best friends are Mexicans.

Now, this leaves me pretty cold because, first of all, I don't like Tequila. I like scotch, and second, I don't like bull fights. I like a good professional football game, the Washington Redskins. But I must confess that I love Mexican food and Mexican women.

The point I'm trying to make is this, that—and we have heard this many times—that we are proud that we are Americans, but we are also proud that we are Mexicans and don't let anybody forget that.

We've got to learn how to identify as a group

because when you do this, then you're going to find out that we're going to have more unity. My friend, Maury Maverick, Jr., told me one time, he said, you know what's wrong with you Mexicans and I said, what, "They made white people out of you and now you don't know what the hell you are." Well, we ought to know what we are. We ought to identify with our people. We ought to identify as Mexicans and the problems that are peculiar to Mexican Americans in the United States.

I would like to also mention just for a few minutes the significance of the Delano grape strike and the significance of the Valley farm march here in Texas.

Here in Texas, I know that the Valley farm marchers that marched from Rio Grande City to Austin had more impact than all the groups, LULAC, GI Forum, PASO, and what have you. I'm not criticizing them because I belong to all of them.

But this march had more impact in those few weeks than all the other things we've been trying to do. Why? Because they not only spotlighted the problem in Rio Grande City but they spotlighted the overall problem of the Mexican American in Texas and throughout the Southwest. And recognition of our problems has been a long time coming. So these are crucial times for us. These next eight or nine or ten or eleven months are very crucial for us. Maybe we should all have stayed home and helped you just a little bit more, Mr. Shriver, and helped with our voter registration drives. This is important. Maybe we could do more good back home today going door to door and knocking on doors and registering people in the barrios because they are the people, these are the unorganized people and we must see that they vote. . . . The only way that they're going to be heard is through the votes. The only thing politicians understand, and I know because I'm one, is votes. They'll talk to people who have votes. And I think here in Texas, and there in Washington, they only understand votes. We need more understanding politicians. The only way that they are going to understand is for you to vote and register everybody in your communities. That's the only way that you're going to do it. It's the only way you're going to do it.

The Valley farm march spotlighted the problems we've been talking about, the high illiteracy rate, job and wage discrimination, the high tubercular rate in our communities, high infant mortality rate in our communities, poverty and injustice, all of these things were spotlighted. This is why it was so important. But there are solutions. I'm confident that there are solutions.

Think, for just a minute, and just imagine an island ninety miles off the United States, not Cuba, with eleven million people of Mexican descent dedicated to our democratic principles and way of life, and they had all these problems that we talk about, illiteracy and poverty and injustice, lack of jobs and high unemployment, all of these things. What would the United States do? They would give them foreign aid. They would give them massive sums of money to take care of that. This is the type of programs we need for the Mexican Americans. We need a Marshall Plan for the Mexican American throughout the Southwest.

These are the only things that I have reduced to writing and I'll try to explain here what I mean by this Marshall Plan.

What South Texas needs, what the land all along our Southwestern border needs, is a new climate, a political, social, economic climate in which the people, the Mexican Americans, can live decently. We need new outside capital to create new jobs. We need new education systems. We need new faces on the political scene and we need ideas. How are we to obtain this change? I'm not sure but I do know that unless the Federal Government begins soon to take unbreached steps towards creating the new climate, something is going to happen. It is inevitable that things will change. Hopefully, change would be orderly. I don't see how this would be possible without the massive assistance of the Federal Government. The State Government, particularly here in Texas, cannot, will not do the job. Most of the local governments up and down the border have but one function, to protect the status quo. In the past, I have called for a Marshall Plan for South Texas with massive aid, with massive loans, with massive technological assistance. What we got was the war

on poverty, too little and too late. I'm not criticizing the war on poverty. What I'm saying is, this is an extension of the war on poverty.

For example, we have some very fine programs in San Antonio. I think we have one of the finest youth organizations, SANYO.

We have the greater San Antonio Federation of Neighborhood Councils and ... they are beginning to do battle with the power structure, so I am not criticizing. I'm saying that the war on poverty as it exists now is not enough. We need to create a new climate.

The Federal Government certainly has the resources to change the atmosphere in the border lands. We saw, after World War II, the demonstration of this when the United States Government converted the economically, politically, and morally destroyed people of Western Europe and Japan into democratic prosperous allies. Why not this for the Americans who live along the border?

I said we need capital. We need it to create jobs which would create the resources for educational and political changes which would pull South Texas and the border land up and we need the capital on this side of the border. If we can subsidize American capital flowing into Mexico, why can't we subsidize American capital flowing into South Texas?

If we can create jobs for Mexicans in Mexico, why can't we create jobs for Americans in America? If we can fight a fifty billion dollar a year war to free the Vietnamese in Vietnam from political tyranny, why can't we do the same for Americans in America?

I want to conclude by outlining what I think the role of government should be, what I believe is the philosophy of *la causa*. I delivered this to a SANYO meeting and also to a PASO convention.

My philosophy, and I am sure that most of yours, are the results of two great men. These two men were dedicated men. They were sincere men. They were good men. They were religious men. One was the leader of a great nation and the other was the leader of a great religion. One died a very young man. The other died a very old man. And both their names were John. One was John Fitzgerald Kennedy and the other was Pope John XXIII. The two Johns wrote many things and they said many things. Pope John wrote *Pacem in Terris*. John Kennedy wrote *Profiles in Courage*. And basically, they believed this. They believed, first, that all men are created equal in the image of God. They believed that every man was entitled to a good job, decent wages, an education, medical care, and decent housing, but more important than that, they believed that every man should have the equal opportunity to obtain these things and such was the impact of the two Johns that when John Kennedy died, even Republicans, conservatives who never voted for him, cried unashamedly, and when Pope John died, Protestants and Jews declared a week of mourning. Such was the impact of the two Johns. Both said, in different ways, that this generation of Americans has been handed the torch of freedom. Think about that for just a minute. You have been handed the torch of freedom but you're not going to get it until you stop asking for it and demand it.

Ralph Guzmán

Ralph Guzmán (Associate Professor of Politics and Community Studies, University of California at Santa Cruz) is co-author of THE MEXICAN-AMERICAN PEOPLE *(1970) as well as many other studies in the area. He served as associate director to the Peace Corps in Venezuela. For Dr. Guzmán the question is not "whether Mexican Americans will riot," but whether violent confrontation will become a permanent fixture on the socio–political landscape. Dr. Guzmán also raises the haunting spectre of a white middle-class riot which could indeed prove more violent than anything previously experienced.*
By permission of the author.

Mexican Americans In The Urban Area: Will They Riot?

Magic was the means by which primitive man made the world meaningful to himself. Modern America is on the verge of resorting to magic because the ideas and information available to it no longer explain the reality of its own life. Part of this phenomenon reflects an attempt to explain urban complexities with agrarian symbolism and value systems.

The real revolution of our time is not only the upsurge of the Negro toward dignity; it is not merely the rebellion of children against their parents; it is not just the erosion of eternal verities; it is not even the fantastic rate of technological development and redevelopment. The real revolution of our times is all of these, in juxtaposition to one another, and more.

One of the sad features of our modern society is that those who gained the most from this age of affluence have never asked: "Who lost?" In a sense, most of the facets of this age of unlimited expectations, this age where nothing seems impossible, is that the revolutions of our generation seem to be separate and apart from one another. But, the distance between the middle-class American who complains about his teen age children and says: "We don't speak the same language" is about the same as that of the Mexican American parent who regrets that his child refuses to learn Spanish. The distance is more apparent than real.

The arid phrases, normally used to describe the transformation of American life in the last decade, obscure rather than reveal the remarkable impact this revolution has had on individual lives and destinies. To say that this revolution has technological aspects does not explain to a 45-year-old man with family responsibilities that he is too old to learn a new trade and too young to vegetate for the rest of his life. Technological unemployment reveals nothing of the despair of an illiterate adolescent when he finds that he is economically irrelevant— or in short that he can't get a job. The words generational gap fail to convey the dilemma of a man who has sacrificed everything to give his children security only to find they reject it.

Fundamental anti-intellectualism in American society has over-shadowed the fact that in the arts, the sciences and the humanities, every tradition has been toppled and supplanted. The fight between college and town is a reflection between different views of the universe. In California the insistence that the university conform to the taxpayer's idea of a university stands in direct contrast to the idea that a university should be a place for the search of truth, however outlandish and antagonistic to the interests of the taxpayer.

Our society has still not assimilated the full implications of the change of the role of the government from that of the necessary evil to that of a force for positive good. This leaves liberals with visions of omnipotence and conservatives with nighmares of disaster. Neither view, of course, accords with reality. Governmental activism cannot resolve all problems; for these are problems that are rightfully beyond the reach of governmental

purview. Neither is governmental intervention an automatic evil; for there are some problems that only government can reach.

Even as the churches have up-dated their rituals and theology, America is long overdue in renovating its supply of ideas. Symbols and values relevant to an agrarian past must be re-cast for our urban present. Notions of community solidarity; I-thou relationships; salvation through work; the Horatio Alger myth must be discarded. We must recognize and cope with the solitude; the privacy; the mobility and the restlessness of the city. For the city is not just a network of freeways. It is not just the decisions of the zoning commission. It is not merely a marble and concrete mechanism. It is a totally new way of life; an organism of immense complexity. It teems not with millions of cogs and wheels but with millions of people.

And for those millions of people the revolution of our time has been dangerously encapsulated in the equation; Negro equals riot equals revolution. For above all, minorities in these United States have been affected adversely by the onslaught of this new age of affluence. Both its victims and its prisoners; they have been the forgotten losers in the game of material acquisition. In the miles and miles and acres and acres of housing developments, few minority members are found. In the myriad expansion of services and luxuries, few minority people benefit. In the explosion of information and learning that circles the earth our ethnic minorities remain a mystery. They have been the most conspicuous of those who have not shared in this era of plenty. But along with the majority they have shared the loss of those psychic comforts associated with a simpler society. For, if the sense of rootlessness afflicts the Negro, it also afflicts the inhabitants of split-level ranch houses. If the loss of identity causes anxiety for the Mexican American he shares that problem with the bulk of American youth. If the break-up of the family exacerbates the problem of the poor let it be known that homes for the aged are not filled with the elderly of the poor and of the minorities.

This community of concern, that faces all Americans, has been strangely twisted into the problem peculiar to the racial and ethnic minorities of our country. Nowhere is the lack of intelligent comprehension of what this nation is, more evident than in the utter lack of knowledge shared by the majority and the minority about each other. Because of this simplistic equation, the search for concepts and solutions has been the province of a thin strata of the American establishment.

No one can say that the problems of the poor have not been researched, studied, examined, handled, committee-ed, anachronimed, and sloganed. There is hardly a letter of the alphabet that has not been used to form an abbreviation for an agency. Government has created OEO, CAP, EDA, MDTA, and HEW. All of these are part of the vast arsenal that comprise the invested personnel and resources in job training programs designed to diminish poverty. Church groups have been conspicuous in the attempt to enliven the conscience of the country about conditions related to poverty and race. In the 1930s the Rockefeller Foundation could deny a grant to aid the Mexican American poor on the grounds of insufficient data about these people. Today, it and other foundations eagerly encourage innovative programs to alleviate poverty and prejudice. But, let there be no mistake, this activity, this flood of concern engages but a minute percentage of the total population. This empathy is restricted to the elite of the American establishment. Between the vast majority and growing minority there exists a gulf of understanding, of information and knowledge that will never be bridged by the jargon of the elite.

Let there be no mistake. Programs designed to help the poor and the deprived have been the product of the top layer of American society. These programs have been created by them, administered by them, supported by them and, in some instances, even thwarted by them. They have been a meager response to the threat of violence. Their existence is predicated upon that threat. Consequently, they have no roots beyond this threat of social disruption. Therefore, the vast majority of the American people have absolutely no involvement intellectually or emotionally in any program designed to aid minorities that is not based on force and the restoration of the old order. This antipathy, on the part of the overwhelming majority, can be directly laid to blame at the door-

step of American leadership. For if one of the functions of leadership is to educate; to help make understandable the events of a nation's life, our leadership is largely talking to itself.

Perhaps this is most evident in the employment of a special new language devised by the elite and debased in popular usage. A term such as "hard-core unemployed" means to the elite an individual who lacks the necessary skills to perform minimum tasks in a highly developed technology. It also includes assumptions about value orientations and environmental disabilities. To the poor it means they can't get a job. Surprisingly enough, they knew this before someone told them they were "hard-core unemployed." But, to most Americans hard-core unemployment means: "to lazy to work." Another term that indicates myopia of the elite is "culturally deprived." One suspects that 97 percent of the entire population of the world would fall into that category. It is a term with meaning only to those who assumed that they have culture. Lumped together, as beyond the pale, are both those with a different culture and those without season tickets to the opera. The net result has been to increase the ignorance of various sectors of American society about each other. In a way the elite have ministered to the poor in a fashion not alike preachers riding circuit in the past. By day they travel to the ghettos of despair and at dusk they return to the security of their suburban retreats. They have become the buffer between the miserably poor and the misunderstanding many.

For the poor the application of terms to their economic circumstances does not increase their ability to escape. For if the poor really knew the causes and remedies for their poverty they would surely choose them of their own accord. Instead, however, they become cases, objects and problems. They themselves are called upon to play a passive part in their own rescue. The traditional values of the poor: suspicion, hostility, mistrust, doubt, hopelessness—all of these are re-enforced by the paternalism of the elite and the contempt of the majority.

The fact that so many of the poor are also ethnic and racial minorities has consequences for both the elite and the white middle classes. For the elite the reigning paternalism is increased by the fear of the mob. Thus what started out as a response to a single aspect of violence has become a defensive maneuver designed to maintain the urban peace; to preserve law and order; to keep the people quiet. For the white middle classes contempt has mingled with fear producing a tension level unparalleled in recent history. For the white middle classes are scared. They expect violence and their only substantive response, thus far, is repression. This misunderstanding of the revolution of our time; by all participants; by the elite; by the poor and by the white middle classes; has produced an atmosphere of terror and anxiety that certainly does not augur well for the future of our democracy. In the effort to repress violence the poor will never miss traditional civil liberties; for they have never had them. And it is increasingly clear that the white middle class will gladly trade traditional liberty for false security. Moreover, this dangerous equation: Negro equals riot equals revolution, has left many groups of people, who are part of this revolution, with neither the benefits of those efforts that have been made nor the goodwill of the society. The Indian and the Mexican American are the preeminent examples of the lost children of the urban revolution.

Right now no one knows exactly how many Mexican Americans there are in the Southwest. Estimates range between six and seven million. We do know that the median age of this group is 19.5 years; that the average family size exceeds that of the white majority and the Negro minority. However, modern statistics cannot reveal the context in which this group has developed. To the people of the Southwest the region itself is a closed book. Movies and television have projected an image of the Southwest in which numerous Nietzchean supermen constantly ride off into the sunset, clutching their saddles, after another sortie against savage Indians and/or villainous Mexicans. We Americans are a strangely historic people. By this I mean that the actual history of the Southwest; the history of violence and exploitation; the lessons of the conqueror and the conquered; the harsh combat of all against an inhospitable land— all these are forgotten, if they were ever known.

Conflict and guile guided the development of this area. Law was the weapon of the strong against the weak. And few people confused law with justice. In their role as conquered, Mexican Americans became prisoners of a popular stereotype of a triumphant and rampant mythology. They became a sideshow; a humorous diversion in the struggle of the victor against nature. Considered as foreigners they were excused their ethnic eccentricities. As peasants they were not supposed to be too bright. As idol-worshippers they were an American brand of basically inferior heathens. Even today the legend persists in the minds of many southwesterners, and practically all who are not from the Southwest. Despite the popular stereotype, however, the Mexican American has felt the urban revolution of our time—no less than his Anglo counterparts.

Technological developments have reduced his employability. First, the increased emphasis on formal language and social skills has erected a formidable barrier to upward occupational mobility. Second, the concommitant decrease in the need for unskilled labor has created a surplus of Spanish surnamed unemployed. Thirdly, mechanization in the agricultural sector has augmented the surplus and the exodus to the urban ghettos. Thus, while fewer jobs are available to the Mexican American in the cities hundreds of thousands stream toward the large metropolitan centers in search of non-existant, unskilled jobs.

With more than a four hundred year history in the Southwest—more than European immigrants, only recently, in the last 25 years, has the majority of the Mexican American people become a part of the urban reality of this region. Long a rural people, this minority is today 87 percent urban.

Many now live in these cities armed with inadequate attitudes and social skills of an agrarian past. Desperately, against tremendous odds, many seek to maintain crumbling idylls that have no roots in the urban reality. Such is the impact of the social forces within the city. Nor have ethnic intellectuals been much help. First, because their numbers are limited. Second, because many are ideologues who look to the restoration of a lost grandeur while obsessively denying the presence of ragged poor. Every day the irrelevance of the latter becomes more apparent. For the Mexican American population of the Southwest is not foreign and archaic but overwhelmingly American by birth, young and grossly disadvantaged.

Moreover, the generational problem in the majority society is more than matched among Mexican Americans. If the old ideologues have little to say to their peers they have nothing to say to the young. Young Mexican Americans are living the urban revolution thus the values of the parent generation and the visions of the offsprings are as sharply contrasted within this minority group as they are in the larger society. The neglect of the young by both the old ideologues and the larger society has left them disillusioned, bitter and deeply resentful. While some may seek an artificial identity with the Che Guevarra and Negro militancy, others withdrew into an anguished apathy. Still others, the majority of the young, await viable direction for their destiny. The majority of them ignore their parents and await for one of their own to articulate grievances and direct social energy.

We cannot expect the young to remain polite and powerless. We cannot expect them to continue saying thank you for nothing. Social disorder is a function of the young. They question contracts established before their birth. And they challenge forces applied to maintain these contracts. The whole litany of inherited problems will never again be accepted as part of the natural order of things.

Still many Mexican American leaders bring up these problems in the same strident tones of their Negro opposites. They call for caution and patience; for thought and logic, and for ethnic unity built upon deference to age. All this is rejected by the young, particularly those who stand in envy of the Black Power movement. For most of the young want to escalate the drive for social change.

The question: "Will the Mexican American riot?" is probably irrelevant. Answering the affirmative or the negative sheds no light on the problems of this minority or this nation. Regretfully, present programs, conceived merely as a response to a threat of social disruption, whether continued or expended, probably will not prevent violence in the streets. For, given the rapidity and intensity of the revolution convulsing our country, the question is not *whether they will riot or when they will riot.* For all of us the question is: "Will riots become a permanent and enduring part of our national existence? Will riots become the only means to affectuate meaningful social change? Or, because of intelligent and reasoned application of resources will urban anarchy pass away into a footnote to history?"

Finally, there is one group that is not well-known. It has not been well-studied, but we do know that it has a propensity for violence exceeding that of either the Negro or the Mexican American. It too, has been equally a victim of revolutionary developments in our history. Any total response to the urban revolution of our times must include programs to assuage the fears of the white, middle-class American who has not yet rioted in full force. For it is this sector of our society whose history of hysterical outburst portends tragic consequences for the future of this country. We would be unwise and unrealistic: all of us Americans, minorities and non-minorities, if we ignore the white, middle class. After all, most members of this strata of our society have rarely displayed either the rural patience of the Negro or the agrarian politeness of the Mexican American.

Richard Griego + Gilbert W. Merkx

Gilbert Merkx (Assistant Professor of Sociology, University of New Mexico) and Richard Griego (Associate Professor of Mathematics and former director of Chicano Studies, University of New Mexico) delivered this paper at a session on Mexican American Life at the 1971 Rocky Mountain Social Studies Convention. In this paper the authors discuss the effects of cultural disintegration in the Mexican American communities and the Chicano response to this loss; in terms of both what has happened, and what may well happen if the Anglo community continues on its present course. The student should note that this paper was written before the 1971 riots in Albuquerque. From Norman R. Yetman and C. Hoy Steele, MAJORITY AND MINORITY: THE DYNAMICS OF RACIAL AND ETHNIC RELATIONS. © copyright 1971 by Allyn and Bacon, Inc. Reprinted by permission of the publisher and authors.

Crisis In New Mexico

Amid the breathtaking sweep of New Mexico's mountains, deserts, and river valleys the grim final stages of a long tragedy are unfolding. Sunshine and scenery in this "land of enchantment" are the setting for the death of a people and their way of life. These people are Mexican-Americans, bearers of an Indo-Hispanic culture that is older than the United States, older than Mexico itself, and far older than "New" Mexico. They are the victims of economic and social forces alien to them and of little concern to other Americans.

New Mexico is the heartland of Mexican-American society. Nearly six million Chicanos or Mexican-Americans live in the Southwest, distributed from California to Texas. But only in the geographic center of this region, which lies in northern New Mexico, are Mexican-Americans still a majority of the population, owning and working

145

land of their own while maintaining Chicano culture in non-ghetto circumstances.

Despite the legal fiction that New Mexico is the nation's one officially bilingual state, this *patria chica,* or little homeland, is rapidly disappearing. Anglo-Americans who pride themselves on New Mexico's "tradition" of cultural pluralism conveniently ignore the fact that they are presiding over a cultural destruction less violent but no less effective than that perpetrated against American Indians. Mexican-Americans are being driven from their rural homeland into urban slums and migrant labor camps throughout the Southwest.

Six counties lying north between Albuquerque and the Colorado border are still largely Spanish-speaking: Santa Fe, San Miguel, Guadalupe, Taos, Mora, and Rio Arriba. The most Chicano county of these is Mora (85 percent of the people were Spanish-surnamed in 1960), and the least is Santa Fe (54 percent). A seventh northern county, Sandoval, lost 37 percent of its Mexican-American population during the 1950s, dropping from 52 percent Spanish-surnamed in 1950 to 32 percent in 1960. The region as a whole lost 15 percent of its Chicano population during those ten years because of a disintegrating rural economy. This exodus began during the Second World War and has been accelerating in recent years. Mora county alone lost 45 percent of its population between 1940 and 1960; between 1960 and 1968 it lost an additional 13 percent.

The impact of this emigration has been felt in the urban centers of New Mexico, particularly Albuquerque, as well as in the area losing people. Albuquerque has grown from 35,000 in 1940 to 310,000 in 1968, partly due to an influx of Anglos attracted by the climate and defense employment, but also due to the yearly arrival of thousands of displaced Chicanos from the northern counties. Albuquerque now has large and growing barrios or slums sprawling along the banks of the Rio Grande and afflicted by considerable poverty. A recent sampling of Albuquerque residents designed by one of the authors found that 60 percent of the Chicanos had moved to Albuquerque from rural counties, 15 percent were from out of state, and only 25 percent were born in Albuquerque.

The destruction of the rural base of Mexican-American society and the proliferation of urban slums are two sides of the same coin, or two different aspects of the social inequity which characterizes the American Southwest. This inequity, which has been rapidly worsening in the period since the Second World War, is the underlying cause of the militant Mexican-American protest movements which have attracted so much public attention in the last three years. Chicano militancy takes several forms, which we will attempt to explain, but all represent a desperate attempt to save Indo-Hispanic culture from disappearing into a dominant "American way of life" which many Mexican-Americans find distasteful and with which they are ill-prepared to cope.

The ecological base of Mexican-American society in the northern counties is a mixed rural economy of small farming, orchards, and small-scale sheep and cattle raising. Unlike the Anglo or "Texan" ranchers and farmers who are competing for the same land, the Chicanos do not live on their land, but in small communities located in river valleys, which date from the days in which land was chartered to such communities by the Spanish Crown. Life in these villages is so attractive to the residents that they will stay under conditions of extreme poverty, and the dream of most migrants in the cities is one day to return to their community.

Nevertheless, the Chicanos are losing their lands to Anglos, and increasing numbers of Mexican-Americans find it impossible to survive in their homeland. Between 1949 and 1964 the acreage under crops in New Mexico declined 45 percent, while about the same area of land was added to Anglo ranches. In the seven northern counties the total number of farms dropped from 4,302 to 2,614 in only five years between 1954 and 1959. Small farms of under 10 acres almost cease to exist (in 1954 there were 2,025, but by 1959 only 662 remained.) Yet at the same time large enterprises of over 1000 acres actually increased in number from 769 to 835.

The tragedy of this destruction of small farming in New Mexico is that it represents not only the passing of inefficient economic units, but also the disintegration of a society and the creation of another urban underclass. As long as their communities are even marginally viable, Chicanos will remain. Some have stayed by taking employment in the cities, commuting long distances so as to live with their own people. Too few are able to find such employment, however, and the result is that these villages contain poverty, malnutrition, and a hopelessness made heart-rending by the stunning beauty of the region and the dignity and warmth of the people.

Some idea of this poverty can be gathered by looking at family income. Median income of Chicano families in six of the counties ranged in 1959 from $1,951 in Mora County to $2,864 in Guadalupe. Only in Santa Fe county, which contains the state capital, did median family income exceed the $4000 poverty line, and there it reached only $4,062. In contrast, Anglo median family income was $6,592 in Santa Fe, $4,605 in Guadalupe, and $3,463 in Mora. These median figures, which represent families in the middle of the income range, do not reflect average income, which is probably lower for Chicano families and considerably higher for Anglos, a number of whom are millionaires.

Those public officials on a local, state, and federal level who might contribute to the economic revitalization of Mexican-American society have done the opposite. New Mexico politics are dominated by a coalition of ranching and oil and gas interests which accept some progressive influence from military-industrial enterprises in Los Alamos and Albuquerque. Politicians of Mexican-American ethnicity are usually committed to these interests or do not challenge them in return for control over patronage in their shrinking local fiefs. Thus the political structure in New Mexico encourages ranching and mineral extraction in the countryside and aero-space and scientific investment in the cities. Anglo leaders in the state are either openly hostile towards Mexican-Americans or regard hastened destruction of small farming and the emigration of Chicanos as an ultimately beneficial phase of modernization. Should their vision predominate, New Mexico will soon resemble Arizona and lower California, where urban slums

in the center cities house a marginal underclass which provides servants and menials for the endless acres of ranch-house suburbia.

The claim that Mexican-Americans in the state are sharing in the benefits of modernization is demonstrably false, despite the existence of a fair percentage of assimilated middle-class Mexican-Americans (the self-styled "Spanish"). Overt discrimination against Chicanos in the south and east of New Mexico, known as "little Texas," resembles the most vicious practices of the American South. Even Albuquerque, the most modern city in the state, evidences social inequalities that are as dramatic as those in rural counties.

Unemployment in Albuquerque has been the lowest in New Mexico for years, fluctuating between 4.1 percent and 4.8 percent from 1963 to 1968, while median family income nearly doubled between 1950 and 1960 (increasing from $3,451 to $6,621). But these figures conceal the increasing relative deprivation of the Chicano population. Employment opportunities have benefited highly skilled Anglos, not the native New Mexicans (43 percent of the Anglos in Albuquerque have been there less than 10 years). The harsh reality of Chicano life in Albuquerque can be seen in the fact that in the sample of Mexican-Americans, 20 percent of the heads of Mexican households were unemployed.

Not only are nearly a fifth of Albuquerque Chicanos unemployed, but also those who do find employment do not do very well. While 44 percent of the Anglos have professional, business, or managerial occupations, only 11 percent of the Chicanos have such employment. Most of the Mexicans are either unskilled manual laborers (41 percent) or machine operators (13 percent), while only 21 percent of the Anglos fall in these two categories combined. Essentially, the Albuquerque pattern is that Anglos are the bosses and Mexican-Americans the workers; Anglos work with their minds and Mexicans with their hands (when they find work).

This state of affairs reflects the inherent discrimination of a state educational system that operates exclusively in English despite a constitutional requirement that teachers be bilingual. The disregard for Chicano language and culture are such that most Mexican-Americans are, in the words of political scientist Ralph Guzmán, "force-outs" rather than drop-outs. Only 12 percent of Anglo heads of households in Albuquerque had not completed high school, compared with 60 percent of the Chicano heads of household. Over half (52 percent) of the Anglos had some education beyond the high school level, as opposed to only 15 percent of the Mexicans.

These depressing statistics are summed up in the figures for the income earned by Anglo and Chicano heads of household, which are shown in Table 1.

Table 1.   Annual Income of Albuquerque Heads of Household, 1967

Income	Anglos	Spanish Surnamed
Over $7,000	57%	20%
$4,000–$7,000	30%	47%
Under $4,000	13%	33%
Total	100%	100%

Source: "A Demographic and Attitudinal Study of the Albuquerque Standard Metropolitan Statistical Area," (Operation SER, Santa Monica, California), Advance Report No. 1, p. 12.

While only 13 percent of Anglos earned under $4,000 annually, 33 percent of the Chicanos were below this poverty line. At the opposite extreme, 57 percent of the Anglos earned over $7,000, as compared with only 20 percent of the Chicanos. Per capita income figures are even more skewed, since Mexican-Americans have larger families than Anglos. It is small wonder that 80 percent of the Chicano respondents agreed with the statement that "Mexican-Americans have to work harder than Anglos to get ahead."

The impact of 124 years of United States rule over New Mexico can therefore be summed up as follows. The original inhabitants of the state have been driven off their land except in a handful of counties where Chicanos still cling to an increasingly marginal existence. Those Mexican-Americans who have emigrated to New Mexico's cities are condemned to slums and unskilled, unsteady employment. Cast out from an Anglo-oriented school system, they are often functionally inadequate in two languages and lacking the skills necessary to benefit from the economic development of the region. Unless an economic and cultural revitalization of New Mexico is undertaken in the next decade, there may be nothing left to save of what was once heralded as a mutually-enriching combination of two cultures and two ways of life.

THE MILITANT REACTION

The exacerbation of social inequity and the deterioration of Chicano society in the last few years have touched off a major wave of Mexican-American militancy. The nature of the militant reaction varies from group to group according to whether the members are rural or urban, middle or lower class, youth or adults. But the common thread running through all militant organizations is belief in the cultural integrity of the Mexican-American people. They view the Spanish language, a close-knit family structure, a sense of interdependence, and an emphasis on human values rather than on money as aspects of the Mexican way of life that should be maintained. The militants are unanimous in their contempt for what they consider to be the sterility of middle-class Anglo values.

The Alianza Federal de Mercedes (Federal Alliance of Land Grants) is the main vehicle of Mexican-American protest in New Mexico. The issues and attitudes projected by the Alianza closely reflect the history of Indo-Hispanic culture in New Mexico. Elder Alianzistas still remember the times when their people had an economically marginal but stable life and were free to graze sheep on their forefathers' land. They have seen gringos come with fences and legal entanglements to cut them off from their grazing lands; the elders recount the disintegration of a way of life in bitter detail and their message is not lost on younger Alianza members.

The issue of land is at the very heart of rural New Mexican problems, since loss of the land destroyed the economic base of most northern villages. The Alianza was organized in 1963 by its leader, Reies López Tijerina, to press for the return of or compensation for millions of acres of land which it claims were wrongfully acquired by the federal government. The Alianza bases its claims on the Treaty of Guadalupe Hidalgo of 1848 which ended the war between Mexico and the United States. The treaty gave citizenship to Mexicans who stayed in the conquered territories, and it stated that land grants given to New Mexicans by the Spanish and Mexican governments were to be "recognized in the tribunals of the United States." Those tribunals invalidated 94 percent of the land claims made by Mexican-Americans, opening the way for their expulsion from the land. The Alianza is primarily concerned with the village land grants owned communally by the heirs of the original grantees. It does not lay explicit claims to land grant acreage now in private hands, but focuses on land appropriated by the federal government, much of which has been declared national forest.

Frustrated in attempts to get recognition for its claims, the Alianza turned to a strategy of direct confrontation with the federal government. The Alianza planned to reoccupy various land grants, in effect seizing what the U.S. government considers federal property. After all, according to Tijerina, the land grants had not ceased to exist; they were real entities that the Alianza would merely reactivate. This device was to bring the government into court, thus forcing recognition of Alianza claims. The strategy brought the Alianza into conflict with the government on several occasions. It culminated with the famous raid on the Tierra Amarilla courthouse in June, 1967, when Alianzistas attempted a citizens arrest of a district attorney who had allegedly violated the rights of Alianza members. In the trial which followed, Tijerina won acquittal on kidnap charges while acting as his own attorney. Since then, however, Tijerina has been convicted on a number of lesser charges related both to the citizens arrest and to the burning of a sign on national forest land. He is now in federal prison.

Unlike the Alianza, the Brown Berets deal with problems of urban Mexican-American poor and draw their members from youth in the city barrios. Brown Berets were organized in Los Angeles, but similar organizations now exist in cities throughout the Southwest.

The Brown Berets in Albuquerque were organized mainly through the efforts of Gilberto Ballejos, an articulate spokesman from the barrio who identifies closely with other *batos* (guys) in the barrio despite the fact that he is a college graduate. These *batos* find it hard to identify with the heritage of land the Alianza emphasizes, and they do not remember rural life as do the Alianza members. The Berets concern themselves with typical problems of the urban ghetto such as police brutality and education. They are currently active in organizing Chicano high school students. Nevertheless, while the Berets do not internalize the values of the Alianza, they generally support the goals of the Alianza. They too are concerned with restoring cultural dignity to la Raza, and chose the color of their berets to symbolize the brown skin of their people.

The Brown Berets' organizational structure is more sophisticated than that of the Alianza. The Alianza has been largely a one-man operation; everything revolved around Tijerina and sometimes it was difficult to separate Tijerina, the man, from the movement he led. The Brown Berets are careful to point out that there is no single leader of their organization. Ballejos, the current spokesman, was chosen by a six-man board that coordinates activities of the individual Brown Beret barrio organizations. Each board member is the equal of the others and each board member is responsible for organizing his own barrio. The individual barrio organizations are somewhat autonomous and the details of membership are known only to the organizers of the individual groups in an effort to guard against infiltration. Despite such efforts, police success in using informers has tended to drive the Brown Berets further underground and to intensify their suspicion of outsiders.

The Berets gained recognition in Albuquerque when they protested the killing of a Chicano youth by an Anglo policeman. The Berets and other groups demanded a police review board to handle complaints from the community. The review board was not accepted by the city commission, but a three-man police community relations task force was set up consisting of an Anglo, a Chicano and Black policeman.

A third militant organization, the United Mexican-American Students (UMAS), consists of Chicano college students from more middle-class urban backgrounds. The students in UMAS are capable of "making it" in American society, and are to a large extent acculturated to American ways. They are the hoped-for products of their parents' striving to be accepted in American society. But these sons and daughters of la Raza refuse to be absorbed. They insist on the viability of Mexican culture in modern America and openly identify with their Indian heritage, emphasizing the fact that they are not "pure white Spaniards." Their use of the term "Mexican-American" is itself controversial, since the word "Mexican" has had derogatory connotations in New Mexico. UMAS students embrace "Mexican-American" and even "Mexican" as cultural terms which accurately describe who they are, despite their parents' preference for the term "Spanish-American."

UMAS has mounted a campaign, already partly successful, for the inclusion of more Mexican and Indian studies in the curriculum of the University of New Mexico. They forced the student government to "Mexicanize" the annual student festival, ironically called "Fiesta." Students in UMAS also joined the Black Student Union in a controversial clenched-fist salute during the playing of the national anthem at a basketball game, as a protest against the allegedly racist policies of Brigham Young University. When the University of New Mexico president suspended a Black teaching assistant who was under community attack for using supposedly obscene poems in class, UMAS was the first organization to ask the President's resignation (acting before such militant organizations as the Black Students Union and SDS).

Following the poem controversy, UMAS touched off another major dispute by alleging university discrimination against Chicano physical plant workers. Despite administration denials, an HEW investigation of UMAS charges found them to be substantially correct. The university was forced to order changes in its personnel policies.

Probably the most significant long-term achievements of UMAS has been their successful drive to establish a Chicano Studies program at the University of New Mexico. This program has recently begun operation under a faculty coordinator but retains extensive student participation.

The differing social bases of the Alianza, the Brown Berets and UMAS help explain the differences in issue-emphasis between each group, as well as differences in style of articulation and approach.

The Alianza draws rural-based, northern New Mexican adults for its membership. They represent some of the most traditional elements of Chicano society in New Mexico. The Alianzistas are closely tied to the land as shown in their slogan *La Tierra-Nuestra Herencia, La Justicia-Nuestro Credo.* Outside a typical meeting at Alianza headquarters in Albuquerque numerous pick-up trucks of *campesinos* will be parked. Spanish is the language of the meetings, although some English will be heard, especially among the members' children. Tijerina is a dynamic speaker. His green eyes flash as he exhorts his audience in the style of his Pentecostal upbringing. Frequent applause and exclamations from the audience punctuate the proceedings. After the speeches, refreshments and Mexican food are served, and a *norteño* band plays ranchera music for dancing. The atmosphere is one of a church rally or family reunion.

Most of the Brown Berets would be called "hard-core ghetto youth" by Anglos. Some are high school drop-outs and others are Vietnam war veterans. But all are from the barrios, children of the working and welfare class. The Berets say they are willing to try nonviolent means to achieve their aims but if that fails they will be forced to revolutionary alternatives. In the words of James Kennedy, a regional SDS organizer, the Brown Berets "come closer to forming a revolutionary vanguard organization than any other group I have seen or talked with or studied in this country."

Few of the families of UMAS students are well off financially, though they come from the middle and lower middle strata of Mexican-American society. These strata are more economically insecure than their Anglo equivalents. Nevertheless, UMAS students have middle-class educational values, viewing higher studies as a vehicle of improvement for themselves and their people. UMAS students are likely to be willing to work within the system, since their education gives them the means to address Anglo society on its terms. The Brown Berets do not have access to such means and hence are more ready to attack the system and force change by radical methods. On a cultural level UMAS and the Brown Berets have much in common. Their members are products of the Chicano urban culture. Their Spanish is liberally sprinkled with *pachuco* expressions. The *pachucos* were Mexican-American urban youngsters of the 1940s and 50s who were caught between traditional Mexican-American society and Anglo-American life. They responded by rejecting both societies and forming a subculture of their own, complete with slang, unusual dress, and a unique life style. Although the pachucos no longer exist as an identifiable group, they passed on a heritage and spirit of rebellion to contemporary Chicano youth.

The term "Chicano" is another word that implies rebellion against the older generation. "Chicano" is a transformation of "Mexicano" and it has not until recently been accepted as a formal or "nice" term to describe Mexican-Americans. The more traditional Alianzistas prefer "Mexicano" or "Indo-Hispano" to describe themselves in Spanish. "Indo-Hispano" is a term popularized by Tijerina, who uses it to emphasize his people's Indian heritage, thus further legitimizing their claim to the land by linking them to the original inhabitants. Perhaps the only term accepted by all Spanish-speaking people of the Southwest (indeed by all of Latin America) is "La Raza." It carries a deep feeling for the blending of Spanish and Indian cultures which produced a mestizo race. The concept of la Raza in a real sense represents all those elements which unify the militant movements of New Mexico.

CONCLUSION

The desperate efforts of Mexican-American militants from the rural heartland, the urban barrios, and the university to save what remains of the Indo-Hispanic culture and the New Mexican way of life constitute the last chance for the United States to undo the destructive results of its acquisition of the American Southwest. Chicano leadership now exists in varied forms, and this leadership offers the promise of combining the traditional strengths of Indo-Hispanic culture with economic viability in contemporary America. But such a promise cannot be realized without an active response from Anglo-American leadership.

The choice which confronts the United States in New Mexico is very similar to that which faced Sweden and Norway in the decades following the First World War. The Scandinavian rural economy, based on small mixed farming like that of New Mexico, began to disintegrate rapidly, and urban planners found themselves faced with massive emigration from the countryside. As in New Mexico, this exodus was even more disturbing since the nexus of Scandinavian folk culture lay in the rural heartland.

The Liberal-Labor governments of Sweden and Norway chose to disregard conventional economic wisdom by investing heavily in the deteriorating areas. Schools and public services were upgraded, and small industry was introduced and encouraged with government aid, which included cheap electricity and transportation as well as massive credit. The rural population was given an opportunity to supplement farm income with factory work and other employment. Even today the usual pattern in rural Scandinavia resembles that which is incipient in New Mexico: a farmer is likely to combine his agriculture with several supplementary incomes from fishing, forestry, manufacturing, and civil service employment. Like the rural Chicanos, rural Scandinavians forego the various advantages of life in the cities in favor of an economically inferior but culturally more rewarding life in the countryside.

The rural way of life in Sweden and Norway remained economically marginal in the Sixties, even as it was marginal in the Twenties. Nevertheless, it is *successfully* marginal, and in real terms the quality of life has greatly improved. The benefits of this rural viability to Scandinavia have been great, though not in the American sense of providing massive agricultural surpluses. The slowdown in rural emigration permitted Scandinavian planners to eliminate slums and absorb the marginal underclass. Perhaps even more important, the maintenance of vital culture in the countryside has done much to give Sweden and Norway their uniquely egalitarian and Scandinavian way of life, so different from that of the more centralized and industrial German state.

The choice in New Mexico seems all too clear. If present trends continue, the last remaining basis for a viable Indo-Hispanic way of life will disappear. The American Southwest will be characterized by an urban underclass of second-class citizens, Mexican-Americans lost in a cultural limbo. Crammed into the ghettos of the cities, Chicanos will cling to an ethnic identity that serves only to stigmatize them and add to their inability to escape the too-well-known vicious cycle of urban poverty. The chasm which already separates prosperous suburban Anglos from barrio Chicanos will become unbridgeable.

On the other hand, a program of economic investment in the Chicano heartland of New Mexico, where both a population majority and a land base continue to exist, offers the very real possibility of saving the *patria chica,* given the determination of Mexican-Americans to remain there if they can find any way of doing so. Reduction of the rural exodus would then offer the chance of improving conditions in the urban barrios and reorganizing educational curricula so as to treat Spanish fluency as an advantage rather than a defect. The current generation of Mexican-American militants could be given the opportunity to take their rightful place as leaders of a cultural and social revitalization rather than being forced to become bitter and defiant organizers of desperate guerilla movements.

Perhaps most important, such a program would offer the United States one more chance to realize that ethnic differences can be a source of strength, not a weakness, that cultural diversity enriches rather than impoverishes, that pride in a people's heritage is a better basis for citizenship than flight from identity. New Mexico stands as an indictment of the United States, but it might still become a source of national hope. To bring this about we must recognize the gravity of the crisis in New Mexico and begin to act while time remains.

Elroy Bode

Elroy Bode (Author, El Paso, Texas) is a well-known author in Southwestern literary circles. This excellent account of the cultural impact of changing population patterns on a former upper-middle class Anglo high school won a 1971 Texas Institute of Letters Award.

Requiem For A WASP School

They stand in their tall, glassed-in picture frames, looking out from the uncomplicated 1940s to the crowded main hallway of El Paso's Austin High School. Small gold plates beneath the frames give the identifications: Walter Driver, State Champion, Boy's Single Tennis 1940; Billy Pitts, State Championship, Declamation 1942; Robert Goodman, First in State, Sliderule 1948. Holding their rackets and winners' cups, wearing their double-breasted suits with wide lapels and wide pants that sag around their shoes, they are reminders of the Days That Were: the days of Admiral Nimitz and General Patton and Ernie Pyle; of Glenn Miller and the Andrew Sisters and "Kokomo, Indiana"; of Jarrin' John Kimbrough and Betty Grable and "One Man's Family." They remain there behind glass, representing the Jack Armstrong-Henry Aldrich-Elm Street America that is gone forever.

It is easy, of course, to understand how rich in memories, how painfully nostalgic, these and other hallway pictures are to an old-timer at Austin High. Why, to him the 1940s mean—well, just about everything that was decent and sensible in American life. They mean kids who weren't perfect, of course, but who nonetheless respected rules and obeyed adults and knew how a human being cut his hair; they mean juke boxes and soda fountains and hayrides on Saturday night. They mean getting a lump in your throat listening to a glee club sing "The Halls of Ivy" because even if you weren't Ronald Coleman standing before a fireplace in college you understood exactly what that kind of song was saying: it was saying that Our Country Was a Grand 'n Glorious Place and Our Youth Were the Hope of Tomorrow. . . . And such an old-timer only has to turn from the pictures on the wall and gaze about him to feel an even

153

greater sense of pride, and of loss. For can't he look at thirteen showcases full of cups, plaques, statues, medals that have been earned by the hard-working students of Austin over the years? And over there—although no one ever stops to read them anymore—aren't those still the bronzed words of Theodore Roosevelt: "What we have a right to expect of the American boy is that he shall turn out to be a good American man"?

... "The American boy," the old-timer can muse: that's the key to the glory that once belonged to Austin, and to our country. And now look who we have filling these sacred halls: Mexicans.

Austin High School—the name is rich with associations for many El Pasoans. Over the past 40 years it has been a symbol of quality education, of good students from good homes, of traditions to be proud of. Students in nearby elementary and junior high schools looked forward to their freshman year at Austin with a certain amount of trembling, respect, and awe, for Austin meant everything a high school was supposed to mean: a long, elegant, two-story stone building for unsure freshmen to get lost in; teachers who presided over difficult courses that "prepared you for college"; a Panther football team that everyone could get excited about in the fall; homecoming assemblies and class officers and DAR essays and clubs and honors and prestige. Austin was the kind of all-around good school that lawyers, architects, businessmen wanted their sons and daughters to attend.

And then it happened. The '40s and '50s wandered innocently into the explosive '60s, and Austin High found itself with a problem on its hands: social change. The image of an Anglo-American, college-oriented student body began blurring into the image of a racially-mixed, academically varied student body that was more than half Mexican-American. A highly regarded middle-class WASP high school was becoming a gathering place for *chicanos.*

To understand this change it is necessary to know something about the geography of El Paso and the location of its high schools. Juarez, Mexico, lies south of the Rio Grande from El Paso; thus traditionally the heaviest concentration of Mexican-Americans has always been on the South Side.

Jefferson and Bowie High Schools, located in South El Paso, have for years been comprised mainly of Mexican-American students. In contrast, El Paso and Austin High Schools, located in the central part of town, have largely had Anglo enrollment along with a scattering of typically middle-class Mexican-American students. The newer suburban high schools—Andress, Irvin, Burges, and Coronado have also had, with the exception of Burges, relatively few Mexican-Americans. Technical High School, in the center of town, was changed this year to Technical Center—a school which next year will no longer offer academic courses or a high school diploma. Thus, since regular classes were being phased out, a number of students—largely Mexican-Americans from south El Paso wanting to enter "A Tech"—were forced into the halls of Austin High School last September even though they wanted to go elsewhere.

Here they came, the slow-walking girls of the freshman class. They moved along sidewalks toward a building which they had always considered "the gringo school on the hill," the snob school with its fancy golden dome, the school that—so rumor had it—didn't really like Mexicans. They came with their dukes up, not willing, in 1969, to let anyone put them down. They walked onto the campus in groups, they ate lunch in groups, they shouted in Spanish at boys from crowded doorways in groups, they waited in groups for whatever action might develop at the nearby Dairy Queen. And they were not Americans, in their own minds: they were Mexicans, they were *la Raza.* Their ties were to Mexico—its language, its culture, its dress and mannerisms.

They were the first class ever to enter Austin High expressing openly the attitudes and behavior patterns of a subculture world (and there seems to be little reason for their younger sisters and brothers to be thinking any differently in '71 and '72). They were not concerned with their "future," these stubborn, defensive South Side girls. Why should they be? They had on their block-heeled shoes, a transistor radio was pressed against their ear; their hair was hanging long and black and loose past their shoulders. Their skirts—brief triangles and handkerchiefs of color—revealed a long, mod stretch of legs halfway up the body.

They were like aliens in a hostile territory, not bothering to care about Austin's Most Beautiful Girl (—it certainly won't be a Mexican, they told one another) or the Select Scholar's list or the "Let's Really Yell it Now, Y'All" that the blonde cheerleader was getting red in the face about down on the gym floor. And they didn't care when they were warned during the morning p.a. announcements that they would "seriously jeopardize future freshman assemblies unless their conduct was more in line with that Austin expected of its student body."

They weren't interested in what Austin expected of them any more than they were interested in diagramming or reading *The Odyssey*. They were simply prisoners being held in an Anglo jail and they would continue to stare out sullenly through their granny glasses until the sentence was lifted.

It has long been the custom of school boards to select principals and other administrators from the ranks of coaches. It is not unusual, therefore, that the principal of Austin High is a former football coach; that the coordinator of instruction and guidance—presumed by many to be the successor to the principal when he retires—is an ex-coach also; and that the counselor most influential with the Austin administration is a former basketball coach. (Indeed, Austin is such a sports-and-coach oriented school that teachers in the good graces of the administrators are likely to be addressed by them as "coach." Thus the most unathletic math or government teacher finds himself being called "coach" as he requests an overhead projector or discusses a class load, for *coach* is the official password, the casual sign of camaraderie, the measuring stick of status).

It is safe to say that the principal and coordinator love Austin High School—that they consider it to be at the core of their life's work. It is also safe to say that both are sincere, intelligent men who are doing their jobs as they see them and who want perhaps more than anything else to keep Austin's image as a Good School from being damaged.

But sincerity, intelligence, and love-of-school—certainly adequate equipment for administrators during the less complex era of the '40s—are not enough to cope with the unsettling seventies. What is also needed are a high degree of flexibility in responding to potentially explosive situations which did not exist thirty years ago; a willingness to understand and trust student leaders who ask for change; and perhaps more than anything else, empathy with persons of minority groups—especially, in El Paso, Mexican-Americans.

High school administrations are generally conservative by nature; Austin's administration is perhaps more conservative than most. It thus views hippies, Reies Tijerina, César Chávez, black militants, anti-war demonstrators, college long hairs, etc. with a wholly unfriendly eye. The faculty, however, shares in large part this same conservative view. (Austin's Teacher of the Year for 1969–70—selected by Austin Teachers—had a sticker on his car reading "Register Communists, Not Firearms"). Whether the teachers' conservatism is directly related to age is conjectural, but the fact that out of a staff of over 100 probably less than half are under the age of forty does suggest that the majority of the faculty is far from being attuned to the strident harmonies of today—especially those voiced with a Spanish accent.

During the past year there was mild racial tension—mainly in September when a *chicano* walkout was threatened and Mexican and Anglo groups fought several afternoons after school; there was an awareness that the "melting pot" togetherness which Austin had begun priding itself on during the last few years had gradually begun to disappear; there was a feeling among many of the Mexican-American students—not just the reluctant freshmen—that they were the Unseen and Ignored Majority as far as honors, offices, awards, etc. were concerned. There was also a grim little war concerning censorship of the student newspaper, the *Pioneer*.

At the beginning of the year an administrative staff member had been assigned the extra duty of censoring the *Pioneer*. (Such censorship by an administrator rather than the journalism teacher was a city-wide policy). In October the administrator censored a letter-to-the-editor by junior journalism student Cecilia Rodríguez. The letter which dealt honestly with Mexican-American experiences and attitudes in typical school situations, was subsequently printed in the UT-El Paso college newspaper, the *Prospector*.

In April, a group on the *Pioneer* staff wanted to devote a entire issue to the concerns, problems, and culture of Mexican-American high school students. After much discussion—in which a few of the more secure Mexican-American students themselves balked at being singled out for special attention ("We're all Americans, aren't we?")—it was agreed that a single page of Mexican-American features would be run. When copy was submitted to the administrator, he cut the four lead articles: "Brown Misery"; "La Huelga," an article about César Chávez and the California farm workers' grape strike; an article on the origin and significance of the term *chicano;* and "the Race United," an article on the newly formed political party in Texas for Mexican-Americans.

It was a typical student-administration conflict. The administrator, in keeping out of the *Pioneer* what he considered to be extremist or inappropriate material, felt, one can be sure, that he was fulfilling his role as censor and was doing what was best for Austin High. What he did also, of course, was frustrate—once again—the efforts of some of the most creative, conscientious, and morally sensitive students at Austin—both Anglo and Mexican-American. ("Change this school?" said one depressed student afterward. "Never. You see how much trouble we had getting just one lousy, watered-down page in the *Pioneer.*" Another student added: "They say their doors are always open—yet every time you go to see them their minds are always closed. You can just see *No* staring at you before you even open your mouth.")

Thus the staff member added another footnote to an already familiar tale: high school administrators ironically helping to create the very college radicals whom they dislike, as well as stimulating the possibilities for an underground press. For the students finally end up believing what they really, at first, do not want to beleive: that the administration *doesn't* really care to understand what they are trying to say, *doesn't* realize that times have drastically changed, *doesn't* care about the quality of people's lives if those lives are led by blacks or browns; *doesn't* care to admit to the reality of a world which exists right outside the classroom doors in the streets, on the television sets, in the books available at every drugstore. Such students who try to express their idealism, and fail, simply resign themselves rather bitterly to their high school fate and wait for college—when they feel they can get rid of all their pent-up frustration in orgies of action.

Thus, at a crucial moment in its history; Austin seems to be maintaining a steady course of drift. Apparently, the official policy is: Business as usual. Don't rock the boat if you want to be considered a good fellow. And don't stir up any trouble about problems which you feel are mounting—wait and see if they don't go away as they always have in the past.

But what is buried at the heart of the problem? Why *should* Austin teachers sigh at the prospect of their high school being filled with Mexican-Americans? Why, really, should Mexican-Americans be less academically capable than Anglos? Who is to blame?

The problem is many-rooted and complex, of course. Yet if there is an answer to the question, Who has been at fault, it should be arrived at after considering these points:

1. For too long Mexican-Americans have been offered the least and the worst of everything that is available in Texas, from jobs to housing to education to social status. They have been forced to live on the bottom rung of society and adopt the survival rules of what Daniel Moynihan has called the "underclass." They learn at a very early age not to believe in the "better tomorrow" of America's Protestant ethic. They learn not to believe they will get ahead by merely studying hard and saying yes-sir and going by all the rules. They learn not to hope, or to save up nickels for a rainy day. They learn not to be open and trusting and optimistic. Indeed, they learn many things which do not help them get A's in government or spelling.

2. A study of underprivileged children, by Norma Radin (condensed in the September-October, 1968, issue of *Children*), has this to say about the "hidden curriculum" which is available in middle-class homes but which is generally absent from homes of the disadvantaged: "Shapes, colors, numbers, names of objects, words on signs, etc., are part of the continuous input to the child. . . .

Books are read, stories are told, intellectual curiosity is rewarded, and efforts perceived as school-oriented are praised. These activities are not part of the mother's role in the lower-class home." The study also states: "A large fraction of the intelligence of a child is already fixed by the age of five. No amount of environmental change beyond that point can affect the intellectual capacity to any significant extent."

3. Granting the difficulty of trying to do alone what society as a whole should do, and granting the possibility that some Mexican-American children by age five are already too severely handicapped to compete on an equal basis with Anglos, the public school administrators of El Paso should nevertheless be held accountable for failing to implement—years ago—a program of bilingual education for elementary grade Mexican-American children. Chances are the school system will not remedy these children's needs until officials decide to give them massive assistance and the highest priority: until they decide that not only the bright Debbies and Bills from middle-class homes have the right to become surgeons and bankers and civil engineers but also the Rogelios and Alicias from south of Paisano Street who have typically grown up not able to read and not seeing much point in learning how to anyway.

The school system must try bold new approaches in order to break the miserable chain of failure which has linked each successive wave of Spanish-speaking students. The traditional methods have not worked, and Head Start—which gets children after the first crucial five years—is simply not enough. Therefore, if the school system does not wish to perpetually deny children from Spanish-speaking homes a chance at the greatest possible success our society offers, then it must implement programs which will allow a child who speaks no English in the first grade to nevertheless become proficient in writing and reading English in a reasonably short time.

4. The voting public bears part of the blame for school ills: One group generally wants "safe" school board members—those who will go slow—instead of concerned, progressive individuals who understand the need for change. The other group refuses to vote at all: it always lets conservatives have their way at the polls and determine important elections with a few hundred votes.

5. Many nervous parents transfer their children from the inner city schools to those in the suburbs —leaving the inner-city schools to become, finally, all Mexican-American. This happens because the typical middle-class Anglo parent is unwilling to run the risk of having *his* child receive less than what he conceives to be the best education—that is, the parent refuses to let his child pay the penalty for society's failure to educate Mexican-American children so that they are on a par with Anglos. Thus he sends his son to the suburbs— hoping the kid won't get on pot or acid—and leaves such schools as Austin and El Paso High to sink or swim with the many black eyes and brown skins. (Classic example: For many years El Paso High School was attended by students from the affluent Kern Place and Rim Road sections "on the hill" above the school, as well as by students from modest homes in the flatland below. It was a relatively successful mingling of rich, poor, and middle-class. Then Coronado High School was built in northwest El Paso, and school authorities gave parents the choice of sending their children to Coronado or El Paso High. The Anglo rush toward a lily-white school began and thus El Paso High— finally cut off from the Rim Road and Kern Place areas through obvious gerrymandering—has had its enrollment to drop by approximately 1,000 students.)

If school administrators genuinely want to educate students for the lives they will be leading in the '70s and '80s—rather than just keeping them quiet and off the streets—they must provide courses and teachers that are meaningful to both the highly motivated academic students and the indifferent, withdrawn couldn't-care-lessers. They must also determine which teachers do the incredibly difficult job of plunging into their subjects and making them exciting, challenging, alive—and which teachers merely show up for work, "keep order" with a deadening fervor, and then go home again.

And the principals: they should be energetic, widely read men who are conversant with the issues of the times and the problems which face students in their schools. They should be men who are constantly mingling with the students—staying in touch, hearing what they have to say in this era of intense social concern and audacious questioning of the status quo—rather than presiding over their desks in their offices. They should be "shirt-sleeves-rolled-up" administrators of the '70s, moving among students the way Mayor Lindsay moves through the people of New York. They should be courteous, open-minded, contemporary men whom the students feel are on their side—which of course, they will be if they are successful principals.

. . . The pictures on the wall at Austin High will continue to look out from a simpler time. Whether it was also a better time more just, more democratic—more American—time is still to be decided. If we truly wish to educate everyone and not just an elite—and if we find ways to turn that wish into a reality—then the glory that was yesterday will pale beside the glory of today.

James Officer

James Officer (Coordinator of International Programs and Professor of Anthropology, University of Arizona) studied urban Chicanos in the barrio of Tucson. In this excerpt from his Ph.D. dissertation, "The Joining Habits of Urban Mexican Americans" (1964), Professor Officer evaluates from his personal experiences the leadership and reasons for the Tucson Chicanos' considerable influence in local elections. Professor Officer has a good deal of knowledge of politics and government, having served both as Assistant Commissioner of Indian Affairs (1962-1967) and as a special assistant (1967-1969) to the then Secretary of the Interior Stewart Udall.
By permission of the author.

Politics And Leadership

During the period of my fieldwork, representatives of the Tucson Mexican colony were successful in winning election to two of Pima County's most important political offices. A Mexican-born lawyer in 1958 was named one of four judges to the county superior court and another young lawyer in 1960 was chosen as one of three county supervisors. The Mexicans had never before had a county judge and only one other member of the colony (Mariano Samaniego) had ever been a county supervisor. However, through the years Mexicans, at one time or another, had occupied most of the other county elective offices; had served on the city council and on the school board of Tucson District No. 1. The Alianza during its early history, and later, the Spanish-American Democratic Club, served the colony well in helping it to become politically sophisticated and aiding it to organize in such a way as to make its influence felt at the polls. Interest in politics among Tucson Mexicans was quite high, even the women taking part in political campaigns.

For many of those in the colony, politics was not so much concerned with choosing the candidate most qualified for office, as with selecting the one most likely to fulfill patronage promises. There was an expression which was frequently used to describe the plight of the individual who had aided a politician and got nothing in return. He was said to have been *muy mal paga'o* ("very poorly paid") for his efforts. Tucson's Mexican-Americans were not the only ones who were guided by such a philosophy, but they were more likely openly to acknowledge the motivation which underlay their voting behavior.

Feeling that Mexican votes, through patronage promises, could be "purchased," Anglo politieians literally swarmed through the *barrios* in election years seeking out the centers of influence and authority. During the election campaigns of 1958 and 1960, I was privileged to have a ringside seat in the *cantina* operated by one of the small Mexican political *jefes* in South Tucson. Anglo office-seekers who would not have deigned to enter his establishment in the "off" years all but established headquarters there while running for office.

Except for rare occasions when a severe crisis confronted the colony, it was split into many factions and no single individual or group could properly presume to speak for all. During the 1960 elections, there were at least five recognizable political factions within the colony, all related to the Democratic Party. At the outset of the campaign, Faction "A" led by the Anglo who held the county's most important political post appeared to be the most powerful. The nucleus of Mexican membership in this faction came from county employees and their families, and its focus of operations was the Latin-American Social Club. (Several of the former leaders of the Spanish-American Democratic Club had been associated with Faction "A", but by 1960, one of the most important had died and another was in such poor health that he could not make much of a contribution.)

Faction "B" was headed by a Mexican notary public who had formerly served in the state legislature. This man was a highly controversial figure in the total community, having attracted much attention to himself through publishing a small pamphlet in which he attacked the editor of the morning newspaper, the chairman of the county board of supervisors, the mayor, and several other Anglo notables. He drew most of his support from disgruntled lower class elements in the *barrios,* and received financial assistance from wealthy individuals, both Mexican and Anglo, who were opposed to the city and county administrations in power.

Faction "C" consisted of a small handful of the most loyal followers of the supreme president of the Alianza. In previous elections, this faction had supported many of the candidates endorsed by Faction "A", but, feeling that the influence of this group was waning, the supreme president in 1960 put up a separate slate of candidates. He was not seconded in this decision by all of the Aliancistas, since some of the candidates he chose to back were running against members of the Alianza lodges.

Faction "D" also included as its nucleus a small group of leaders from the Alianza. These were young men in their late 20's from the Alianza lodge known as the Monte Carlo Men's Club. They were mostly veterans and university graduates and their greatest political strength came from the Menlo Park district, and the *barrios* of El Río and Hollywood. They concentrated much of their attention on electing Mexicans to the state legislature and on capturing control of the county machinery of the Democratic Party.

Faction "E" was a coalition group, including among its organizers several small *jefes* who had defected from factions "A" and "C". Some were dissatisfied county employees and others were individuals with an extreme dislike for the supreme president of the Alianza. They gave their support to a young Mexican lawyer in the race to overthrow the Anglo head of Faction "A".

In the 1960 elections, the honors went to Factions "D" and "E." The Anglo who headed Faction "A" was soundly defeated by the young lawyer, and many of the candidates supported by the Alianza president also lost.

Through the years Mexicans had been less successful in winning elections than in helping elect Anglos who could be relied upon to fulfill campaign patronage promises. Many Mexican *jefes* concerned themselves less with the ethnic and racial backgrounds of candidates than with the likelihood of the latter to provide jobs for chicanos. The feeling of these politicos was summarized for me early in 1961 by the man who had been the leader of Faction "B." (At the time he had just been convicted in Federal court of falsifying an immigration document.) According to his observation: "It doesn't make much difference whether a candidate is a *gringo* or a *chicano.* One can screw you (*Uno le puede chingar*) just as bad as another. The thing that counts is whether he'll deliver what he says he will when he gets into office."

Although a woman of Mexican descent had been the Pima County Recorder for many years, women from the colony did not often seek political office. However, many contributed to the political life of the community and several, through politics, had moved into important city and county offices. For example, the city clerk was a Mexican woman, as was the clerk for the county board of supervisors and one of the deputy county attorneys. Those men from the colony who involved themselves in politics often called upon their wives and other female family members for aid. "Women have the time to work," one of the Mexican *jefes* told me in 1960, "and without their aid a Mexican candidate hasn't got much chance." Several of my informants reported that during the elections of 1958, a prominent U.S. Senator on a visit to Tucson sought out and spent several hours with two middle-age Mexican women who were *madrecitas* of large families.

Just as it was important in other areas of colony life, the kin group played a significant role in the realm of politics. Family members were expected to stand together in support of a candidate (they did not always do so,) and the Mexican political chieftains tried to enlist the support of persons from large extended families whenever they could do so. An informant reported that during the 1958 elections a Mexican who had previously supported one of the prominent Anglo politicians switched his allegiance to another candidate and brought with him the votes of more than 100 close relatives.

Those who played major roles in colony politics were not the only individuals of influence. A survey which I conducted during 1958-59 revealed several other areas of leadership. One of the most important of these consisted of the Spanish-language radio announcers of the city. One man especially had a tremendous following among the lower middle and lower class Mexicans. An immigrant from a small mining town in the state of Zacatecas, he had come to Tucson in the 1930s after working previously in the copper mines at Jerome, Arizona. In addition to mining, he had conducted a radio program in Spanish on one of the Jerome stations, and was able to arrange a similar broadcast in Tucson. Despite the fact that he was an "outsider," he quickly gained a following among Tucson Mexicans, and the volume of advertising handled by his program helped the radio station to survive the depression. By the time I began my fieldwork in 1958, this man had become a local legend and was doing both radio and television broadcasts.

Two other radio announcers were also very influential within the *colonia* at the time of my research. Both were immigrants, one being from Nogales, Sonora, and the other from Ciudad Juárez, Chihuahua.

Either individually or collectively, the radio announcers often sponsored *colectas* (fund raising campaigns) on their programs to aid colony residents faced with crises of various kinds. In this endeavor they were often helped by the Mexican formal voluntary associations.

The successful Mexican businessmen constituted another influential element of the colony's population. To the Anglos, these men symbolized the Mexican upper class, and although some ignored the daily round of the colony, when they did become interested in its affairs, they could quickly find followers. Among the most highly respected and influential of the Mexican businessmen was a bank vice-president who had served on the city school board a few years before I began my study. This man's father had continued to reside in Barrio Libre despite his sons's prominence and success.

Several Tucson druggists were men of influence. Foremost among these was the Anglo-Mexican who for many years had owned the city's largest drug chain. Although he had sold his business and retired a few years prior to the beginning of my fieldwork, he was still being sought out for advice on matters of particular interest to the Mexican population. Another prominent druggist, whose store was located in the downtown district, was the community's principal supplier of medicinal herbs and was much respected by the lower class population of the colony. He was one of the few Mexicans who took an interest in such groups as the Tucson Council for Civil Unity.

Barbers, butchers and bartenders also contributed importantly to the formulation of opinion within the *barrios*. The latter especially were influential with working class males who spent much of their leisure time in the *cantinas*. Politicians were well aware of the role of the bartenders *(cantineros)* and devoted much attention to winning them over in election years.

Apart from the church, the beauty parlor was a significant moulder of opinion among the women of the colony. Two such establishments which were especially influential came to my attention in 1959. One, located at the edge of Barrio Libre, was owned and managed by a woman from a pioneer Mexican family, whose husband was a druggist. She had been president of the Drachman School P.T.A. and of the Club Camelia. She was also active in the auxiliaries to a veterans' organization and an occupational association.

Another beauty parlor which played an important role in opinion making among the women of the colony was located in Barrio El Río, and managed by a young woman whose brother was an official of the Democratic Party. As I was completing my fieldwork, this woman and her Anglo sister-in law were talking about relocating their business to an Anglo neighborhood, a move which certainly would have reduced its influence on colony affairs.

Some years prior to my study, the newspaper *El Tucsonense* went into a majority of the Tucson Mexican homes and may be presumed to have contributed significantly to the thinking of the *colonia*. However, it was forced to discontinue publication in 1959 upon the death of its elderly editor. Another paper, called *La Voz,* was put out by the head of the *Sociedad Mutualista Porfirio Díaz* who owned a small printing shop. It was an advertising "throw away" and not widely circulated throughout the community. For a short time during the period of my fieldwork, the head of political faction "B" prepared and distributed an inflammatory pamphlet of political tone known as *Arizona P-M.* Its greatest appeal was to the lower class families of Barrio Libre. Just beginning to emerge as I finished my research was a paper called *La Prensa,* published by a young Mexican-American university graduate from California. Its influence on the thinking of the colony remained to be determined.

Despite the fact that its affiliated lodges did not always follow the leadership of its supreme president, the Alianza was unquestionably the most influential Mexican formal voluntary association. On political matters the Latin-American Social Club had been influential with many males of the lower middle and lower classes, but following the defeat of its candidate for county supervisor in the 1960 elections, its future role remained to be determined. With certain groups, the *Sociedad Mutualista Porfirio Díaz* and the *Cocío-Estrada Post* of the American Legion were important opinion-making collectivities.

Probably the most influential of the women's associations were the Club Camelia, the Ladies' Auxiliary to the Club Comwolei, the *Damas Auxiliares de la Logia Fundalora* (the women's auxiliary to the founding lodge of the Alianza,) and the Ladies' Auxiliary to the Benefit Sportsmen's Club.

Prior to World War II, the Mexican Consul had been a major influence on the Mexican Colony, but this was not so in 1959. The Consul's closest friends in the community were the persons who retained the greatest patriotic interest in Mexico and these were declining in numbers at the time of my study.

DONALd FReeMAN

*Donald Freeman (Chairman of Political Science
Department, University of West Florida, Pensacola, Florida)
has co-authored a textbook,* POLITICAL PARTIES AND
POLITICAL BEHAVIOR *(1966) on the workings of the
American political system. In this paper read at the
Southwestern Social Studies Association in 1967, Professor
Freeman uses the tools of the political scientist to attempt to
determine the political patterns of the large Chicano
population in South Tucson.
By permission of the author. From a paper prepared for
the Annual Meeting of the Southwestern Political Science
Association, March 1967.*

Party,Vote,
And The Mexican American
In South Tucson

South Tucson is an incorporated city, completely surrounded by the city of Tucson. The little municipality (population of 7,004 in 1960, and about one square mile in land mass) is now twenty-seven years old, and apparently South Tucsonians continue to enjoy their separate existence. Incorporation was a tactic to avoid the taxes and regulations of Tucson. Over 60 percent of the population of South Tucson is Mexican-American, and Mexican-Americans dominate the government of the city today.

South Tucson was chosen as the universe for study because of the concentration of Mexican-Americans there, because the land area of the city could be covered easily in a survey, and because of its location only a few miles from the campus of the University of Arizona. Since South Tucson is relatively small, we were able to use a two-stage, strict random sample. The research design and supporting interview schedule for the study were prepared to replicate substantial portions of the Voting Studies of the Survey Research Center of the University of Michigan and the study of Southern voting behavior done by Matthews and Prothro at the University of North Carolina.

THE SAMPLE AND OPERATIONAL DEFINITION OF "MEXICAN-AMERICAN"

Largely this paper is based on simple descriptive and comparative analysis, describing the political behavior of the Mexican-American and comparing it with the political behavior of known populations and a control group. There is little bivariate analysis presented here, and no multivariate analysis. The number of respondents in the sample produces very small "N's" in cells if very elaborate analysis is used. This study was designed and carried out as a pilot project, with hope that a much larger sample would be secured in a more extensive research project at a later date.

The sample is, I am convinced, an excellent sample of South Tucson. According to the 1960 census, 61.1 percent of the residents of South Tucson had Spanish surnames. The proportion of Mexican-Americans in our sample of South Tucson is 64.9 percent. One major fear of survey sample designers is an over-sampling of females, especially in marginal communities like South Tucson where the interviewer may be misperceived as a bill collector or a policeman. Our sample is composed of 53 percent females and 47 percent males, a remarkable balance when you consider that a number of the households in South Tucson are headed by women.

One of the most difficult tasks faced in drawing up the research design was defining the term "Mexican-American." Interviewer observation would ask the interviewer to make a very doubtful and difficult judgment. A direct question about ethnic background might offend the respondent, and Spanish surnames are not always indicative of Mexican-American stock. Therefore, we have used the following operational definition: any respondent is Mexican-American if he or she, or his or her spouse, or any parent or grandparent of either the respondent or the respondent's spouse was born in Mexico. We also collected an interviewer perception of the ethnic background of the respondent, and this agreed with the operational definition in 185 of the 188 cases. On the basis of interviewer perception, three respondents were classified as Indian though they were born in Mexico. Operationally we have included them in the Mexican-American group. Our sample breakdown was as follows:

Mexican-American	64.9%	(122)
Anglo	27.7%	(52)
American Indian	4.3%	(8)
Negro	2.7%	(5)
Oriental	.5%	(1)
TOTAL	100.1%	(188)

In the balance of this paper we will group the Anglo, American Indian, Negro, and Oriental components of the sample together as "Others." The "Others" grouping is obviously a heterogeneous one, but it has a certain unity about it in being the non-Mexican-American population of South Tucson, and as such, is the best control group, based on similarity of setting, which we could use.

The major problem faced in the fieldwork for this project was the nature of the community to be studied. South Tucson is made up almost entirely of low income people who are largely outside the social mainstream of middle class America. The political world of such people is a limited world. As voting studies have demonstrated, most American voters live all their political lives with a limited awareness of issues, parties, politics, and governmental operations. The people who exist at the bottom of the status ladder (of whatever sort of measure you wish to use) attain a level of political knowledge far more limited than that of the mass public. Awareness of functional specialization within the world of politics may well escape the deprived and disinherited in our society. How meaningful are issue questions to these people? Are interviewer and respondent communicating with each other? Are concepts taken for granted by the research designer understood by the respondent? We were very conscious of this problem. We worked hard to gain complete acceptance in the South Tucson community, used screening questions on all major issue and behavior items, and had available to the interviewer check boxes for "didn't understand" in many sections of the questionnaire. In large part, we feel that we were able to measure lack of understanding and avoid incorporating it as a bias into the survey results.

SOCIAL CHARACTERISTICS OF SOUTH TUCSON

A drive through South Tucson will quickly convince a social scientist that he is observing a distinctive sub-population in society. One strip of retail and service establishments runs right down through the middle of the city. The balance of South Tucson is probably best described as humble, simple, or marginal housing. There is a substantial number of trailer-dwelling units in South Tucson. The motels have mixed temporary and permanent residents. There are many small houses in South Tucson which would never pass the building inspection laws of a modern city, but the city should not be described as a slum and a ghetto. It is more appropriate to think of it as a predominately Mexican-American enclave, with a number of substandard dwelling-units. Some houses in South Tucson that would have a very low tax evaluation are kept so well that they have a neat and attractive appearance.

Ninety-one percent of the Mexican-Americans in South Tucson are Catholics, compared to 37.9 percent of the Others category. One National Opinion Research Center sample taken in January of 1964 found the American general public to be 26.0 percent Catholic. The commitment of the Catholics in South Tucson to their church is not as great as you would find among Catholics in New England: 31.9 percent said they seldom or never attend church, and 37.7 percent said they are not strong Catholics.

Relying on the three best objective measures of socioeconomic status, we can draw a more detailed picture of the social and economic opportunities available to Mexican-Americans. Using

occupation of the head of the houshold we find that only 3.3 percent of the Mexican-Americans hold white collar jobs (professional and technical, managers and officials, self-employed businessmen, clerical and sales), while 24.2 percent of the Others in South Tucson hold white collar jobs. The largest single occupational category for Mexican-Americans is unskilled labor, 28.7 percent. Eighty-two percent of the Mexican-Americans hold blue collar jobs, compared to 63.7 percent of the Others grouping.

The opportunity to break out of the blue collar occupational category is simply not available to the Mexican-American, since the educational background to make the move has not been acquired. Slightly over 10 percent of the Mexican-Americans have had no education at all, and a total of 57.4 percent of this ethnic group in South Tucson has had no more than a seventh grade education. The lack of education at the higher levels for Mexican-Americans is even more striking: no Mexican-American in our sample has completed college. If you add together all categories of education from completed high school on up, you find that just under 10 percent of the Mexican-Americans have a high school education or better. The Others grouping has been considerably more advantaged in education level. Only 25.7 percent of the Others have seven or less grades of schooling, and 30.3 percent of the group has a high school or better than a high school education.

There is no statistically significant difference between the Mexican-Americans and the Others on the basis of total family income. Twenty to 25.0 percent of the respondents did not give information on family income, which makes it impossible to do an accurate comparison between these and other sets of data from national studies. Most of the non-responses were "don't knows" and appeared to be genuinely based on an inability to determine the family income. Roughly one-third of the Mexican-American families have a total income of less than $3,000 a year, and over two-thirds of the families earn less than $7,500 a year.

The Mexican-Americans are quite aware of their social and economic condition. One fifty-three-year-old, second generation Mexican-

American, who had five grades of school was described by the interviewer in these terms:

Respondent had strong feelings about any inequality because of race or wealth. She kept remarking about how no one cares about the poor—they are thrown into jail. And she was often not hired because she was Mexican. 'But we are free and have our health, so I can't complain.'

She is a housewife and a hospital kitchen aide; her husband is a laborer with Southern Pacific Railroad. For another example, a second generation Mexican-American male, forty-five-years-old, with one-half a year of education was described by the interviewer in this quote:

Respondent had very strong opinions and was quite articulate, but he kept apologizing about how he talked. Said he wished he could express himself well, but didn't go to school and felt his English was poor. It really wasn't. He used some words like cooperate, etc., and used them properly. He said the fellows where he worked kidded him about how he talked. Really, most frustrated he was. Said he would like to tell a lot of people how he felt, and was glad to have this interview, but thought he still wouldn't get across what he meant. He is very bitter about government in a way. Said he used to be quite interested, but not any more—all he gets is promises and nobody will help.

In the party response section of this same interview, the respondent was asked "Is there anything in particular that you don't like about the Democratic party?" His answer speaks of his economic condition and reveals something of the operations of the Democratic party in South Tucson:

Nothing to say against them—But, the guys after us for voting—get elected, and all that you just talk to me and we'll fix you up—get you work—8 to 10 days a month. They never did—I went to talk to [Mexican-American South Tucson Democratic Councilman]— out of work one and one-half years—losing

house—sorry nothing for laborer. What's the use of voting if they won't help us—even if he is Mexican, I'd rather go for white people even if I'm a Mexican.

In sum, there is ample evidence to convince the social scientist that the Mexican-American is disadvantaged socially and economically by his ethnic status.

POLITICAL PARTIES IN SOUTH TUCSON

The two great political parties in the United States are venerable institutions, with rich images and traditions which permit the voter and even the non-voter to relate through them with the world of politics. In *Political Parties and Political Behavior* this description of the mass public's image of parties appears:

The images of the Democratic and Republican parties have remained rather stable for three decades. The Democratic party is the party of prosperity, war, creeping socialism, bureaucratic red tape, the little man, the laboring man, the Negro and minority groups generally, the welfare state, Franklin D. Roosevelt and John F. Kennedy, the South, and internationalism. The Republican party is the party of peace, responsible administration, depression, free economy, the businessman, the better classes, the white Protestant of English origins generally, Dwight D. Eisenhower, and Herbert Hoover, "Americanism," and cautious internationalism.

The images of the two political parties for Mexican-Americans and South Tucsonians generally fit rather well into research findings on the mass images.

The image of the Democratic party for South Tucsonians and for Mexican-Americans is quite positive. For South Tucson as a whole, 181 favorable comments were made about the Democratic party and only 49 unfavorable comments were made, a ratio of better than three favorable to one unfavorable comment. Mexican-Americans volunteered 112 favorable remarks to 22 unfavorable ones, a positive Democratic ratio of five to one.

Group Related responses account for 31.9 percent of South Tucson's image of the Democratic party. Traditional ties with the Democratic party (personal, family ties or affective comment) account for 24.5 percent of the remarks, and the Domestic Policies of the party account for another 14.1 percent. It is rather remarkable that Party Leaders drew only 10.1 percent of the volunteered remarks. Government Management is a cipher in the image, evoking about an equal number of positive and negative comments, while the Democratic party's Foreign Policies are a clear liability for its image.

For Mexican-Americans only, the image is even more clearly dominated by the Group Related, Traditional, and Domestic Policy components. Slightly over seventy percent of the Mexican-Americans volunteered positive remarks falling into these three categories. Only 21.3 percent of the Mexican-Americans volunteered remarks falling in all the other four categories.

The image of the Republican party among people in South Tucson is much weaker in detail, and substantially negative. The number of volunteered negative remarks is greater than the number of volunteered positive remarks, 72 to 50 for all of South Tucson and 35 to 22 for Mexican-Americans only. However, the negative feeling toward the Republican party appears to lack intensity—there appears to be an abbreviated or disinterested view of the Republican party. For South Tucson as a whole, the three leading components of the anti-Republican image are Group Related (11.7%), Party Leaders (10.1%) and Traditional (6.9%). Only the order changes when we talk about Mexican-Americans alone: Group Related (9.8%), Traditional (5.7%), and Party Leaders (4.9%). The pro-Democratic and anti-Republican views are not mirror images of each other; because Domestic Policy is supplanted by Party Leaders when you move from the pro-Democratic to the anti-Republican side of the data. An overwhelming proportion of the Group Related responses favoring the Democratic party and opposing the Republican party were couched in these terms: the Democratic party is the party of the common man, lower income people, working-class people, and the average man, while the Republican party is bad for these groups or good for big business, the upper classes, the rich and the powerful.

More than a few Mexican-Americans have no knowledge of political parties and politics—they are apolitical. One eighty-one-year old lady who was born in Sonora, speaks only Spanish, is not a citizen, and is a widow, could not distinguish between parties and government. We asked her what she likes about the Democratic party and she replied: "I am very happy in this country. I'm an immigrant and they have treated me with kindness." And some have only a limited view of the parties. For example, here are the statements from a twenty-seven-year old, second generation Mexican-American (he had seven grades in school, works as a dishwasher in a drug store, and there are eight adults and seven children in the household he heads):

Like about Democrats: "Some people say it's better than Republicans. I feel the same way as others."

Dislike about Democrats: "Seems all right to me."

Like about Republicans: "No."

Dislike about Republicans: "Just don't like them."

The affection for the Democratic party, and the positive image of the Democratic party, transcends generational and social differences among the Mexican-American people in South Tucson. Below I shall quote the party responses from several Mexican-Americans of different circumstances.

A. Female, forty-nine years old, she and her husband are second generation Mexican-Americans, nine grades in school, and she has voted.

Like about Democrats: "Democrats are mostly the poor people—they are more interested in helping the poor people—lots of Spanish-speaking people get jobs from the Democrats—not from the Republicans."

Dislike about Democrats: "No, nothing."
Like about Republicans: "No, I really don't like the Republican party very well."
Dislike about Republicans: "They are the party of the big fish; we are the little fish."

B. Male, fifty-seven years old, he was born in Arizona but his wife was born in Mexico, three grades of school, speaks only Spanish, has voted.
Like about Democrats: "Always provides jobs and supports."
Dislike about Democrats: "No, no idea."
Like about Republicans: No response.
Dislike about Republicans: "Yes, the Republican president in 1929 allowed the people to starve. Ever since then I have always disliked [them]."

C. Male, eighty-three years old, born in Mexico and came to this country in 1890, has been a citizen since 1946, two years of school in Mexico, retired from Southern Pacific Railroad, and has voted. Respondent speaks only Spanish.
Like about Democrats: "Democrats working man's party. Republicans for the rich. Democrats best for him because he is a working man."
Dislike about Democrats: "Nothing in particular."

Like about Republicans: "I don't like a thing. Some speak well of them, but I won't change my affiliation." All candidates promise much but do nothing. Once in office won't comply with campaign promises. All parties' candidates do this, no exceptions."
Dislike about Republicans: "Nothing in particular except they are the party of the rich."

D. Male, thirty-eight years old, he and his wife born in Mexico, is not a citizen, is trying to learn to speak English but now speaks only Spanish, has six grades of education, he is a laborer with a construction company, and has not voted.
Like about Democrats: "Its more on the side of the poor—makes a better chance for one."

Dislike about Democrats: "No."
Like about Republicans: "I don't know. The Democrats pull a little more to the side of the poor—it is convenient for one."
Dislike about Republicans: "No."

E. Male, twenty-nine years old, he was born in Mexico but his wife was born in Arizona, he is not a citizen, speaks only Spanish, has seven years of school, is a mechanic, and voted in Mexico but not in the United States.
Like about the Democrats: "They give more opportunities to the worker. They help."
Dislike about the Democrats: "No."
Like about the Republicans: "No. They don't help as much."
Dislike about the Republicans: "No."

Political Scientists have attempted to measure the voter's relationship with his political party in a variety of ways since the earliest voting behavior research. The most successful technique of measuring the voter's psychological relationship to his party is that designed by the Survey Research Center at Michigan. The SRC party identification scale classifies the voter at one of seven points along a continuum running from Strong Democrat through Independent to Strong Republican, or, if the person completely rejects party as a meaningful concept to him, he is designated as Apolitical. Party identification, as measured by the SRC scale, is a powerful independent variable which explains a substantial proportion of a person's partisan political behavior.

The party identification of Mexican-Americans in South Tucson is distinctively pro-Democratic. About one-half of all American voters are strong or weak identifiers with the Democratic party, but roughly two-thirds of all South Tucsonians are strong or weak Democrats. The Mexican-Americans are significantly stronger in their identification with the Democrats when compared to either a national sample or the Others group from South Tucson. Forty-three and four-tenths percent of the Mexican-Americans are strong Democrats, while only 0.8 percent of this group are strong Republicans. The proportion of weak Democrats to weak Republicans is 23.0 percent to 1.6 percent. As might be expected, given the Mexican-Americans' background and lack of socialization in this political system, 13.1 percent of the group is Apolitical, a figure much larger than one could find in a national sample.

The voting consistency of Mexican-Americans in all presidential elections reinforces the picture we are drawing of this group's attachment to the Democratic party. Thirty-six and one-tenth percent of the Mexican-Americans always vote Democratic in presidential elections, compared to 0.8 percent of the group that always votes Republican and 8.2 percent which votes for different parties. Mexican-Americans are distinctively more Democratic in the consistency of their voting than either the 'Others' group or the SRC 1964 national sample, and they are substantially under the 'Others' group and the SRC 1964 national sample in voting Republican and voting for different parties. The significantly large proportion of Mexican-Americans voting Democratic over the years is made even more remarkable by the fact that 47.5 percent of the Mexican-Americans have never voted and were thereby not distributed in the party voting frequency cells.

The extensive literature on American voting behavior that has developed in the last twenty years has revealed that party attachments for the individual voter are largely inherited from the voter's parents. We asked our respondents about the voting behavior of their parents and found that 72.1 percent of the Mexican-Americans either had parents who did not vote or they didn't know whether their parents voted. The socialization literature largely rests on parental party identification, not voting behavior, however there is an indication in our data that much of the party identification of Mexican-Americans cannot be attributed to parental political orientation. Only 23.0 percent of the Mexican-Americans had one or both parents who voted Democratic. As our party identification data would predict, only 2.4 percent of the Mexican-Americans had one or both parents voting Republican. The Others group divides much as you would expect a low-income population to divide: 45.5 percent had one or both par-

ents who voted Democratic, 6.1 percent had parents who voted for different parties, and 12.1 percent had one or both parents who voted Republican.

There are actually more strong Democrats, 44.4 percent, among those Mexican-Americans who said their parents did not vote or didn't know whether their parents voted than there are among those who said that one or both parents had voted Democratic, 42.9 percent. This would lead us to minimally hypothesize that the strong ties of Mexican-Americans with the Democratic party flow in part from the ethnic group to which they belong.

VOTING BEHAVIOR IN 1964

The most important observation one can make about Mexican-American voting behavior in 1964 is that 51.6 percent were not eligible to vote and 13.9 percent who were eligible did not vote. In other words, roughly two-thirds of the Mexican-Americans in South Tucson did not vote. Johnson outpolled Goldwater among Mexican-Americans 30.3 percent to 0.8 percent. About one-fifth of the Others group was ineligible to vote and another fifth was eligible but did not vote. The Others group divided its vote in favor of Johnson, 47.0 percent to 9.1 percent.

If we consider the voting decision of voters only in 1964, the distinctiveness of the entire South Tucson support for Johnson is quite clear. Johnson drew 97.4 percent of the Mexican-American vote and 83.8 percent of the Others vote in South Tucson. The comparable percentage from SRC's post-election reported vote from the nation as a whole was 67.5 percent. At least in South Tucson, Mexican-Americans voted for Johnson about as heavily as Negroes across the nation. Even allowing for an over-reporting of vote in favor of the winner in a post-election survey, this is a remarkably high level of support for President Johnson.

When voting behavior in 1964 is checked by party identification, there appears to be a clear relationship between the two variables, however, one must be very careful about interpreting these data since most of the cells in the table are empty or contain very small frequencies. Johnson received the votes of 43.2 percent of those Mexican-Americans who identified themselves as either strong or weak Democrats, 11.2 percent of the votes of persons who identified themselves as independent Democrats, Independents or independent Republicans, and none of the votes of the three persons who identified themselves as weak or strong Republicans. The persons who identified themselves as weak or strong Democrats appear to be more clearly integrated into the political system; of all the party identification categories, they have the smallest proportion who did not vote. All of the Apoliticals were ineligible to vote, as might be expected.

POLITICAL PARTICIPATION IN SOUTH TUCSON

One of the simplest measures of the voter's involvement in the political system is the voter's level of interest in politics. The low level of interest in politics on the part of all South Tucsonians is only one indication, among several which we shall now marshall as the conclusion of this paper, of their lack of integration into the American political and party system. There is no statistically significant difference between the Mexican-American and 'Others' categories; both have a low level of interest in politics. Just under one half of both groups say that they are "somewhat interested" in politics. Roughly four Mexican-Americans say that they are "not interested at all" in politics to every one who says that he is "interested a great deal" in politics. The Others group does have a substantially larger proportion saying they are "interested a great deal" in politics.

We have checked Mexican-Americans against Others in South Tucson on six types of political activity. In every case the Others group has a larger proportion of persons saying they have engaged in the activity. Because of the small frequencies involved in the cells of tables under analysis, there is no significant statistical difference between Mexican-Americans and Others in two of the six activities, however, the overall difference between the two groups is impressive. Only 52.5 percent of the Mexican-Americans *have voted* at some time in their lives. Eighteen per-

cent of the group have *attended political meetings and rallies.* The same proportion of the Mexican-Americans, 13.1 percent, say they have *made a financial contribution to a party* and *worked for a political candidate.* Fifteen and six-tenths percent of the Mexican-Americans *have tried to influence another person's voting decision,* and 2.5 percent *have held a government or party office.* The level of political participation of Mexican-Americans is quite comparable to the level of political participation of Southern Negroes in 1961 on three of the activities: attending meetings and rallies, making a financial contribution, and working for a political candidate. In 1961 only 41.0 percent of Southern Negroes said that they had voted at some time in their lives, significantly lower than the comparable 52.5 percent for Mexican-Americans in South Tucson.

The cause of the large non-voting population in South Tucson should be explored, since 47.5 percent of the Mexican-Americans and 19.7 percent of the Others group have never voted. Some non-voting exists all through our political system, and the traditional explanations one receives from the non-voter are: illness, not old enough before, military service interfered, work interferes, or my religion forbids any political activity. Only 17.2 percent of the non-voting among Mexican-Americans can be explained by one of these traditional "excuses," and the comparable figure for Others is 46.2 percent. Students of voting behavior also expect to find a segment of the public which lacks interest in politics or can give no reason for not voting; 22.4 percent of the Mexican-Americans and 30.8 percent of the Others give these explanations. The largest single explanation for non-voting given to us by Mexican-Americans is tied directly to the group's ethnic status; they say they are not citizens of the United States, they are immigrants and they don't relate to the system, or that they do not speak English. One of these statements explained non-voting for 41.4 percent of the Mexican-American group. Another 3.4 percent are illiterate.

The research design for this study was drawn up with the expectation that Mexican-Americans had been barred from the ballot box and had been victims of discrimination against them in the political system. A battery of questions to measure political discrimination in voting used by Matthews and Prothro in their study of Southern politics was included in our questionnaire. Not one indication of discrimination is to be found in our interviews. Throughout the interview schedules the respondents say they were treated well, fine, or great when they went down to register. Some respondents indicated that the mobile registration unit had come to their home to register them because they were not physically able to go down to register. In the language of one Mexican-American respondent, they treated him "well—they gave him full honors—first class." The precincts which serve South Tucson overlap areas of Tucson as well and may be staffed by non-South Tucsonians, however there is excellent evidence here that Registrars have not discriminated against Mexican-Americans.

There is ample evidence in the data we have already presented to demonstrate that Mexican-Americans are poorly related to and only partially integrated into the political system. There is every reason to expect that the Mexican-American in South Tucson lacks information about the political system and that the government and its leaders are vague, only partially understood referents in their lives. We sought to test this hypothesis by including a simple political information test in the interview schedule. Six of the seven items used in our test were replicated from the Matthews and Prothro Southern political behavior questionnaire.

On five of the seven questions in the test a substantially smaller proportion of the Mexican-Americans answered the questions correctly compared to the Others group in South Tucson. On the other two questions, the proportion of both groups answering the questions correctly was small, and the margin of the Mexican-Americans over the Others was one and two percent. A summary table was prepared comparing the scores of the Mexican-Americans and the scores of the 'Others' group. Three Mexican-Americans for every one 'Others' group member answered none correctly, and more Mexican-Americans than Others answered one correctly, but at each of the other levels, from two correct to six correct, the Others group had a larger percentage of its members answering questions correctly than had the Mexican-

Americans. The mean score of correct answers for Mexican-Americans is 2.025; for the Others the mean is 2.939.

In each of the six directly comparable political information questions asked to Mexican-Americans and to Southerners, the proportion of Mexican-Americans answering the question correctly is smaller than the proportion of Southern whites answering the question correctly, and, in general, the Southern Negro scores higher than the South Tucson Mexican-American. The proportion of correct responses to the question "Do you happen to remember whether Franklin Roosevelt was a Republican or a Democrat?" was 54.0 percent for South Tucson Mexican-Americans and 57.0 percent for Southern Negroes. Forty-three percent of the Mexican-Americans could name the governor of their state, compared to 68.0 percent of the Southern Negroes. Only 18.0 percent of the Mexican-Americans could give the length of their governor's term of office, whereas 65.0 percent of Southern Negroes could give this information. Eight percent of the Southern Negroes and 4.0 percent of the Mexican-Americans knew that there are nine Justices on the United States Supreme Court. The two items on which the Mexican-Americans in South Tucson did better than the Southern Negro were: length of term of United States Senators (12.0 to 8.0 percent) and naming the last two states to enter the union (45.0 to 35.0 percent). I am hoping that our coders did not code as correct the several responses we received that a United States Senator must serve for a long time or life because "Hayden there always." This response does have a ring of truth to one who has lived in Arizona. It is likely that the Mexican-American margin over Southern Negroes on the last states entering the union is due to a passage of time and the greater proximity of Arizona to Alaska and Hawaii physically and historically in statehood.

CONCLUSION

We have only begun, in this brief paper, to sketch the broad outlines of the political behavior of Mexican-Americans in South Tucson. These sketches have been basically descriptive and comparative. Explanatory models of any level of sophistication are absent from this paper.

The picture we have drawn is of a people who are economically and educationally deprived, who see the Deomcratic party as an aid to the underprivileged and poor, who have a strong commitment to the Democratic party demonstrated in psychological identification with it and in a strong tendency to vote for it, and finally, who reflect their ethnic background and lack of integration in the political system through low levels of political participation and low levels of political information. All of these components of our picture are true despite the fact that these Mexican-Americans have their own city, governed by Mexican-Americans, and that there is no indication whatsoever that they have suffered discrimination at the ballot box. Mexican-Americans have held public and party offices at every level of Arizona state and local government, but probably not in proportion to their potential or real voting power.

Our data describe South Tucson. Do they describe all of the 3,344,000 Mexican-Americans in the Southwest? We don't know. Our social and economic data have been confirmed in other studies, but there has been a fantastic lack of attention to Mexican-American political behavior. The behavioral sciences must, in my opinion, turn their research attention to this ethnic group. Research using aggregate data on a large scale is underway; a few small-scale studies based on survey research have been conducted; large-scale, significant research on Mexican-American political behavior, using the most powerful research tools and techniques available (and of course calling on our foundations to open their coffers) is certainly in order at this time.

Ralph GUZMÁN

Dr. Guzmán in the following essay discusses the softening of political campaigns for limited ethnic goals. Professor Guzmán then turns to seven selected organizations that work for The Mexican American's assimilation into American society and politics.
Ralph Guzmán "Politics and the Policies of the Mexican-American Community." From CALIFORNIA POLITICS AND POLICIES, *Dvorin-Misner, (eds.), Reading, Mass.: Addison-Wesley, 1966. And by permission of the author.*

Politics In The Mexican American Community

POLITICAL PARTIES

Like voting, political party membership before World War II was not well understood. Mexicans were not voters and they were not involved in party politics. Consequently, contact between the Mexican people and the two major parties was insignificant. Without contact, conflict did not exist.

Nevertheless, Mexicans who lived during the 1930s held definite images of each party. The Republican Party was the party of Hoover, and the Democratic Party was that of Roosevelt. Beyond this, Republicans were often identified with the heavy hand of authority that denied food and demanded conformity. On the other hand, Democrats always conveyed an image of liberalism, generosity, and understanding. The generalizations, while not always correct, remained as myths through the war years, to be revived in the late 1940s and the 1950s.

Political party recruitment in the Mexican communities of the Southwest was unknown and unnecessary, again with the possible exception of the

173

State of New Mexico. Mexicans had neither votes nor money. When the direct efforts of groups like the Community Service Organization (CSO) gave thousands of Mexicans the voting privilege, Republicans and Democrats took note of the political emergence of the Mexican people. In 1965 an important member of the hierarchy of the Los Angeles Democratic Party raised the question, "How can the Democratic Party become more effective in the Mexican community?" A Republican official commented: "If you try to move in, you meet a great deal of resistance, whether you are a Protestant missionary or a Republican. Mexicans really couldn't care less. . . . they just don't want to get involved politically."

METAMORPHOSIS

World War II accelerated the change from a predominantly rural to an urban orientation. Many of the young people had gone off to war. Those who stayed behind included young and old, men and women as well as citizen and noncitizen. Almost all of these people found employment in defense or related industries. The rural pursuits of the past were abandoned for better paying urban jobs.

In East Los Angeles, the *enganches,* contract labor crews, frequently organized among members of only one family, became less evident during the war. The migratory worker cycle that started in areas like Belvedere, and went north to the prune and grape country and back again to the walnut orchards of Southern California, was gradually brought to an end. The new caravans were exclusively male and were composed of Mexican nationals, contracted in Mexico under an international labor agreement between Mexico and the United States. For years to come, Mexican nationals, popularly referred to as *braceros,* were to dominate the agricultural fields where Mexican-Americans once labored.

Throughout the Southwest, the war fever of the majority group was picked up by Mexicans. War songs, the counterparts of famous American World War ballads, were composed in Spanish. One song, with an improvised arrangement of taps, the evening bugle call, began: *"Vengo a de-cirle adios a los muchachos porque pronto me voy para la guerra . . . "* ("I come to say goodby to all my friends because I shall soon be going off to war . . . "). When the New Mexico National Guard was trapped in Corregidor, the war was brought closer to many Mexicans. Thousands of youngsters volunteered for combat. The Marine Corps and the Paratroopers, in particular, attracted Mexicans from the urban slums of the Southwest. In California 375,000 Mexicans joined the Armed Forces during World War II. In Los Angeles, where Mexicans made up 10 percent of the total city population when Pearl Harbor was bombed, Mexicans accounted for 20 percent of all names on the war casualty lists.

Both new-found urban employment and involvement in the armed forces contributed to the change from rural to urban life. Within the postwar urban *barrios, colonias,* or ghettos, further changes took place. Increased social interaction with non-Mexicans opened new social vistas and new ethnic goals. Unknown to many members of this minority group, the process of acculturation had increased its effect on the members of the urban Mexican community.

Social change seemed to be greatest in residential areas where Mexicans were well-integrated with other peoples, including so-called Anglos. On the other hand, neighborhoods that were predominantly Mexican reflected less rapid social change during the early postwar years. East Los Angeles provides a graphic illustration. The first significant postwar political activity took place in the Boyle Heights community, where Mexicans lived side by side with other minorities. On the other hand, social change came about more slowly in the predominantly Mexican enclave of Maravilla, located on the outskirts of the Los Angeles urban area.

THE GAME OF POLITICS

Increased contact with Anglo society during the War, together with the new-found urban status of the Mexican, gave rise to commensurate political activity throughout the Southwest. However, most of this activity was local and of a protest nature. Often, discrimination and other majority group pressures forced the creation of new organizations that were later to reach national prominence. One such organization was the American G.I. Forum organized in Corpus Christi, Texas after a local cemetery refused to accept the body of a Mexican serviceman who died during World War II. In California, Pomona and San Bernardino Valley veterans, ranch hands, industrial workers, and railroad laborers formed Unity Leagues in order to deal with local problems, e.g., street lighting, sanitary conditions, street repairs, and politics. Throughout the Southwest, both old and new organizations emphasized the ballot as the most important method for bringing about social change.

Political organization was rarely exclusively Mexican in plan and execution. Considerable financial and organizational support was given to the Mexican people by sympathetic Anglos. Anglo groups like the Race Relations Council, the Industrial Areas Foundation, the Fund for the Republic, the Marshall Trust Fund, and many labor and church groups made substantial contributions. In addition, minority group organizations like the Legal Redress Committee of the National Association for the Advancement of Colored People (NAACP), the Urban League, the Anti-Defamation League of B'Nai B'rith, the American Jewish Committee, the Japanese-American Citizens' League (JACL), and several other groups provided funds and/or organizational knowledge to Mexican groups, particularly to the Mexican-American members of the Community Service Organization (CSO).

Mexicans were a disadvantaged people who recognized their social problems but who knew little about means for solving those problems. The concept of community organization, working together and finding allies among non-Mexicans, was not a familiar one. Invariably, community goals were defined with great difficulty. And when agreement did prevail, the implementation of proposals suffered from lack of full-time personnel and funds with which to pay them.

In California, the efforts of the American Council on Race Relations, and later the program of the Industrial Areas Foundation, emphasized (1) voter registration of Mexicans by Mexicans, (2) articulation of community needs by members of the community, and (3) continuous participation at the polls. The task was *not* how to induce a sense of community (an ethos), but rather how to organize Mexicans so as to recognize and achieve a priority of goals.

Voter registration of Mexicans by Mexicans forced community people to articulate organizational goals at the screen doors of their neighbors. Mexicans learned to walk the pavements and to ring doorbells. Many learned to sell American democracy at the doorstep in both English and Spanish. Mexican voter registrars were best equipped to establish instant rapport in the Mexican *barrios,* thus helping to bring about permanent social change.

Whereas, in the past, social workers and well-meaning private citizens had tried to articulate the ethnic goals of Mexicans, the Race Relations Council and the Industrial Areas Foundation emphasized indigenous expression. Mexican Laborers, their wives, and their children learned to speak up at community meetings.

Organizational efforts were not always successful. Enormous apathy and self-denunciation blocked early postwar attempts to organize the Mexican community. Heavy clouds of cynicism, distrust of the Anglo, and fear of other Mexicans enervated the Mexican people. Anglos were suspected of ulterior motives, of trying to use the Mexicans, and of being insincere. Mexican leaders, on the other hand, were equally suspect. Too many of our leaders, the people said, betray us once they are in power.

Ultimately, post-war organizational efforts in California and in other parts of the Southwest resulted in improved relations between the Mexican people and governmental agencies, other minorities, and with the majority group. Ethnic goals became more clearly defined.

ETHNIC GOALS AND ANGLO POWER

After World War II, Mexicans tested the boundaries of the Anglo political world. Some, like Gustavo Garcia in San Antonio, ran for elective office in the school system and won. In other areas, Mexicans filed for political office, ran, and lost. Few had precinct-level experience and fewer still knew how to deal with "entrenched" Anglo politicians. Like Don Quixote, postwar Mexicans were convinced of the "justice of our cause." However, pure ethnic politics was seldom successful. Invariably, Mexicans were confronted by the majority group's political power structure, which was not always understanding and accommodating. In 1963, the Mexican community of Crystal City, Texas, aided by the Political Association of Spanish Speaking People (PASSO), the Teamsters Union, and other groups, won control of the home town's political system. Two years later, in 1965, a coalition slate of Mexicans and Anglos defeated the all-*chicano* group.

In California, two political campaigns, both organized in East Los Angeles, reveal how campaign strategy was adjusted in order to achieve limited ethnic goals. The campaign of Edward R. Roybal, when he first ran for Councilman in the Ninth District of the City of Los Angeles, is one example. A second is Leopoldo Sánchez' campaign for Municipal Court Judge in the East Los Angeles Judicial District. Both candidates were resisted by Anglo politicians. And both men wore the ethnic label. Yet each resolved the conflict of ethnic goals and Anglo power in different ways.

Roybal's effort was set in Boyle Heights, an east side community where there was much interaction between Anglo and Mexican and also a substantial amount of conflict. On the other hand, the Sanchez judicial campaign was launched in Belvedere, where there was little Mexican-Anglo interaction but a great deal of conflict. Another important difference is time. The Roybal campaign was initiated shortly after World War II, when Mexican social issues, sometimes provoked by the Los Angeles police, were immediate and urgent. By contrast, the Sánchez campaign took place in the late 1950s after great political momentum had been gathered and when police brutality, discrimination in housing, unequal educational opportunities, and other social problems seemed less urgent. However, it is in the area of ethnic goals that the greatest disparity between Roybal and Sánchez is seen. Roybal, recruited by a group of Mexican businessmen as an ethnic can-

didate to replace an aging Anglo in City Hall, dispensed with pure ethnic politics early in his campaign. Sánchez, on the other hand, maintained an ethnic platform in which he stressed that the majority of the people who came before the east side judiciary were Mexican, and that a Mexican from the local area could best administer the law for Mexicans.

While Roybal's district was heavily Mexican, the Mexicans were widely interspersed with other minority groups. Consequently, victory for Roybal depended on the successful blending of minority voting blocs (i.e., Mexican, Jewish, Negro, Oriental) along with pockets of Anglo votes. The Roybal strategy, to which no Mexican Democratic Party campaign organizer contributed personally, deemphasized the image of a Mexican politician.

Sánchez' East Los Angeles Judicial District included a heavily Mexican section (around Belvedere and Maravilla), several neighborhoods where Mexicans were interspersed with Jews, and a heavy concentration of Anglos in the Montebello area. In terms of voting blocs, Sánchez faced a more difficult path to victory than Roybal.

Ethnic goals in the Sánchez campaign, while clear from the beginning, were placed in sharp relief by opposition from Governor Brown. And, unlike Roybal who had the invaluable services of a professional Anglo organizer, Sánchez counted on a few friends, mostly from the American G.I. Forum, a Mexican civic action group. Reconciliation of ethnic goals with Anglo political power came early in the Roybal campaign because the issues were specific, e.g., discrimination in housing, in employment, and before the law. For Sánchez, the issues were vague, e.g., the need for Mexican representation and the need for justice. Sánchez noted that "bread and butter issues are not at stake in a judicial campaign." In the Roybal effort the issues concerned a candidate for a legislative post.

Today, several years later, both men remain important ethnic symbols. However, neither seems exclusively concerned with the ethnic goals that appeared sharp and urgent at the outset of their campaigns. Both seek effective involvement of Mexicans in the American political system.

ETHNIC GOALS AND ETHNIC ORGANIZATION

Civic organizations have been vehicles for the accomplishment of minority goals. However, American society has changed, and so have the goals of the minorities. The result is that new models of the vehicles of social change have emerged.

The following typologies of Mexican organizations is useful to the understanding of the creation of Mexican organizations and of the shifting patterns of ethnic goals: (1) assimilation into American society, and (2) participation in the American political system. Seven selected organizations illustrate this pattern of changing group goals. These organizations, arranged chronologically in terms of the period in history when they were created, are as follows:

1. The Mexican Liberal Party (MLP), organized September 28, 1906;
2. The Order of Sons of America, founded circa 1920;
3. The League of United Latin-American Citizens (LULAC), established in 1927;
4. Community Service Organization (CSO), chartered in 1947;
5. American G.I. Forum, organized in 1948;
6. Mexican-American Political Association (MAPA), founded in 1959;
7. Political Association of Spanish Speaking Organizations (PASSO), founded in 1960.

Concern for social assimilation as expressed in the constitution of the organization, recruitment pamphlets, house organs, news releases, and public statements by elected officials are used to classify organizations in terms of high, medium, or low intent to become socially assimilated. Some groups, for example, express organizational goals of complete integration into American society, with small concern for retention of things Mexican or a Mexican way of life. At the other extreme, some organizations emphasize retention of things Mexican or a Mexican way of life and only small concern for integration into American society.

In addition to general social goals, all organizations seem to have a high, medium, or low intent

to become politically partisan. Some groups, for example, are highly active politically. On the other hand, some organizations are studiously nonpolitical.

THE MEXICAN LIBERAL PARTY (MLP)

Organized in St. Louis, Missouri, the Mexican Liberal Party of 1906 was oriented toward Mexico. Like the Cuban expatriate organizations of today that plan for the recovery of their island homeland, Mexican refugees established centers of resistance in the United States. Assimilation within American society was not a group goal. Nor was political participation in the American political system. The MLP exemplifies a Mexican organization functioning within the United States with little or no intent of belonging to American society or of participating in the American political system.

When members of the MLP intervened in the politics of Mexico, the neutrality laws of the United States were breached and MLP members were placed on trial in a Los Angeles Federal Court. Mexican residents, according to McWilliams, demonstrated great interest in the legal proceedings. Each day, supporters of the MLP would appear in court wearing the red arm band, the symbol of the organization; the visual effect was that of a solid phalanx of red. However, no evidence exists that the MLP's completely Mexico-oriented goals survived the trial and later the death of Ricardo Flores Magon, the principal defendant.

THE ORDER OF SONS OF AMERICA

During the early 1920s, a number of Mexican organizations had goals whose social intent seemed to be complete assimilation into American society, accompanied by some disturbance of the political seas. The Order of Sons of America *(Orden Hijos de America),* organized in Texas, was such a group. They did not demand "a complete equality either among the Mexican-Americans themselves or between them and the Anglo-Americans." Group goals for the Order of Sons included:

1. Elimination of racial prejudice;
2. Equality before the law;
3. Improved educational opportunities;
4. A reasonable share of the political representation in the affairs of the community, State, and Nation.

In order to achieve these social and political goals, the organization placed great emphasis on learning the English language and on the acquisition of naturalization papers. Indeed, the Order of Sons of America declared that their membership was restricted "exclusively to citizens of the United States of Mexican or Spanish extraction, either native or naturalized."

LEAGUE OF UNITED LATIN-AMERICAN CITIZENS (LULAC)

By 1927 the Order of Sons of America split and the League of United Latin-American Citizens, commonly referred to as the LULAC organization, emerged in the State of Texas. Like the Order, LULAC reflected a serious intent to become assimilated into American society and moderate concern for political participation. LULAC documents from this founding period are difficult to obtain. Douglas Weeks reports LULAC goals which reflect high intent to assimilate into American society. However, little is said about political intent. The following assimilation goals seem designed to reduce potential Anglo apprehension:

1. To develop within the members of our race the best, purest, and most perfect type of a true and loyal citizen of the United States of America.
2. The acquisition of the English language, which is the official language of our country, being necessary for the enjoyment of our rights and privileges ... we pledge ourselves to learn and speak and teach same to our children.

Other LULAC goals similarly focused on ultimate assimilation. Unlike the Mexican Liberal Party, the LULAC organization did not create conflict between Anglo and Mexican. Whereas members of the MLP invaded the Mexican Republic from bases in Los Angeles, the LULAC

and its antecedent, the Order of Sons of America, were concerned with peaceful entry into American society.

The MLP attracted intellectuals and individuals whose interest in the United States was transistory and based on the hope that they would someday return to Mexico. On the other hand, both the LULAC group and the Order of Sons of America had a permanent interest in the United States and, at best, only a casual concern for Mexico.

COMMUNITY SERVICE ORGANIZATION (CSO)

The aftermath of World War II brought with it the first significant alteration of previous sociopolitical goals. Throughout the Southwest, marked emphasis on political participation was seen. New organizations like the Community Service Organization (CSO) in the State of California called for increased political involvement of "the masses." "the grass roots," and the people of "the *barrios*" in American democracy. CSO organizers talked in terms of "the people in city hall" and the "need for more Spanish surnames on the voter registration lists downtown." Beginning on an intensely high level of political participation, as the partisan supporters of Edward R. Roybal's campaign for City Councilman, CSO members reduced their activity to nonpartisan civic action. The CSO focused on the community and less on individual candidates. Though members had once seriously considered calling their organization the Community Political Organization (CPO), they agreed that the connotations of this name were "too political."

Significantly, the social intent of the CSO seemed to balance the political intent. CSO members selected a name for their organization that did not have Mexican connotations. Social assimilation, therefore, clearly seemed a concomitant goal with political participation. Indeed, CSO campaigns for integrated public and private housing supported an implicit intent to assimilate into American society.

Whereas the Order of Sons of America and the LULAC organizations had earlier pointed to goals similar to those of the postwar CSO, the older organizations had couched their sociopolitical intent in more cautious phraseology. An early preamble of the CSO constitution (1949) set the following aims:

1. To guard and further our democratic rights.
2. To become aware of our responsibilities as citizens.
3. To better discharge our civic duties.
4. To coordinate our efforts for the common good of the community [12, p. 2].

Unlike earlier organization, the CSO did not restrict membership. Use of the English language and American citizenship were not prerequisites to membership. The CSO focus was on an economically and socially deprived sector of American society that happened to be Mexican, and all persons with concern for the people who lived in these deprived sectors were accepted as members. Consequently, the membership base became vast and heterogeneous. Members ranged from the very old to the very young, and from the recent immigrant from Mexico to the highly acculturated Mexican-American professional. When necessary, the Spanish language was used in order to improve communication, not to preserve a culture.

Like the Order of Sons of America and LULAC, the CSO also stressed American citizenship. When the Japanese Americans Citizen League (JACL) succeeded in its efforts to include a section in the Walter McCarran Immigration Law of the early 1950s that would enable immigrant "old-timers" to become naturalized in the language of their birth, the CSO launched a highly successful citizenship drive. Classes in Spanish, taught by CSO members, brought full American citizenship to thousands of old-timers in their sixties.

THE AMERICAN G.I. FORUM

The changing context of American society affects the goals of minority groups. It may be hypothesized that minority communities in the United States organize because (1) they want something, e.g., increased sociopolitical involvement, or (2) they want to defend themselves against an immediate majority group threat. In both instances undercurrents of conflict are present, the heritage of the past.

The genesis of the American G.I. Forum in Three Rivers, Texas supports the hypothesis of defense. In this respect, the American G.I. Forum, in large part a veterans' organization, is singular among Mexican organizations. Like the Order of Sons of America and LULAC, the American G.I. Forum was formed in an area of the Southwest where the heritage of conflict was severe and omnipresent. Unlike the Community Service Organization in California, the American G.I. Forum's home grounds appeared to be much more hostile.

In 1947, when the body of a Mexican-American G.I. was returned to Three Rivers, the use of local mortuary and cemetery facilities was refused. Mexican-American G.I.'s met to protest the discrimination. Telegrams and letters were sent to Congress and to the press, making the case of the deceased Private Felix Longoria well known throughout the country. Ultimately, Private Longoria was buried in Arlington, Virginia, through the intercession of then U.S. Senator Lyndon B. Johnson. Months later, Mexican-American G.I.'s met again to protest discrimination and poor service at a veterans' hospital in Corpus Christi, Texas. At this second meeting, identified as a public forum for the discussion of problems facing Mexican-American G.I.'s, the American G.I. Forum of Texas was born.

In spite of the fact that it had been organized out of urgent necessity and in response to restrictive pressure from the majority group, the ultimate social goals of the Forum reflected a balanced image which seems to be at once very American and very Mexican. For example, the format of American G.I. Forum meetings, the ceremony and the dialogue, is not unlike what is seen at an American Legion meeting or at some other veteran groups, Forum members wear campaign caps with the rank and home town of the wearer embroidered in gold lettering.

Unlike other veteran organizations, the language of American G.I. Forum members occasionally lapses into Spanish. A casual visitor to a Forum function may get the impression that the Mexican personality of the Forum is more pervasive when the meetings adjourn and informality returns. Politically, the American G.I. Forum goes to the brink of partisanship. Like the CSO, the Forum is explicit about its political intent. It calls for increased political participation and openly encourages potential leaders to run for office or to seek political appointments. Though professing political neutrality, it is a predominantly Democratic organization. Many Forum leaders enjoy close personal friendships with members of the hierarchy of the Democratic Party.

While skirting the edge of total partisanship, the Forum ranks high in political participation in the American political system. Unlike other organizations, it has a full-time lobbyist in Washington, D.C. and a monthly newspaper that constantly emphasizes social legislation on the State and Federal levels. In 1960, Forum members figured prominently in the Viva Kennedy Club movement that helped to win the Mexican vote for John F. Kennedy.

Where other organizations have failed to weld regional interests into functioning national organizations, the Forum has succeeded. Forum chapters exist in every southwestern state, and several more groups have been organized in other states of the Union.

The American G.I. Forum's sociopolitical goals are partially reflected in recruitment literature that pledges to

1. Develop leadership, by creating interest in the Mexican-American people to participate intelligently and wholeheartedly in community, civic, and political affairs.
2. Advance understanding between citizens of various national origins and religious beliefs.
3. Present and advance the basic principles of democracy.
4. Aid needy and disabled veterans.

THE MEXICAN-AMERICAN POLITICAL ASSOCIATION (MAPA)

The balance between social and political goals achieved by organizations like the American G.I. Forum and the Community Service Organization

(CSO) after World War II kept both organizations on the edge of partisanship. A curious political contradiction emerged during the 1950's. Organizations like the Forum and the CSO armed the Mexican people, a predominantly Democratic electorate, with the franchise, thereby increasing the Democratic Party's strength. Yet few effective efforts were made by Anglo Democrats to integrate the emerging Mexican community into the formal structure of the Party. For years, Democratic Party organizations throughout the Southwest appeared unable or unwilling to reach Mexican political activists. Consequently, many Mexican organizations and Mexican individuals remained outside of the organized life of the Democratic Party. Mexicans with political experience in labor unions, civil rights groups, and civic organizations sought participation in the formal structure of the Democratic Party. They considered this a logical move for a minority group emerging within the American political system. Unsuccessful efforts to open gateways into the Party structure convinced some ethnic leaders that "we are taken for granted." Meaningful participation in politics thus became a matter of paramount concern.

In 1959, after Henry P. Lopez, a Harvard-trained Mexican-American lawyer, became the only casualty on an otherwise victorious California slate of Democratic candidates, a convention was called in Fresno to consider means of protecting Mexican political interests. At that convention, the Mexican-American Political Association (MAPA) was formed.

Unlike other ethnic organizations, MAPA made explicit its serious political intent and small concern for social assimilation. MAPA members chose an ethnic organizational name that was clearly Mexican. The organization's political goals were similarly stripped of ambiguity. Mexican candidates were sought and heartily endorsed. Public positions were taken on issues affecting Mexicans. Other forms of political participation included voter registration drives, get-out-the-vote campaigns, and visits to elected and appointed officials to lobby for Mexican political interests. Within a relatively short time, the politically militant tactics of MAPA made it well known in California politics.

To judge from public positions taken, MAPA focuses more on politics and less on the sociological question of acculturation. Nevertheless, MAPA's name and political stance make it appear highly political within the American political system, and yet distinctively Mexican within American society.

POLITICAL ASSOCIATION OF SPANISH-SPEAKING ORGANIZATIONS (PASSO)

The genesis of PASSO reflects political change within the Mexican minority and the Anglo majority. By 1960, most Mexican organizations were involved in politics. Political activity ranged from cautious support of voter registration efforts to explicit advocacy of particular campaigns. In California, old-line organizations supported the nonpartisan recruitment of new voters. At the other extreme, the Mexican-American Political Association (MAPA) urged the voters to vote and to be partisan.

MAPA's activity attracted attention throughout the Southwest. In Victoria, Texas in 1960, a group of individuals organized a Texas counterpart of the California MAPA. The Texas organization was called Mexican-Americans for Political Action; its initials, of course, were also MAPA. The Victoria, Texas MAPA was overshadowed by a sudden mushrooming of *Viva Kennedy Clubs* after the late President won the Democratic nomination in Los Angeles. The *Viva Kennedy Clubs,* organized outside the regular framework of the Democratic Party, drew members from most of the active organizations of the Southwest, and captured the imagination of the Mexican electorate everywhere in this region. Apparently, both the widespread attraction and the intense political activity of the *Viva Kennedy* movement coopted the Texas MAPA's purpose and area of action.

After John F. Kennedy's Presidential triumph, *Kennedy Club* members and representatives of the California MAPA gathered in Phoenix, Arizona. Political activists from each of the five southwestern states met for the purpose of form-

ing a national organization. *Viva Kennedy Club* members included political activists who were also members of other Mexican organizations. Some of those other organizations were the League of United Latin-American Citizens (LULAC), the Community Service Organization (CSO), the Alianza Hispano-Americana (AHA), and the American G.I. Forum.

Throughout the convention, the California members of MAPA urged that the format of the proposed national body be comparable to that of MAPA, and recommended explicit identification as a *Mexican* political organization. The MAPA position was, however, rejected.

A consensus prevailed that Puerto Ricans and other Latin Americans who, it was argued, lent significant support to the *Viva Kennedy Club* movement merited some concern. Opponents of the MAPA strategy, which called for clear ethnic identity, suggested that a less ethnically partisan name could conceivably reattract non-Mexican Latin-Americans. Ultimately, the Political Association of Spanish-Speaking Organizations (PASSO) became the name of the new national organization. In California, however, both MAPA and the CSO refused to subsume their activities beneath the PASSO label.

Today, PASSO maintains a high level of political participation, mainly in the State of Texas. Like MAPA in California, PASSO concentrates on direct political action. Recently, in 1963, PASSO, joined by the Teamsters' Union and other organizations, helped to elect a completely Mexican slate of city officials in Crystal City, Texas. The Crystal City victory appeared to be a high-water mark of political activity for PASSO.

Like MAPA, the Texas-based PASSO does not seem to have much concern for social assimilation. PASSO, again like MAPA, reflects explicitly partisan political goals, in spite of the apparent ambiguity that its organizational label proclaims. A woman orator at a PASSO rally said:

Los Mexicans han estado en el back seat for *muchos años* (The Mexicans have been in the back seat for many years.) Let's get in the front seat and go. We, the Mexicans, deserve a few paved streets and a little self-dignity, and we're going to get it.

PORTENTS OF CHANGE

It has been said that the majority group determines the behavior of the minority. This relationship is evident in the politics of the Southwest. The California context is different from that of Texas. In California, Mexicans were able to organize the Mexican American Political Association, an unquestionable Mexican organization with untarnished ethnic goals. On the other hand, a clear ethnic identity in Texas was possible only briefly, when the Mexican-Americans for Political Action was formed. In California, prejudice against Mexicans is considerably less than it is in Texas and in other parts of the Southwest. It is easier (and safer) to say "Mexican" in California than it is in other states. In Texas, for example, "Mexican" has unmistakable pejorative implications derived from a heritage of conflict.

POLITICS

The political effectiveness of MAPA and PASSO is much debated by Mexicans and non-Mexicans alike. Among Mexicans it seems generally agreed that both MAPA and PASSO perform an essential gadfly function that has on occasion caused the donkey to bray and the elephant to trumpet. However, a significant section is concerned lest the image of a stoical, uncompromising Mexican supplant that of the docile *bracero*. One non-Mexican, a defeated officeholder in Mathis, Texas, said:

I don't know what it is they want. These people on the other side have got so bitter. I asked one of the Mexican leaders, "What are you people up to? What have we done?" All he could say was, "We want to get on top."

VOTING

Mexican leaders at a 1965 meeting in Los Angeles said: "The Mexican vote, once a monolithic Democratic vote, has shrunk and so has our political effectiveness." The voting strength of the Mex-

ican in California has, indeed, dropped. Massive voter registration drives, once common in East Los Angeles, have been replaced by occasional specialized and narrowly focused efforts in selected Spanish-surname precincts. Out of a 1960 potential voting population of more than 600,000 Spanish-surname people in California, less than 20 percent were registered voters, and fewer yet were brought to the polls. In Los Angeles County a potential Spanish-surname vote of 256,000 was never activated. An estimate of comparative voting strength between Negro and Mexican voters (U.S. citizens only), based on 1960 Census data, suggests a potential Negro vote on the State level of 454,000 and a Mexican vote of 633,000. In Los Angeles County, the population of U.S. citizens in both groups is more nearly equal. Negro voters are computed at 243,400 and Mexicans (Spanish surnames) at 256,800. The combined potential of these two enormous minority groups has long been a prominent point in majority group conversation.

RACE RELATIONS

Substantial support has been given to the Mexican people by other minority groups and by members of the Anglo majority. That Jewish organizational know-how and Jewish funds have helped the Mexican people of California is slightly known. Less known is the political and financial aid that was rendered by the Negro community.

In California, there have been two examples of Negro cooperation and assistance to the Mexican community. One involved a group of Mexican and Negro citizens from El Centro, California who, in 1955, jointly filed a class suit in a Federal district court in an effort to end school segregation in California. The case, called *Romero vs. Weakley,* was sponsored by the Alianza Hispano-Americana and the National Association for the Advancement of Colored People (NAACP). Several other organizations, among them the American Civil Liberties Union, the American Jewish Committee, and the Greater Los Angeles CIO Council, filed an *Amicus Curiae* (Friend of the Court) brief supporting the Mexican and Negro plaintiffs. A news release from the Alianza Hispano Americana announced:

This *case* marks the first time in U.S. history that the Negro and Mexican communities have joined hands, as American citizens, to fight for a common social problem.

Three years later, in 1958, a Negro woman lawyer, representing a coalition of Mexican and Negro politicians, nominated Henry P. Lopez, a Mexican Attorney, for the office of Secretary of State at a convention in Fresno, California. That same year the Democratic Minority Conference, a predominantly Negro association, organized and financed an intensive voter registration drive among Mexican and Negro voters that netted 25,-000 new voter registrations within a three month period.

Comparable cooperation between these two massive minorities no longer prevails. Mexicans and Negroes have long shared similar economic and social distress in the large urban centers of the Southwest. And yet today, meaningful dialogue between responsible Mexican and Negro leaders is not heard. However, with the increasing pressure of the Negro Civil Rights movement, it seems likely that Mexicans will eventually seek renewed contact with the Negro people.

IMMIGRATION

Outside of the Southwest, majority group members view Mexicans in the same way as they do other American immigrant groups. For example, at the 1965 White House Conference on Education a participant commented that "Mexicans will cease to have problems when they become better acculturated, just like the Poles, the Italians, and other immigrant groups." This facile solution, unfortunately incorrect, ignores the historical factors that differentiate the Mexican from other minorities: the symbiotic relationship between American Southwest and the Mexican northern area, and the difficulty of guarding the border. Most of all, it ignores the millions of Mexicans who have long had roots in this country. Given these conditions, it seems highly probable that the Mexican community will for a long time remain an emerging social complexity with a very real, and unresolved, heritage of conflict.

3.

CONCLUSION

FeRNANdo PeÑAlosA

Fernanado Peñalosa (see p. 15) expresses satisfaction that no longer will sociological studies of Mexican Americans be done exclusively by Anglos. But he warns, too, that before the Mexican American sociologist begins work in this nascent field he should try to define the extremely varied and complex nature of the group. Then Professor Peñalosa asks several questions about the Mexican American population and offers very tentative answers to the student. Reprinted from AZTLÁN-CHICANO JOURNAL OF THE SOCIAL SCIENCES AND THE ARTS, *Volume 1 Number 1, (Spring 1970), Aztlán Publication's, Chicano Studies Center, UCLA, pp. 1–12.*

Toward An Operational Definition Of The Mexican American

The sociological study of the Mexican American, until very recently almost the exclusive province of Anglo sociologists, is about to be launched into a new period of development that should certainly produce more fruitful, more realistic, and more relevant data and conclusions than have previously been forthcoming. Before we move into this new period, however, we would be well advised to map out somewhat more carefully the population

we are going to study. In developing a relatively new field it is not so important to attempt to produce immediately the right answers as it is to ask the right questions. If we ask simple questions we may get simple and probably misleading answers, particularly since our subject is not at all simple, but exceedingly complex. Mexican Americans may constitute one of the most heterogeneous ethnic groups ever to be studied by sociologists. With reference to the scholarly study of the Mexican American we would be well advised to stop trying to find the "typical" or "true," and seek rather to establish the range of variation. Generalizations extrapolated from the community in which a Chicano writer happened to grow up or which an Anglo sociologist or anthropologist happened to have studied can be particularly misleading.

It is furthermore essential that we avoid simplistic either-or types of questions, such as, are Chicanos a people or not?, do they have a distinctive culture or not?, or is there such a thing existentially as the Mexican American community or not? Realistically we are handicapped in attempting to answer these types of inquiries in which the alternatives are already implicitly limited by the question itself. A much more productive approach might be rather to consider prefixing our questions with a phrase such as "to what extent . . ." so that we ask to what extent Mexican Americans constitute a stratum, possess a distinct subculture, etc.

Scholars, both Chicano and Anglo, have furthermore spent countless hours debating the question of the correct name for our group, and then attempting to define the entity for which the supposedly correct name stands. Perhaps the time has come to move beyond terminological and definitional polemics to an examination of some of the dimensions along which we might explore our subject in an attempt better to understand its character.[1]

The method of procedure in this paper will be as follows: A series of questions will be asked about the Mexican American population. An attempt will be made to answer each one, based on the writer's admittedly limited perception of the current state of knowledge, and to point out some possible lines of future research along that dimension. *Some* day, when we have approximately adequate answers to the questions posed, we *may* have a more of less acceptable operational definition of the Mexican American. By way of overview, these are the questions which will be discussed:

1. To what extent do Mexican Americans constitute a separate racial entity?

2. To what extent do Mexican Americans conceive of themselves as belonging to a separate ethnic group?

3. To what extent do Mexican Americans have a separate or distinct culture?

4. To what extent do Mexican Americans constitute an identifiable stratum in society?

5. To what extent is it realistic to speak of Mexican American communities?

6. To what extent are differences in historical antecedents reflected among Mexican Americans?

7. To what extent are regional socio economic differences significant among Mexican Americans?[2]

Let us then direct our attention to each of these questions in turn.

To What Extent Do Mexican Americans Constitute a Separate Racial Entity?

A goodly number of Mexican Americans and others are confused as to the biological nature of this particular group. An Anglo American may carelessly divide people into whites, Negroes, and Mexicans, or a Chicano may assertively speak of "La Raza."[3] The recently increasing use of the term "brown" similarly represents pride in the group's presumed racial distinctiveness, analogous not only to the Negroes' newly-found blackness but also to "La Raza Cósmica" of José Vasconcelos. Although most Mexican Americans are of mixed Spanish, Indian (both Southwestern and Mexican), and Negro descent, a large proportion are not physically distinct from the majority American population hence the group as a whole cannot be characterized in terms of race.[4] "Race" is essentially furthermore a nineteenth century notion which is rapidly becoming obsolete in physical anthropology and related disciplines. In any case biological differences as such are no concern of the sociologist; only the ways in which notions of race influence people's behavior concern him. The topic of our discussion is therefore what social scientists refer to as socially supposed races. Regardless of whatever mythology may be involved, however, if the majority group considers Mexican Americans as a race, and insists therefore on continuing to treat them in a discriminatory fashion, then the consequences are nonetheless real: not only the deprivation and segregation, but as the progress of the Chicano movement has shown, racial pride. Not all the consequences of racism are necessarily negative.

Some historical perspective is needed here. With reference to color discrimination it was noted by Manuel Gamio that in the 1920s dark-skinned Mexicans suffered about the same type of discrimination as Negroes, but that medium complected Mexicans were able to use second-class public facilities. Even light-brown skinned Mexicans were excluded from high-class facilities, while "white" Mexicans might be freely admitted, especially if they spoke fluent English.[5] To what extent is such a type of scale still applied in public facilities or in other areas of public and private life, and what social factors affect its application? Furthermore we might well examine the extent to which differences in physical appearances are socially significant to Mexican Americans themselves. The fact that we live in a racist society where the primary factor affecting a person's status and life chances has always been the color of his skin, means that it is unrealistic to attempt to sweep an unpleasant situation under the carpet and pretend it does not exist.

To What Extent Do Mexican Americans Conceive of Themselves as Belonging to a Separate Ethnic Group?

Tentatively at least we might characterize an ethnic group as a sub-population which shares a common ancestry and which is distinguished by a way of life or culture which is significantly different in one or more respects from what of the majority of the population, which regards it as an out-group. Do Mexican Americans conceive of themselves in this manner? If they thus conceive of themselves, what is the degree of separateness perceived? It depends of course on whom you ask. But it may be hypothesized that answers would probably fall along a spectrum or continuum, of which it is not too difficult to identify three principal segments: those at the extremes, and one at or near the center.

These segments can be characterized according to varying self-conceptions and variations in self-identity. At one extreme are those who acknowledge the fact of their Mexican descent but for whom this fact constitutes neither a particularly positive nor a particularly negative value, because it plays a very unimportant part in their lives and their self-conception. At or near the middle of this putative continuum are those for whom being of Mexican ancestry is something of which they are constantly conscious and which looms importantly as part of their self-conception. Their Mexican descent may constitute for them a positive value, a negative value, or more generally an ambiguous blend of the two. At the other end of the continuum are those who are not only acutely aware of their Mexican identity and descent but are committed to the defense of Mexican American subcultural values, and strive to work actively for the betterment of their people. Tentatively I would like to suggest, without any implication as to their "correctness," that the terms "Americans of Mexican ancestry," "Mexican Americans," and "Chicanos," are sometimes used for those who closely resemble the three types suggested.

Research is needed to determine whether indeed such a continuum can be identified, and if so, what are the proportions of persons falling at various points along its length, and with what other social indices these positions are associated. Sample surveys would seem to be one of the most direct ways of attacking this problem.

To What Extent Do Mexican Americans Have a Separate Or Distinct Culture?

Mexican American culture or subculture whatever its precise nature, composition and structure, if such are even determinable, appears to be a product of multiple origins, as one would expect in light of its history. The focus of its synthesis and emergence is of course the barrio and it is here and not toward Mexico where we must focus our primary attention. At the same time we should not minimize differences between the way of life of Chicanos residing inside and of those residing outside the barrio.

Tentatively it may be suggested that the chief sources of Mexican American culture are four in number. First, there is the initially overriding but subsequently attenuated influence of what is usually called "traditional" Mexican culture, the way of life brought by most of the immigrants from Mexico during several centuries.[7]

Secondly there is the initially weak but subsequently growing influence of the surrounding majority American culture. Mexican Americans are subject to approximately the same educational system and mass media of communication as are other Americans and participate to varying extents in the economic, social, intellectual and religious life of the broader society. A careful comparison of the way of life of persons of Mexican descent in the United States with those of Mexico will help substantiate the notion that the former are first and foremost "Americans," and only secondary "Mexican Americans."

A third source of influence upon Mexican American culture is class influence. The fact that the bulk of the Mexican American population has been concentrated at the lower socio-economic levels of the society means that some aspects of Mexican American culture may have their source in behavior characteristic generally of lower-class people regardless of ethnic group. Thus, for example, the alleged relatively high crime rate (at least for certain types of crimes) among Mexican Americans can perhaps best be explained in terms of social class rather than ethnicity, as well as in terms of the relative youth of the group as a whole and differential law enforcement practices. Apart from the question of Anglo discrimination, insensitivity and incompetence, Mexican American problems in education seem to be as much class problems as they are cultural problems. Educational studies comparing lower class Chicano students with middle class Anglos are as methodologically faulty as they are socially pernicious. Neither must it be forgotten that class discrimination is as real in this country as racial or ethnic discrimination.

The fourth source of influence on Mexican American culture results from the minority status of its bearers. The term "minority" is not properly a numerical concept, (Chicanos outnumber Anglos in East Los Angeles) but rather a term suggesting that the group has less than its share of political, economic and social power vis-à-vis the majority population and hence suffers from educational, social, occupational and other economic disadvantages mediated through the processes of prejudice, discrimination and segregation. Inasmuch as the concept of culture basically refers to the sum-total of techniques a people has in coping with and adapting to its physical and social environment, there have been developed some special cultural responses among Mexican Americans to their minority status, as occurs among members of other minority groups. These responses may be viewed as very important components of the admittedly heterogeneous and ill-defined Chicano subculture. An obvious example of this sort of trait is the Chicano Movement itself, which is both a response to the majority culture and society, and an outstanding component of Chicano culture itself. But even here the matter gets complicated, for it is necessary to recognize that the Movement has borrowed at least some of its goals, values, techniques and strategies from both the black and Anglo civil rights Movements.

It is suggested therefore that Mexican American culture is a multidimensional phenomenon and must be studied in terms of these four dimensions at least (there may be more), as well as in terms of its historical, regional, and ecological variants. It is highly unlikely that all the various strands will ever be completely unravelled and laid out neatly side by side for us to see, but neither must we lose sight of the heterogeneous origins of Mexican American culture, the nature of the varying continuing influences on it, and its continuously changing nature, as we seek to ascertain its differential dispersal, influence, and persistence among persons of Mexican descent in this country.

To What Extent Do Mexican Americans Constitute an Identifiable Stratum in Society?

A number of social scientists who have studied the relations between Mexican Americans and Anglo Americans in the Southwest have described these relations as being "caste-like."[8] That is, the nature of interethnic relations was said to bear some resemblance to the relations between castes in India and elsewhere. In the United States the situation which undoubtedly most closely resembles a color caste system is the traditional pattern of race relations in the South, with its supposedly superordinate white caste and subordinate Negro caste.

Although Mexican-Anglo relations have never been as rigid as black-white relations there may still have been a resemblance, particularly in certain communities, strong enough to characterize them as "semi-caste," "quasi-caste," or "caste-like." That is, there would be manifested a strong degree of segregation, blocking of entrance to certain occupations, political impotence, ritual avoidance, and taboos on intermarriage stemming from notions of "racial" or "color" differences. Intermarriage is an important criterion, for marriage implies social equality between partners. The idea that Mexicans and Mexican Americans are not whites was certainly more prevalent before the World War II period, or at least people expressed the idea more frequently without worrying whether or not anyone might take offense. The current situation in this regard is unclear.[9] It may be that the continuing low rate of intermarriage, the tacit or explicit superior-inferior nature of ethnic relations, and the concentration of Mexican Americans in certain jobs and their virtual exclusion from others, means that Mexican-Anglo relations still approximate semi-caste, although increasingly less so.

If Anglo-Mexican relations appear to be moving away from a caste basis to a class basis, and the evidence is definitely pointing in this direction, the internal stratification of the Mexican American population looms increasingly more important. With a few exceptions, our knowledge of Mexican American stratification has had to depend so far primarily on the rather impressionistic accounts of a handful of Anglo social scientists. We know that, generally speaking, Mexican American rural populations have less differentiated social class structures than the urban ones, that is, the status spread is greater in the city than in the country. We know some of the variables associated with socioeconomic status and self and community perception. Much more we do not know.

Impressionistic accounts and reworking of U. S. Census data in the manner of the UCLA Mexican American Study Project have not been enough. Careful original sample surveys to study the inter-relations of "objective" stratification variables as well as the study of the "subjective" perceptions by Chicanos of their own internal stratification systems are urgently needed. Only thus will the myth of the class homogeneity of the Mexican American population be thoroughly discredited and its heterogeneity adequately documented.

To What Extent Is It Realistic to Speak of Mexican American Communities?

One badly neglected area of research is the extent to which Mexican Americans have a feeling of belonging to an identifiable Mexican American community and the extent to which their participation in its organizations and other community activities enable us to identify leadership roles and a social structure as well as a body of sentiment. Regional and ecological considerations are of primary importance here. Degree of community feeling and participation undoubtedly varies as among such places as East Los Angeles, Pomona, Tucson, Chicago, or Hidalgo County, Texas, to mention but a few. It varies between those who live in the barrio and those who live outside. Rural-urban differences are likewise significant. Rural Mexican Americans were never able to establish true communities in California, for example, because of Anglo pressures and because of the migratory work patterns of most of the people, according to Ernesto Galarza.[10] The range and variation of "communityness" must be empirically studied, not assumed a priori, both within populations and among a sample of different locales reflecting the differential impact of relevant regional and ecological variables.

To What Extent Are Differences In Historical Antecedents Reflected Among Mexican Americans?

To a certain extent this question foreshadows the succeeding one inasmuch as the principal regional variations have emerged because of different historical antecedents, and hence it is possible to separate analytically but not empirically the geographical and historical dimensions.

The Mexican American population in the United States from 1848 down to the present has been continually expanded and renewed by immi gration both legal and illegal from Mexico, a continually changing Mexico. Mexican immigrants who came for example, before the Revolution, during the Revolution, shortly after the Revolution, and more recently, each came from a somewhat different Mexico. Those coming in at the present time as permanent residents come for the most part from Mexico vastly more industrialized, urbanized, modernized and educated than the Mexico of our fathers or grandfathers. How well have immigrants from different periods of Mexico's history, and their children, fared in the United States? What have been the differential rates of mobility and/or assimilation? We should also raise questions about generational differences, and with reference to the differential composition of Mexican American local populations in terms of their historical antecedents. How are these kinds of differences associated with significant social indices, rates of acculturation, and self-perception and self-identity variables?

To What Extent Are Regional Socioeconomic Differences Significant Among Mexican Americans?

A number of Mexican American regional subcultures can probably be identified. The historical and geographical factors affecting the emergence of these subvarieties are of crucial importance in understanding their present nature. It is important to realize, for example, that the Hispanos of New Mexico and Colorado evolved their culture in isolated mountain villages fairly remote from Anglo civilization; that the Texas-Mexicans are not only concentrated along the border but are also located geographically in the South with its unique tradition of discrimination and prejudice; whereas the Chicanos of Southern California have been caught up in a changing situation of rapid urban growth.

In all areas of the Southwest, the shift from rural to urban has been a highly significant trend. The overwhelming majority of Southwestern Mexican Americans now live in urban areas. These Mexican American urban settlements have grown primarily through migration from the countryside, so that the bulk of the adult residents of those communities have not yet completely adjusted to urban life. The kinds of problems they face therefore are quite different from those they had to face in the small towns and rural areas from which they came. Simple agricultural skills are no longer enough for the security of employment. The kinds of job opportunities available are primarily of an industrial nature and increasingly require a high degree of either manual dexterity or intellectual skills or both. The needs of automation are furthermore constantly raising the level of skills required in order to compete successfully in the job market. So the urban Mexican American is pushed further and further away from pre-industrial skills, habits, and attitudes and directly into the modern industrial social order with all its complexities and problems.

At the opposite extreme, Mexican Americans in such a place as rural Texas score the lowest on all the social measures. It is in this area where the permanent residences of many migratory agricultural laborers are concentrated. There is perhaps less social differentiation of Mexican Americans here than in any other area of the Southwest, and the most vigorous preservation of so-called tradional Mexican rural culture.

The Spanish Americans, Hispanos, "Manitos," or "mejicanos," are the descendants of the original racially mixed but Europeanized settlers of New Mexico and southern Colorado, when this area was under Spanish rule, but administered and colonized from Mexico. Traditionally most of the Hispanos lived in isolated rural areas and were economically and socially handicapped. In recent years they have become increasingly urbanized as many have been forced off their lands by the more competitive Anglo farmers, or as mines were closed. Many Hispanos left New Mexico and Colorado during the World War II and post-war periods. Many came and continue to come to Southern California and other areas of high urbanization. Here we have another case of attempting to unravel the strands, as Chicano urban populations are increasing in heterogeneity with reference to interstate geographical origins. The sociological study of the Mexican American should include both the *systematic* comparative examination of regional variants of the admittedly hard to define and identify Chicano culture and community (and not just a series of monographic reports, each one on a separate community), as well as the way in which these differences are being gradually obliterated in the urban milieu.[11]

In summary, seven questions were posed with reference to the Chicano population, some tentative answers were given, and some areas for future research indicated. It is not the writer's intention to imply that a series of adequately documented answers to these questions would constitute the corpus of Chicano sociology. There are a number of other extremely important unmentioned questions and topics which are obviously part of such a sociology, such as those relating to family life, value systems, power relations, bilingualism, educational questions, and many others. Rather, the explicit intention and hope is that the answers to these questions will help in the formulation of a sociological definition of our subject population before we tackle the multitude of difficult intellectual and social questions which lie ahead of us.

REFERENCES

1. The terms "Mexican American" and "Chicano" are used here for convenience as equivalent and interchangeable, without any implication of their "correctness" or of the "correctness" of any other term or terms that might have been used in their place.

2. The careful reader will have detected that the writer's philosophical bias is strongly nominalistic, that is, that he conceives of "culture," "community," "ethnic group," etc., not as "things," but rather as labels which refer to abstractions conjured up by the social scientist or others as a convenience in handling the data they are trying to understand. For example, the latest issue of *El Chicano*, a newspaper published in San Bernardino, carries the headline "Mexican Community Demands Dismissal of Judge Chargin." This is a figure of speech, of course, inasmuch as if the community is indeed an abstraction, it cannot demand anything; only individuals or organized groups can demand.

3. Readers of this journal are undoubtedly acquainted with the fact that throughout the Spanish-speaking world Columbus Day is referred to as "El Día de la Raza," the word "raza" in this context referring to all persons of Hispanic culture, as it does in the motto of the National Autonomous University of Mexico: "Por mi raza hablará el espíritu." Nevertheless, in matters social, words mean what their users *want* them to mean.

4. Cf. Marcus Goldstein, *Demographic and Bodily Changes in Descendants of Mexican Immigrants.* Austin: Institute of Latin American Studies, University of Texas, 1943, and Gonzalo Aguirre Beltrán, *La Población Negra de México 1519-1810* (México, D. F.: Ediciones Fuente Cultural, 1946).

5. Manuel Gamio, *Mexican Immigration to the United States* (Chicago: University of Chicago Press, 1930), p. 53.

6. The writer is currently carrying out a random-sample survey of the Mexican American population of San Bernardino, California, with reference to internal social stratification, self-identification, and perception of community and subculture. Hopefully the results will throw some light on these questions.

7. The pitfalls of stereotyping in this area are very great, as so ably pointed out by Octavio I. Romano-V., "The Anthropology and Sociology of the Mexican Americans," *El Grito,* II (Fall, 1968), 13-26.

8. Walter Goldschmidt, *As You Sow* (New York: Harcourt, Brace and Co., 1947), p. 59; Paul Schuster Taylor, *An American-Mexican Frontier, Nueces County, Texas* (Chapel Hill: The University of North Carolina Press, 1934); Ruth D. Tuck, *Not with the Fist: Mexican-Americans in a Southwest City* (New York: Harcourt, Brace and Co., 1946), p. 44; Thomas E. Lasswell, "Status Stratification in a Selected Community," unpublished Ph. D. dissertation, University of Southern California, 1953; Robert B. Rogers, "Perception of the Power Structure by Social Class in a California Community," unpublished Ph.D. dissertation, University of Southern California, 1962; James B. Watson and Julián Samora, "Subordinate Leadership in a Bi-cultural Community," *American Sociological* Review, 19 (August 1954), pp. 413-421; Ozzie Simmons, "Americans and Mexican Americans in South Texas," unpublished Ph. D. dissertation, Harvard University, 1952; William H. Madsen, *The Mexican-Americans of South Texas* (New York: Holt, Rinehart & Winston, 1964).

It may be argued that since the authors of all these studies are Anglos they may have had a slanted view of the situation, yet it should be understood they are reporting Anglo residents' perceptions of the social barriers they themselves have set up.

9. After the 1930 Census, in which Mexicans were listed as a separate "race," persons of Mexican descent were subsequently put back into the "white" category largely because the Mexican American leaders of that time insisted Mexicans were "white." Similarly the Chicano population is substantially the same as the 1950 and 1960 Census category "White persons of Spanish surname." Understandably therefore the recent emphasis on "brown"and "La Raza" has some Anglos confused. With reference

to the possible relevance of the caste model, it should be pointed out that the nature of the discrimination against Chicanos has been primarily social rather than legal, as has been the case for blacks in the South.

10. Lecture in the University of California Extension Series "The Mexican American in Transition," Ontario, California, Spring, 1967.

11. One of the findings of the writer's "Spanish-surname" sample survey of Pomona was that in every case in which a household contained a "Spanish American" adult, that person was married to a "Mexican American." It may be hypothesized on the basis of this admittedly flimsy evidence that in urban Southern California Hispanos are more likely to marry children or grandchildren of Mexican immigrants than they are Hispanos because there are no real barriers between the two groups and the statistical odds are therefore against the endogamy of the smaller group. To what extent this may be true of other areas of the country it would be hazardous to guess.

Joseph NAVARRO

*Joseph Navarro (currently working for the doctorate in
history at The University of California, Santa Barbara)
surveys the present state of Mexican American History,
evaluates the need for further research, and discusses some
of the problems "inherent in the study of Mexican American
History."*
By permission of the author and THE JOURNAL OF
MEXICAN AMERICAN HISTORY.

The Condition Of
Mexican American History

Unlike the Anglo, the Spanish-American or
Mexican-American is likely to be strongly
oriented toward the present or the immediate past. He is not a visionary, with his eyes
on the golden promise of the future. Nor is he
a dreamer brooding over the glories of the
past. Rather he is a realist who is concerned
with the problems and rewards of the immediate present. The past, since he comes from
a folk culture with no tradition of writing,
was not carefully recorded, contained little
that was sufficiently out of the ordinary to
justify recording, and has been almost forgotten. The future, since for hundreds of years
it brought almost nothing different from

what he already had, offers no particular
promise and is neither to be anticipated with
joy nor feared. But the present cannot be
ignored. Its demands must be coped with, its
rewards must be enjoyed—now.
(Lyle Saunders, *Cultural Difference and
Medical Care.*)

INTRODUCTION

The purpose of this paper is to examine the condition of Mexican-American history, which in this
paper is defined as the history of Mexicans in the
United States in the period from 1848 to the
present. More specifically, this paper will consider

problems inherent to the study of Mexican-American history, and examine the most useful and representative literature. This report makes no claim to finality, but is offered for consideration in the hope it will stimulate thought, profitable dialogue, and relevant criticism.

To begin with, very little has been written about the history of Mexicans in the United States, and almost no effort has been made to tap and index primary sources in the archives and wherever else they might be found. These serious limitations explain why teachers are plagued by problems of organization and periodization: they want to know when their subject begins and what to include. Some students have asked if some distinction should be made, in the study of Mexican-American history, between history and social science, and whether some distinction should be made between history and journalism. These questions are raised not only because some writers have failed to make a distinction between history and other branches of knowledge, but have gone so far as to obscure the difference between history and social science, and also, the difference between history and journalism. It is true that bibliographies of Mexican-American history contain more works in social science than history, and more works of current events or journalism than developments which took place before World War II. In part, this is because little Mexican-American history has been written, because more Mexican-American literature is found in the social sciences, and because publishers and the news media have given increasing attention to current Mexican-American history, especially the Mexican-American Civil Rights Movement led by César Chávez and Reies Tijerina. Nonetheless, it should be made clear why social science studies and journalism are included in a bibliography pertaining to Mexican-American history. If Mexican-American history is to advance professionally, it must not only be defined clearly but it must also be made clear how Mexican-American history as history and as a specialized area of history, is related to other branches of knowledge, and also, how it is different from them. This is not to say that the serious student has to become deeply involved in the controversies over history and social science, in epistemological questions in the philosophy of history, etc., but he should know what most historians recognize as the distinguishing essentials between history and other studies of man.

The foregoing generalizations and problems will be examined and discussed further in the following manner: first, a discussion of the problem of defining Mexican-American history and how that problem is related to other fundamental questions; second, a critical review of the most useful and representative works on Mexican-American history; third, a discussion of the characteristics of history generally accepted by professional historians, and a brief comment on how history relates to other branches of knowledge, especially to social science and journalism; and finally, concluding suggestions on how the critical and scholarly study of Mexican-American history can be advanced.

DEFINITION: A PROBLEM OF LABELS, AREA, AND PERIODIZATION.

Since so little has been written about Mexican-American history, those who have to think about the subject for the first time are apt to be puzzled by a number of fundamental questions.

There is, to begin, a problem over what label should be used to refer to all Mexicans in the United States. Those who speak Spanish in New Mexico and southern Colorado prefer to be called Hispanos or Spanish-Americans. This is because they had little contact with Mexico, and because they identify with the early Spaniards. Those Mexicans whose ancestors came to the United States in the 1900s prefer to be called Mexican-American; the word Mexicano is generally accepted even by those who come from Mexico: some Mexicans will fight if they are called anything other than American; the label Spanish-speaking has been used by some writers because to them it appears to be the least offensive label; and the news media has popularized the label Chicano which some Mexican-American activists have adopted. There are other labels and preferences. It is enough here to point out that it is difficult to find a label which refers to all Mexicans in the United States, and which, at the same time, is pleasing to everyone, especially to all Mexicans.

Having noted that the label Mexican-American will not please everyone, it should also be pointed out that the definition of Mexican-American history used in this paper will probably be received with the same lack of unanimity. As already explained, this is because little thought has been given to the questions: What is Mexican-American history? What area(s) and period(s) of time does Mexican-American history encompass? My own experience with high schools, colleges, history conferences, and interviews reveal that teachers, writers, social scientists, and historians have different ideas about the definition of Mexican-American history. Not only do they use different labels to refer to all Mexicans in the United States, but they differ, also, on the proper area(s) of study, and they have different answers to the question of periodization. For example, some present the history of Mexicans in the United States as an extension of the history of Mexico; others organize Mexican-American history around both the history of Mexico and the United States. There are other combinations. This is not to say, however, that because pundits differ over the matter of labels, over the proper area(s) of study, and over the question of periodization, the definition of Mexican-American history must be arbitrary. The serious student will see that the definition of Mexican-American history need not be so arbitrary as to have no basis in history.

As indicated above, the definition of Mexican-American history in this paper is *limited in area to the United States and encompasses the period from the end of the "Mexican War" or more precisely from the signing of the Treaty of Guadalupe Hidalgo on February 2, 1848, to the present.* The label Mexican-American was chosen because it is now commonly known that it refers to "citizens of Mexican origin." Mexican-American history began with the signing of the Treaty of Guadalupe Hidalgo because this Treaty extended citizenship, albeit second-class citizenship to all Mexicans who lived in the conquered territories of the Southwest; prior to this Treaty there were no Mexican-Americans in the United States, at least, as we know them today. Further, in this report, the term Mexican-American refers to all Mexicans in the United States, including those few who are not citizens. It should be made clear that the choice of

terminology and definitions in this paper are conventional or conservative; Mexican-American history is regarded as ethnic history, an area of specialization within United States history. And it is probable that if professional historians ever take interest in Mexican-American history, they will define Mexican-American history along lines which have been expounded in this report. This is not to say that there is no room for imagination. It is conceivable, for example, that some thoughtful student might define Mexican-American history as the history of Mexicans in the Southwest beginning, say, in 1540 when the Spaniards began to colonize the area. In this system, the signing of the Treaty of Guadalupe Hidalgo would mean a continuation of the history of Mexicans in the Southwest under new conditions: the conquest of the Southwest by the United States and the decline of Mexicans from power to cheap labor and second-class citizenship. In brief, the definition of Mexican-American history used in this paper is conventional, unencumbered by exploratory theories of periodization or intricate schemes recommending the study of overlapping areas—happily, this is left to the next generation, which might have more information to work with.

It is important, also, to include with the definition of Mexican-American history given in this paper, some explanation of the value of four histories: the history of the North American Indian, of Spain, Mexico, and the United States. All of these histories are useful as background to the history of Mexicans in the United States. The history of the North American Indian should not be confined to the glories of the Mayas and Aztecs which is often done by popular and superficial writers; special emphasis should be given to the Indians of the Southwest. The Spaniards learned much from the Indians whom they intermarried with to create the Mexican people. The history of Spain should devote special attention to the contribution of the Romans, Moors, and Jews because their contributions were carried to Mexico and the Southwest, where they are permanent cultural features. The history of Mexico is not only useful as background (especially the background to the so-called "Mexican War"), but also because it helps explain why Mexicans are constantly migrating to and from the United States. Moreover, Mexican history sheds light on the social and economic conditions which influence Mexican immigration, and to some extent, how that immigration affects the lives of Mexican-Americans. The political instability of the Mexican Revolution helps explain why large numbers of Mexicans migrated to the United States, and as usual, this immigration affected the lives of Mexican-Americans: in some areas where large numbers of immigrants settled, Anglos became apprehensive and intensified their hostility and discrimination which was not limited to the immigrants only, but extended, also, to the Mexican-Americans. As for United States history, it, too, is useful as background to the "Mexican War." Needless to say, Mexican-American history has been a part of the history of the United States since 1848.

Those who study Mexican-American history in the manner recommended in this paper should be able to perceive that the concept of *mestizaje* applies to Mexican-American history. *Mestizaje* refers to the long history of racial and cultural mixing which Mexican-Americans and their ancestors have experienced in Spain, Mexico, and the United States. *Mestizaje* is the Mexican-American heritage.

In sum, the matter of defining Mexican-American history, at this time is in a state of confusion, owing to the fact that little thought has been given to the subject, or Mexican-American history is just beginning to be studied seriously. To be sure, the matter of defining Mexican-American history is apt to be hotly debated for some time. No doubt, the definition used in this paper adds to the confusion or lack of consensus, but it has to be entered in this discussion for the sake of clarity and to distinguish it from others. Finally, those who are struggling for a judicious definition of Mexican-American history are admonished to treat their terms provisionally, and to treat the definition of their subject like a probable hypothesis, flexibly defined so as to leave plenty of room for improvement.

THE LITERATURE AND ITS LIMITATIONS

The number of useful works on Mexican-American history can be counted on one's fingers, and the number of scholarly histories of Mexicans in the United States is considerably less. With rare exceptions, professional historians have paid no serious attention to Mexican-American history. The bulk of the literature has been written and continues to be written by amateur historians, i.e., journalists and to a lesser extent social scientists. This is probably why Mexican-American history tends to be ahistorical, and why more attention has been devoted to recent developments. From these initial comments, I should like to move on to the literature, beginning with the only general survey of Mexican-American history, and then move on to more specialized works.

The only comprehensive work on Mexican-American history *North From Mexico* (New York, 1948) was written by Carey McWilliams, who is not a professional historian. He is, however, a talented man of letters and distinguished journalist. His books on minorities, especially *North From Mexico*, were destined to have a long life because he was among the first to write ethnic history. It is still largely true that one has to start with McWilliams when undertaking the study of some ethnic groups, especially the study of ethnic groups in California. McWilliams wrote *North From Mexico* as part of the "Peoples of America Series" under the general editorship of Louis Adamic. A brilliant literary form and mastery of the best sources assured the popularity of McWilliams' survey in wide reading circles, especially among specialists and the intelligensia.

Fortunately for Mexican-American history, its only survey has many remarkable qualities. Although the author likes Mexican-Americans, an attitude which easily comes through in *North From Mexico*, he is not blind to problems Mexicans have among themselves. For example, he understands the generation gap between native and foreign-born Mexicans, and how this gap is manipulated by Anglos against the Mexican community. He perceives keenly the tendency of Anglos to work with the least representative or lighter-skinned Mexican; he mentions the frivolous nature of some Mexican organizations; and he also presents some telling facts on the matter of class differences among Mexicans. The book not only appreciates the contributions and cultural influence of Mexicans in the Southwest, but presents also an unusual analysis of the cultural and historical interaction of Spaniards, Indians, Mexicans, Mexican-Americans, and Anglos in the Southwest. There is more to this general history. It is perhaps the first thoughtful exposition on how to organize Mexican-American history. In the Foreword, McWilliams grapples with the question: who are the Spanish-speaking people (Mexican-Americans)? He explains that the Southwest and the relations between Anglos and Mexicans are important parts of the story, but to stress the region and Anglo-Mexican relations would divert attention from "the people, their origins, and ordeals, their struggles and experiences." He, therefore, decided to structure the story of the Spanish-speaking people in terms of a "process" or "movement north from Mexico." This process or movement suggests "an extension of a way of life . . . a oneness of experience if not of blood or language or ancestry; a similar movement within a similar environment." McWilliams is aware of the difficulty of trying to find a suitable label to describe accurately such a diverse ethnic group as the Mexican-American people. He notes that the Mexican border is regarded as "invisible" by Mexicans who are constantly crossing back and forth. He explains that Mexicans are not immigrants: they were in the Southwest long before the Anglos conquered them. *North From Mexico* is an excellent model of how social science and current events can be useful to history. At no time while the author uses information from the social sciences, or when he refers to the present, does he discard the historical perspective. While the movement of the narrative is chronological, the author is able to move back and forth in time; he never becomes topically redundant. It is an excellent balance of chronology and topical analysis. Those interested in research will find in *North From Mexico* numerous suggestions and hints.

Although the author respects Mexican-Americans, he is not as uncritical as Ralph Guzmán suggests when he writes that *North From Mexico* is a "passionate apologia of the Mexican people. And there seems to be some exaggeration in Russell Fitzgibbon's review where Fitzgibbon presents McWilliams as "counsel rather than judge . . . the zealot rather than dispassionate researcher shows up on every page. Flaming indignation is the tone

of the book." Fitzgibbon is probably right when he concludes that *North From Mexico* is a "book to make many of us blush." Nonetheless, the book is not perfect: it is poorly documented and poorly illustrated. For example, McWilliams claims the Treaty of Guadalupe Hidalgo provided for the teaching of Mexican culture to those Mexicans who would become citizens in accordance with another provision of the same Treaty. Yet, despite exhausting efforts, the author of this report has failed to locate such a provision in the various and final draft of the Treaty of Guadalupe Hidalgo. As for illustrations, there is only one map in the whole book.

As one moves away from McWilliams' resplendent general history to more specialized studies, it will become evident that the topics investigated are uneven, that many gaps exist, and that some of the information is only partially relevant to Mexican-American history.

The image of the Mexican as seen by Anglo-American writers is admirably documented in Cecil Robinson's *With the Ears of Strangers* (Tucson, 1963). Robinson has a good sense of history, that is, his study begins with the Conquest of Mexico and moves on chronologically to the present, analyzing the continuity and changing attitudes of Anglo-American writers. Early Anglo-American writers did not hesitate to show their disapproval of Mexicans. They disapproved of the "dirty" Mexican, the Mexican's preoccupation with pleasure, his laziness, the Mexican's technological backwardness, his morbid sense of death, the Mexican's willingness to marry Indians which deprives him of his right to be called "white," his cowardice, his violent tendencies, and several other attributes associated with the early stereotype. But in the early part of the twentieth century, as American Writers became more critical of the pace of American life, of the "rat race" and crass materialism, they expressed a more respectful attitude toward the Mexican life-style. One group of Americans expressed nostalgia for the Spanish past in the Southwest. To be sure, they romanticized the past, and longed for those bygone days which Ray Billington describes as "the charm of life in Mexican California, where a bountiful nature, a genial climate massive nature, and the home government's neglect allowed man to bask in an atmosphere reminiscent of the garden before Adam's fall." In this mission culture fantasy, Anglo readers could satisfy their cravings for a serene pastoral past. At the end of the nineteenth century, there emerged another group of Anglo-American writers, such as Oscar Lewis, whose writings on the Mexicans demonstrated critical and scholarly depth. Despite their new romantic and realistic attitudes, Robinson concludes, North American writers still do not understand Mexicans; they continue to perceive "with the ears of strangers."

Although Manuel Gamio's studies on Mexican immigration are anthropological and have been supplemented by more recent investigations, they are useful and give us insightful information about Mexican immigration before the depression decade. Gamio, a distinguished anthropologist, was selected by the Mexican government to cooperate with Social Science Research Council in undertaking the study of Mexican immigration during the period 1926–27. The first volume, *Mexican Immigration to the United States* (Chicago, 1930), indicates that low pay and unemployment in Mexico encouraged Mexicans to migrate to the United States where they work as cheap labor. Gamio points out that most Mexicans were not at home in the United States, where the hostility and discrimination of the Anglo tends to make immigrants more patriotic. The book has some valuable chapters on the mentality, religion, and songs of the immigrant. It should be mentioned, also, that since Gamio had undertaken a pioneer study, it was necessary for him to engage in extensive field work to obtain his information. The companion volume, Gamio's *The Mexican Immigrant, His Life Story* (Chicago, 1931) is based on interviews collected from 57 immigrants. It indicates that the Mexican Revolution was an important reason for migrating to the United States, that the immigrants distrusted native-born Mexicans, that they were loyal to Mexico, and that they usually planned to return to Mexico. Of interest, also, in these studies is Gamio's underscoring statement that he has been concerned only with the most representative Mexican immigrant or the dark-skinned Mexican with strong Indian features.

Gamio's investigation of immigrants is actually an investigation of Mexicans as cheap labor, a subject which has received more attention than most topics of Mexican-American history. One of the first serious studies of Mexican labor is Paul S. Taylor's series of monographs entitled, "Mexican Labor in the United States." Professor Taylor is an economist who, as we shall see, appreciates the historical perspective, which he uses judiciously in conjunction with field work and statistics. His researches not only tell us a good deal about Mexican farm labor in the Southwest (Winter Garden District, Texas; Imperial Valley, California; and South Platte, Colorado), but also the conditions of workers, on railroads, large industries and steel mills (Chicago and Calumet Region, and Bethlehem, Pennsylvania). His pioneer studies on "migration statistics reveal the difficulty of estimating illegal entries of Mexicans to the United States, and he points out differences between Mexican and United States statistics. Taylor's studies, like Gamio's, are fundamental and provide valuable information about Mexican labor before the Depression.

Recently, the migrant labor movement in the United States has received wide national and international attention. The famous strike in Delano has been covered satisfactorily by such writers as Eugene Nelson, *Huelga* (Delano, 1966), and such journalists as John Dunne, *Delano* (New York, 1967), and Peter Matthiessen, *Salsipuedes* (New York, 1970). In addition to these works, Ernesto Galarza has published several works on farm labor. In *Merchants of Labor* (Santa Barbara, 1965), Galarza presents a good historical background of the Bracero program, and then proceeds to a discussion of its adverse effects on domestic farm labor; the Bracero program prevented farm labor from organizing, the Federal government cooperated with agribusiness at the expense of farm labor interests, and Galarza explains that organized labor has remained remarkably indifferent to the plight and interests of farm labor. This study also describes how braceros were treated by employers, and how the program was administered by the government. Galarza's most recent book, *Spiders in the House and Workers in the Field* (Notre Dame, 1970), despite this funny title, is a fascinating history of the National Farm Workers Union's strike (1947–50) and how it was put down by Di Giorgio Fruit Corporation with the help of the Federal government, that is, with the help of such Congressmen as R. Nixon, T. Morton, and T. Stood, who sat in a committee which investigated the strike and drew up a document which condemned the union and its effort to organize farm labor.

Mexican-Americans, that is, United States citizens of Mexican descent, have not only distinguished themselves as cheap labor, but they have also been good soldiers. Those who read Raul Morin's *Among the Valiant* Los Angeles, 1963) will find out that Mexican-Americans received the largest number of Congressional Medals of Honor than any other ethnic group in World War II. *Among the Valiant* is a colorful book, illustrated with medal winners, and a glowing introduction by Lyndon B. Johnson. Although the author is not a professional historian, he has done extensive research and has been able to present his knowledge lucidly and historically; he notes social and economic changes which have affected Mexican-Americans from the Depression to the post-war period; and Morin gives an historical account of all the major campaigns in World War II and Korea. The author is optimistic about the future of the Mexican-American, and evinces an unusual patriotism. For example, on the last page, he exclaims: "our standard of living has improved 100 percent." This last exclamation is controversial and probably exaggerated. According to Professor Ralph Guzmán, who gave a lecture on the Mexican-American at the University of California, Santa Barbara in 1969, Morin is no longer alive. A member of the G.I. Forum of Santa Barbara has also confirmed that Morin is deceased, and that Morin lived in Santa Barbara. Of interest also is Professor Guzmán's statement that Morin could not understand why young Mexican-Americans did not share his patriotism. In any case, Morin felt that conditions had improved greatly for the Mexican-American since the Depression.

The book by Leonard Pitt on the *Decline of the Californios: A Social History of the Spanish-speaking Californians, 1846–1890* (Berkeley, 1966) is probably the most scholarly work on Mexican-American history. As the title suggests, the book deals with the removal of Mexicans from power

after the "Mexican War," and the Mexicans decline to cheap labor, banditry, and second-class citizenship. This book is based on Pitt's dissertation which he completed in 1958 at UCLA, and bears the title "Submergence of the Mexican in California, 1846–90." Pitt not only details the illegal transfer of property or dispossession of Californios, the lynchings, and other forms of violence, but he also presents a good analysis of the Mexican social structure in California before the Anglos took over: he discusses class differences between the Californios, Mexicans, and Indians. Class differences and relations in Mexican California might be likened to class arrangements in the South: Californios might be likened to the planter class, Mexicans to the poor whites, and Indians to Black slaves. Of great interest, the author notes on page vii that the Californios "even in their heyday ... were numerically too small and culturally too backward to contribute to mankind much that was new or original ... the Yanks beat them badly and all but swept them into the dust bin of history." Moses Rischin, who reviewed the book, observes that Spanish language sources are very scarce and for this reason, Pitt had to limit himself to Southern California. Rischin is merely saying that Mexican sources are rare because the majority of Mexicans, then as now, were extremely illiterate. In any case, Pitt was able to find sources to piece together his story on the submergence of Mexicans to second-class status. He drew substantially from literate Californios whose recollections, memoirs, and accounts are stored at Berkeley in the Bancroft Library. Pitt also drew from a large number of books, newspapers, and some government publications and some theses and dissertations. The last section on the "schizoid heritage," explains lucidly the Anglo creation of a Spanish mythical past which, among other things, diverts attention from the embarrassing discrimination and poverty which Mexicans have been experiencing daily since their conquest one hundred and twenty-two years ago.

Cited in Pitt's bibliography is a very useful book entitled *The Life and Adventures of Joaquín Murieta* by John R. Ridge, who originally published the book in 1854 under the pseudonym of Yellow Bird. The Introduction to the reprinted edition (Norman, 1955), by Joseph H. Jackson, traces the origin and evolution of the Joaquín Murieta myth. Those writers who continue to refer to the existence of a Murieta would do well to read this book.

The historical literature on the Hispanos (Spanish-speaking of New Mexico) compares favorably with that of Mexicans in California, but is about as good as that of Texas and better by far the history of Mexicans in Colorado and Arizona—it would be no exaggeration to say that with the exception of brief mention in the general histories, the history of Mexicans in Colorado and Arizona is nonexistent. Like the Delano strike in California, the land grant conflict in New Mexico, under the leadership of Reies Tijerina, has received wide national attention. And like the Delano strike, Anglo journalists have been busy writing on Tijerina and the land grant conflict: Peter Nabokov's *Tijerina and the Court House Raid* (Albuquerque, 1969); Michael Jenkinson's *Tijerina* (Albuquerque, 1968); and now Richard Gardner's *Grito* (Indianapolis, 1970). All of these works supply a brief historical background and concentrate on contemporary social and economic pi oblems. The same is true of Nancie L. González *The Spanish American of New Mexico* (Albuquerque, 1967) and George Sánchez' *Forgotten People* (Albuquerque, 1940). González' presentation is topical and concentrates on contemporary aspects of Hispano living conditions. She states that Hispanos experience less discrimination than Mexican-Americans in other parts of the United States. Sánchez supplies, in *Forgotten People,* a very brief historical summary, an in-depth analysis of social and economic problems in Taos, and concludes by suggesting that government intervene and solve the problems of his forgotten people. The tone of these studies is one of "flaming indignation," to use Russell Fitzgibbon's phrase: the emphasis is typically on the immediate which is detailed and followed by suggestions for reform. This impatience with the past deprives the reader of what Allen Nevins calls "a bridge connecting the past with the present, and pointing the road to the future."

Several analytic studies of Texas barrios have appeared recently. Their discussion is reserved below in connection with social science. Insofar as the writing of the history of Mexican-Americans in Texas is concerned, there are no good works.

The book by Beatrice Griffith, *American Me* (Boston, 1948) is not history, but it tells us a good deal about the grass roots Mexican-American in California cities during the 30s and 40s. It is unfortunate that this excellent book has not been reprinted, for the questions it raises and insights it gives into urban barrio life make it worthy of mention in any Mexican-American bibliography. Another similar piece, written about the same time, is Ruth Tuck's *Not With the Fist* (New York, 1946), is also out of print. It is a study of a small Mexican community "similar to other cities in Arizona and Texas," a small city with plenty of immigrants. In its introduction, Tuck points out that her book was intended for those who work directly with Mexican-Americans, e.g., police officers and social workers. Ignacio López, who wrote the Foreword, indicated that there has been "an appalling dearth of information" concerning the Mexican. "Of those studies made in years past," wrote López, "some were rigidly scholastic, coldly quantative things of charts and graphs." There was a "Mexican skeleton, but there was no flesh and movement. Still others," continued López, "were narrowly regional. ... Many, far too many, dripped with an overdose of sentimentality. ... much ado about that ... quaint ... Mexican." If this is true, and Mr. López is still around, he might be delighted with recent publications on the Mexican-American by Anglo journalists, having plenty of "flesh and movement."

Stan Steiner's *La Raza* (New York, 1970) is one of these books. There is no question that the author has demonstrated understanding of the contemporary Mexican-American movement, but the haste in which the book was written has led to several glaring errors. In the Bibliography, for example, he accuses professional historians of suppressing Mexican-American history because professional historians fear that if the study of Mexican-American history is undertaken it will disturb the historian's ethnocentricity and belief that Mexicans are inferior. There is no question that professional historians have neglected Mexican-American history, but Steiner should prove that historians have consciously tried to suppress it. It is true that scarcity of sources is one reason why so little has been written about the history of Mexicans in the United States. It may be however, that historians and other groups have discouraged either by silence or other means a vigorous search for documents. A discussion of how Mexican-American history might be abused, once it is written, should have been considered by Steiner. How would *La Raza* use or abuse Mexican-American history? How could Mexican-American history be abused by "Chicano" opportunists in the universities? Steiner might have speculated further and asked this question: How can the realistic study of Mexican-American history be advanced if *La Raza* demands that it be manipulated and used as propaganda? To what extent is this going on in "Chicano Studies" programs? Who in the United States should advance the serious study of Mexican-American history? Steiner of course is wrong in stating that a history of Mexican-Americans has not been written unless he does not regard Carey McWilliams' *North From Mexico* as a history of Mexican-Americans. He is also wrong in writing that a biography of Joaquín Murieta remains to be written. Apparently, Steiner did not look carefully into the Murieta literature, for if he had, he would have discovered that Murieta never existed, and the legendary biography was written for the first time in 1854. There seems to be some exaggeration in the statement that the general public did not have access to the Treaty of Guadalupe Hidalgo until 1967. There are other flaws but the greatest flaw of journalists like Steiner is the tendency to be uncritical and unduly sympathetic toward the Mexican-Americans. In one sense, this new attitude compensates for earlier disparaging attitude of Anglo-American writers, but like the earlier attitude, it serves more the interest of propaganda than of truth.

Although their professional level and scholarly value vary, most articles on Mexican-American history are superficial and poorly documented. The three articles which have been chosen for brief comment in this report were selected because they illustrate the kind of research which can and needs to be undertaken by serious students. Mrs. Jean F. Riss of Costa Mesa, California, was inspired into writing her article, "Lynch Law,

Orange County Style" while reading Carey McWilliams' *Southern California Country.* She came across a passage on the lynching of a Mexican in her county. Intrigued by this local episode, Riss prepared a thoroughly documented paper on the lynching of Francisco Torres, apparently the last Mexican to be lynched in California. Riss' is an original contribution because she is the first to undertake this investigation, the first to bring most of the scattered literature together, and the first to tap primary sources relating to her study. The only major defect of the article is its failure to provide some historical background essential to any study, because it gives the reader what Allen Nevins calls "a sense of continuity."

The next article, "The White Caps in San Miguel County, New Mexico, 1889-91: A Study in Primitive Rebellion" was written by Andrew B. Schlesinger of Harvard University. Since Schlesinger's article will appear in this issue of the *Journal,* all that will be indicated for the moment, is that the article is a brilliant contribution to vigilante history in New Mexico, especially as that history relates to Mexican-American history in the late nineteenth century.

The third article is on the "Zoot Suit" riots of 1943. Ruben Cortez who researched the article has studied most of the available literature about Mexicans in Los Angeles. His investigation of the so-called "Zoot Suit" riots is remarkable not only because it is carefully researched and thoroughly documented, but also because of its keen sense of history: the story of the Riots is woven into the history of Los Angeles; Cortez gives the reader a better understanding of the Riots by reviewing briefly the evolution of the barrio in Los Angeles, and also, by reviewing antecedent conditions of the Riots. He concludes that little changed in Anglo-Mexican relations in Los Angeles, and refers to recent eruptions and the continuing poverty and discrimination.

In the social sciences, there are several studies which can be useful to Mexican-American history. Among the best of these studies are the advance reports of the Mexican-American Study Project, and Leo Grebler's *The Mexican-American,* which has appeared since the fourth draft of this paper one month ago. This bulky volume brings together all the findings of the advance reports, and has some additional topics on the Catholic Church, politics, and a majestic section on the "Historical Perspective." According to forecasts in high places, this handbook is a landmark in Mexican-American literature. The volume is based on over four years of research funded by the Ford Foundation. The information in the advance reports and Grebler's handbook are on the whole, "rigidly scholastic, coldly quantitative things of charts and graphs," lacking what Ignacio López calls "flesh and movement." The section on history (part two) is superficial and is based on old sources. It is not clear why a study which has only one Spanish-surname on its staff bothers to list almost every prominent Mexican-American in Los Angeles and San Antonio. (pp. xiii-xiv) In any case, it is to be hoped that the social science journals will be able to find judicious reviewers to tell us more about the value of this handbook.

Another useful social science study is Celis S. Heller's piece on Mexican-American youth. The book is not notably insightful, and contains only a three-page, poorly documented "Historical Profile." Heller's book, however, is useful because it supplies some basic information about Mexican-American youth. Margaret Clark's study of the San Jose *barrio* in California is also weak, as far as the historical dimension goes, but it provides some useful information on the health habits of that community. Of course, not all social science studies lack a sense of history. For example, Paul Taylor's study of Mexicans in Neuces County, Texas provides the reader with a brief historical discussion before illuminating on social and economic conditions of that area during the 20s and 30s. Another good example of a social science investigation which makes good use of history is Arthur J. Rubel's *Across the Tracks: Mexican Americans in a Texas City* (Austin, 1966). The author devotes a full chapter to what he calls "New Lots in Historical Perspective." Rubel uses good sources to document the history of his subject: dissertations, contemporary accounts, rigorous articles, and the best secondary sources.

There is an urgent need to study the various Mexican-American dialects. Little attention has been given to studies like George C. Barker's *Pa-*

chucho: An American-Spanish Argot and its Social Functions in Tucson, Arizona (Tucson, 1950) which is an effort to understand the vocabulary of a "small minority of Mexican-American youth." Linguistic studies of this kind can be useful in a number of ways: first, it might put an end to some of the petty bickering among Mexicans over the origins and meaning of such words as "Chicano" and "Mexican-American," with or without the hyphen; and second, it could lead to the compilation of a dictionary and history of the Mexican-American language.

Finally, there are studies which justify the complaints which some historians lodge against the social sciences. I refer to the tendency of some social science studies to derive generalizations from a particular situation, and then proceed to apply those generalizations to all situations. For example, Lyle Saunders' *Cultural Difference and Medical Care* (New York, 1954) abounds in controversial generalizations about the Mexican-American; it is enough here to state that Saunders, from time to time, makes curt allusions to history in order to give cogence to his generalizations. Probably the best example, that is, the most odious and reckless example of social science generalization, is William Madsen's *The Mexican-Americans of South Texas* (New York, 1964). The fault of this work is not found so much in Madsen. He is careful enough and makes himself clear: "I will try to describe the socio-cultural condition of the Mexican-Americans in one county on the Mexican border today in order to provide some understanding of the stresses of acculturation process in this area." One could accuse Madsen of insincerity because the title of his study appears to refer to all Mexican-Americans of South Texas rather than those of one county. The fault, however, is found in those who recommend the book and read more into it then is actually there. For example, the Curriculum Guide used in one secondary school makes the following careless statement about Madsen's book: "Extremely valuable because the concepts examined and narrated are very valid and applicable to all Mexican-Americans in the United States." Octavio Romano's scathing critique in "The Sociology and Anthropology of the Mexican-Americans," assumes Madsen is referring to all Mexican-Americans, and reads perhaps too much into Madsen's generalizations.

HISTORY AND OTHER STUDIES OF MAN.

The final observation of this report on the condition of Mexican-American history relates to a subject close to my interests: the definition of history and how history is different from and relates to other studies of man. Specifically, this section is concerned with Mexican-American history as history; how as history it differs from and is related to the social science studies on the Mexican-American, and also, how it is different from and related to journalistic reports on current Mexican-American events. These distinctions and relations have been confused and obscured by several writers, which is one reason I have entered their discussion here. A second reason is to draw special attention to the affirmation that "history has a special mission to perform." If Mexican-American history is to advance from its present nascent stage to professional and scholarly levels, not only must it be defined clearly, but it must also be made clear how it is different from and related to other branches of knowledge. It should be mentioned that this section is not an effort to review every theory and definition of history. It is true that historians have a good deal to debate regarding the definition of history: the interest here, however, is their agreement.

Robin George Collingwood suggested that there are four characteristics of history generally accepted by historians: (1) history is an "inquiry:" (2) history inquires about past human actions; (3) history is a method which interprets evidence; and (4) history teaches "what man has done" and "what man is." Thus Mexican-American history asks questions about the Mexican-American past; in order to answer these questions about the Mexican-American past, it interprets evidence: and it teaches what Mexican-Americans have done and what they are.

This definition of history, however, does not tell us how history is different from other studies of man, especially how it is different from social science and current events. Of several works consulted on this matter, the final comments of T.R.

Tholfsen's *Historical Thinking* (New York, 1967) are useful and illuminating. Recapitulating the virtues of history, Tholfsen affirms "that in studying any human phenomenon it is necessary not only to identify recurring patterns and connected ways." He then tells us how history is different from social science:

> Focusing on the event or idea or institution as it exists at a particular moment, the historian . . . cherishes peculiarities of time and place and resists any tendency to dismiss them as merely peripheral. He urges that general concepts be applied gently, so as not to do violence to the distinctive features of the phenomena. In addition . . . the historian inquires into the relationship between phenomena connected in time. He looks for continuity and change. He seeks the past that lies within every phenomenon. Above all, he analyzes the processes that brought it into being.

In other words, history is concerned with the analysis of change over time; the main responsibility of the historian is to find out what happened, "to identify events in sequence, to analyze the interrelationships among those events, and to discover how they occur in a given order." In this sense, Mexican-American history is an investigation of how things have come to be as they are in the barrios and wherever else Mexicans live in the United States. The subject matter of Mexican-American history consists of events which are worthy of being kept in remembrance, e.g., the Treaty of Guadalupe Hidalgo. Knowledge about these events is obtained by careful examination of surviving evidence. Thus, the explanation of the present condition of the Mexican-American involves a systematic study of the most important events which have taken place in the barrios since Guadalupe Hidalgo, and also the relationship of these events to conditions under which changes have taken place in the past. This means an analysis of the patterns found in the continuity of old forms, e.g., poverty and discrimination, and, also, an analysis of the patterns found in conditions under which changes have taken place. In short,

Mexican-American history is interested in continuity and the analysis of change over time. And it is this interest in the development of man over time which distinguishes history from social science and other studies of man.

There are, however, other characteristics which distinguish history from social science. A.S. Eisenstadt observes that the social sciences seek information for immediate use in solving social problems, and, also, that the social sciences tend to be reform oriented. History, on the other hand, has not traditionally been interested in social ills, and is usually conservative or part of the establishment. Social science is interested in formulating consistent patterns of human behavior while history is interested in differences between individuals and groups. The language of social science is supposedly impersonal, while the language of history reflects the personality of the historian and is, in a sense, a kind of poetry. According to Eisenstadt, both history and social science began in the nineteenth century in search of positive truth. History gave up the search in the twentieth century while the social sciences persist because if "they cannot claim to be furnishing society with certain knowledge arrived at by certain methods, they can claim nothing at all."

Although history differs from social science, it does not mean history cannot use social science information and methods. To be sure, both historians and social scientists agree that they have something to learn from each other. In its bulletin on *The Social Sciences in Historical Study* (New York, 1954), the Committee on Historiography of the Social Science Research Council encouraged historians to make use of the social sciences. *The Modern Researcher* (New York, 1970) claims: "history and social science are true sisters because the historian must again and again rely on the results of surveys, studies, and statistics gathered by his painstaking colleagues in the ologies; and because they in turn cannot breathe or move without adopting toward their material the attitude of history." Economist Paul S. Taylor believes that "history can serve social science—at least under many circumstances; history illuminates the contemporary social science study—and the reverse is also true."

Journalism presents the same problem as social science. For example, the increasing output of works on the current Mexican-American Civil Rights Movement, chiefly the work of journalists, is not history. This literature confines itself to current events with little or no consideration of the historical perspective; the subject is rarely perceived in terms of continuity and the analysis of change over time. More specifically, some writers confuse current events with history, and others cite works on current events in bibliographies of Mexican-American history without explaining how these works qualify as history. As in social science, the historian who uses information from current events or any other source, for that matter, should make clear how that information qualifies as history:

> Hence the historian who borrows most enthusiastically from the sister disciplines will take pains to use what he borrows 'historically' and maintains the identity of his own discipline.

The main point is not that history is superior to social science or any other discipline, but that history has certain advantages over social science—and the reverse is also true. The main point is that some writers have confused history with other disciplines and, also, they have failed to illuminate upon the specific interest of history: the development of the Mexican-American people over a period of time.

CONCLUSION

Although some of the works mentioned in this report have drawn extensively from archives, museums, libraries, field work, etc., it is still generally true that no serious effort has been made to tap primary sources. There are museums, archives, libraries, and other depositories which have never been catalogued and investigators have no way of knowing what sources on Mexican-American history are available. There must be a gold mine of information in the archives of the national, state, and local governments of Mexico and the United States. Further, a search for documents should not be limited to the Southwest because Mexicans also live in other states. It should be mentioned that written testimony by Mexican-Americans is rare, owing to the fact that the majority of Mexicans have been and continue to be extensively illiterate. Fortunately, there are Mexicans still around who witnessed much of their history in the period from 1850 to the present. Some scholars have considered the possibility of obtaining oral testimony from these survivors and utilizing the methods of ethnohistory to corroborate it. The process of searching for documents, cataloguing, indexing, editing, annotating, publishing, and making them available to serious students, if ever undertaken, will be expensive, requiring infinite patience, special skills, and years of labor. And if Mexican-American history is to advance in scholarly depth, it is imperative that this process be undertaken.

In this report, a discussion of the use and abuse of Mexican-American history by civil rights groups has been avoided. This is because sufficient information is not available. A terse comment, however, on the author's experience is perhaps not amiss. First, it is clear that the university which should be the vanguard of serious research, is not going to advance the serious study of Mexican-American history. This is so despite "Chicano Studies" as a publicity gimmick (to let the community know that the college is interested in "disadvantaged Chicanos"), and also, Mexican-American history is threatened in the universities by student politics and some professors who go along for reasons of personal advancement. And it is generally true that:

> When a community is at a crucial stage, just emerging from a time of oppression and second-class status, it is simply going to manipulate the past for its own purposes. One must expect this.

In other words, it is the opinion of this writer that the propaganda of the Mexican-American Civil Rights Movement, especially as it is used by the students is an impediment to the serious study of Mexican-American history. It is also sad, again, in the opinion and experience of this author, that foundations and government agencies also seem more interested in appeasing the vociferous than funding such critically neglected areas as Mexican-American history.

Also, in this report, no effort has been made to accuse professional historians of consciously suppressing Mexican-American history. The reason is simple: there is no evidence for such a charge or suspicion. Stan Steiner, as I briefly indicated, wrote in *La Raza* that "those who have written the textbooks of the Southwest have for one hundred years suppressed the history of La Raza." Steiner did not prove this serious charge. Henry Steele Commager, however, in his book on *The Nature and the Study of History* observes: "Over the centuries history has been written by the victors, not the vanquished. . . . One of the less amiable traits of victors, in the past, has been the deliberate destruction of enemy records and the silencing—often by death—of enemy historians. It is true that documents on Mexican-American history have mysteriously disappeared from certain depositories in the Los Angeles area, but this activity is not so widespread as to justify alarm. And no Mexican-American historian has yet been silenced, owing to the fact that there are none. Presently, it seems difficult if not impossible to train cadres of Mexican-American historians who: (1) are of Mexican descent, and (2) are independent of the politics and propaganda of the Mexican-American Civil Rights Movement. In short, there is no evidence which convicts professional historians of the suppression of Mexican-American history.

Mexican-American history, as defined in this paper, is just beginning to be studied seriously. Professional historians have almost paid no attention to the subject, and the bulk of the literature has been written and continues to be written by amateur historians, that is, by journalists and social scientists. Further, much of the literature has an indignant and reformist tone to it, and the recent literature, mostly the hasty product of journalists, concentrates on recent developments and ignores the historical perspective. The development of Mexican-American history, such as it is, has been far from smooth. It has proceeded unevenly; there are many gaps and most of the topics already dealt with in the literature require more profound study.

Ralph Guzmán

Ralph Guzmán (see p. 140); testifying before the U.S. Inter-Agency Committee on Mexican American Affairs in 1967, charged that scholars more interested in money than truth have taken government grants and reinforced racial stereotypes. The crux of Professor Guzmán's argument resides in what he considers the inability of academe in the pay of the government to look away from the minority group and into the majority society for the source of non-achievement.
By permission of the author.

Ethics In Federally Subsidized Research – The Case Of The Mexican American

All of the recent internal and external challenges to American values and power must not obscure the fact that we are in the midst of a most profound moral crisis. While most analysis of this crisis refer to questions of traditional moral virtues or business ethics or the behavior of the young, a largely unexamined arena is the question of the relationship between the ethics of scholarship and the actions of government.

The importance and influence of governmental actions has been cited so often that it has become one of John Stuart Mills' "dead truths." In the field of minority research it is necessary to reemphasize that the programs of the government, in large part, determine and fix for generations the conceptions, the images, the popular stereotypes of what the majority and the minority think of each other and of themselves. By the concepts it supports, by the programs it selects, and by the values it endorses, the government holds up a mirror of society. To the degree to which that mirror distorts, the society suffers. Society becomes imprisoned in irrationality and illusion. Men turn to magic rather than reason; they seek panaceas rather than programs to solve their problems.

The development of this crisis has been aided and abetted by American scholars; they are partially responsible for it. For American scholars have aborted the ethics of scholarship. They have participated in premature government programs; they have profited from the fears of isolated policy-makers; they have exploited the privation of the poor; in short, too many scholars have succumbed to the lure of profit and power and abandoned the acient obligation of their profession: The unremitting but unrewarded search for valid knowledge. Thus many have forgotten that the search for truth is not the same as the search for solutions of problems. Government operates; it is primarily interested in the question: "Will it work?" It must select among alternatives. But it is not primarily or preeminently interested in abstract truth and unrelated knowledge. As such the interest of government differs from the interest of scholarship. A working relationship between the two must be one of tension and co-existence—not merger. A strange symbiotic relationship has arisen between government officials who use the university as window dressing to validate their predetermined choices and the academics who use government grants, consultancies and contracts to validate their prowess in their pursuit of academic prestige. If this relationship were merely confined to the participants, it would only be sordid; however the ramifications of this symbiosis stretches the length and breadth of the land and as such affects the high and the low; the majority and the minority, in their respective quest for identity and dignity. And this is of particular significance in the Southwest.

Five and one-half million Americans of Mexican descent provide living testimony to repeated failures of the American conscience. The destiny of these people is inextricably entwined in the resolution of our internal moral crisis. The challenge posed by these people to American scholars and American political institutions has been largely unmet. The response has been ineffective, irrelevant and miserly, both in material and spiritual assistance. The consequences to the Mexican-American people echo like a medieval petition to a benevolent despot.

Many government officials and scholars have assumed the ideology of the past. At its highest level of conceptualization this tendency assumes that the problem of a minority group inheres in the minority group. It assumes that the larger society is without fault; if you could only find the fatal flaw in the character or the mores of the minority group the problem would be solved. The real question is not to "know the minority," but to know the failure of societal institutions to relate effectively to members of minority groups. The real emphasis should be placed in the malfunctions in the total system not on some supposed trait—really culpability within the Mexican-American. (It is this basic problem of *where* to focus—on the minority or on the society—that produced the government's agonies over the Moynihan Report.) This first basic error in where to look results in other fallacious assumptions. By this I mean that notions of racial inferiority; low intellectual capacity; social maladjustment; expendability in war and peace permeate official and academic circles. The more sophisticated camouflage these notions with phrases like cultural deprivation, lack of motivation, social alienation; marginality and lack of acculturation. The less sophisticated are more honest in their terminology. They talk about laziness and un-Americanism.

Tragically, these external social judgments have been internalized by many Mexican Americans. Recent surveys in San Antonio and Los Angeles show a tendency for Mexican Americans to agree with the negative judgments that the larger society passed upon them. Surely it is logically evident that if you treat people for generations as if they were inferior some will begin to believe that they are inferior and act accordingly when they are with you: if you treat people as if they were lazy some of them will respond accordingly to your demands; if you treat people as if they were unintelligent some will respond as if, indeed, they were unintelligent in performing your tasks. What this does to the chances of succeeding generations is not only morally but even criminally wrong; for it is a basic offense against human dignity. For scholars to participate in this process is to make them party to the destruction of human values rather than the fulfillment of them. This is a repudiation of their role as validators of the truth.

In another dimension this process generates social and personality patterns founded on fear—fear of the outside world; fear of competition; fear of social change; and fear of self in any but the safe, predictable world of the minority. The assumption that the intrusion of the "outside world" is a hostile event; the creation of categories of "we and they," not bridged by symbols named justice, democracy and consensus—these cripple the community. The young Mexican American scholar who is afraid to leave the *barrio* in order to compete; the immature mind that refuses to explore beyond the comfortable; the young adult that opts for social indifference rather than moral indignation—these are the heirs of the merger of government and scholar.

A romanticized picture of reality has obscured the salient problems of these people. Certain cultural anthropologists, among others, have unduly transmuted aspects of the Mexican-American people into presupposed patterns of behavior. They have swindled the American people into believing that the quixotic and picturesque represent permanent cultural essences. And they have also performed a grave disservice to the government as well as the community of scholars. To establish elaborate exegesis from the fact that some members of this minority group may have a rural sense of time; that some of them may remain dependent upon the local *curandera;* that some males remain obsessed with a notion of *machismo;* and that others have an overriding sense of social fatalism is not only disingenuous it is a cruel hoax. A quest for the quaint is not science; nor is it likely to be service to the United States government.

Having helped to warp the Mexican-American self-image American social institutions have not even been able to project an adequate picture of what the larger society really is. The legitimating myth of the American educational system posits a society in which achievement, loyalty and patriotism are automatically rewarded. No Mexican-American needs a college education to tell him that this is patently false. His own life experiences tell him that economic reward is not commensurate with educational achievement. His observations of the Negro teach him that a firm joining of the thumb to the nose produces more attention than patient supplication. Moreover, he knows that valor in war brings no vantage in peace. Both those who believe in the myth implicity and those who reject it completely share a gross misunderstanding of American society.

In the minority, this misunderstanding contributes to a disposition for unrealistic and irrelevant group goals. For example, the demand of some leaders, supported by some scholars, that the community *must* maintain a high degree of cultural solidarity and yet still be accorded the benefits of the affluent society is obviously impractical and an interference with a basic personal liberty. The Negroes wisely never accepted the idea of separate but equal. After almost sixty years the Supreme Court rejected the idea that separate facilities could ever be made equal. It should not take another sixty years to realize that separate cultural communities cannot be made equal either. Those who would impose group solidarity in terms of cultural pluralism merely re-state the old separate but equal doctrine. The point is that if an individual opts for one cultural identity or another that is *his* privilege, but for a government or its agencies to predetermine that choice is an easy concession to mutual racism. The concelebration of the Chamizal Agreement, and these hearings, presumes and assumes a relationship between Mexican Americans and the Republic of Mexico that exists largely in the minds of intellectual romantics. These El Paso agreements will not affect one school drop-out in Denver; they will not cleanse *Barrio Barelas* in Albuquerque; nor will they desegregate schools in Los Angeles; jobs will still be scarce for Mexican Americans in San Antonio, and houses in Phoenix will still have invisible but real signs that read: "For Anglos Only." In short, the problems that Mexican Americans face relate to the fact that they are American citizens. In the face of these problems of the Mexican Americans the disposition of the Chamizal is unimportant to the people gathered here.

The predisposition on the part of leaders and scholars to assert unrealistic and irrelevant goals naturally produces an excess of sweetheart leaders. Such leaders romance both the larger society and the Mexican-American community in their efforts to preserve the illusion of cooperation. Their concern for preserving this facade is maintained at the expense of genuine progress for all Americans.

All these things sustain a fatal dependency that destroys the effectiveness of legitimate government endeavors and impairs the ability of the Mexican American to enter a meaningful relationship to himself or to American society.

This dependency is fostered by improper and unethical scholarship. Mexican Americans have not been served well by those who purport to interpret them to the larger society. In a sense, they have been the victims of spurious relationships between the scholar, his subject and program builder. Some scholars, blinded by a passionate commitment to methodology or to their own attachments to Mexican Americans fail to see the real strengths and liabilities in the Mexican American community.

Many educators, for example, graciously concede the existence of a representative Mexican-American culture. However, in making this concession they seize the opportunity of defining its content. Naturally they also assume the responsibility for fitting every square peg of a Mexican American into the round hole of culture they have invented. There is no one so totalitarian as an educator confronted by a Mexican-American child who refuses to conform to the educator's notion of what a Mexican American child should be. Unique individuals are assumed to be non-real, non-legal or possibly non-Mexican. This diagnosis is *not* necessary. If necessary, Mexican-Americans can define their own culture.

There is an attachment to the method which sometimes transcends interest in its success. There are some, for example, so committed to adult education television that they discount the weight of any impartial evaluation as to how it might be received in the *barrios*.

In another category are those that have a ready made diagnosis in scholarly findings about Mexican Americans. They admit that they don't know Mexican Americans well but emphasize that they are well-disposed towards them. These same individuals squeeze Mexican Americans into models based on previous ethnic experiences in different times and settings. Well-meaning, well-disposed scholars assume that Mexican Americans are only dislocated Puerto Ricans, merely lower class Cubans, a variant of the Black Power Movement, or simply Spanish-speaking Irish. These scholars suggest programs that have worked for other ethnic groups while ignoring the reality of the Mexican Americans. For example, bussing children into middle-class white neighborhoods may symbolize the aspirations of some parents of middle class Negro children. It does not follow, however, that the same program will cause the parents of Mexican-American children to rejoice.

Others have exploited this minority in the game of government grants-manship. Personnel from school systems that have failed to serve Mexican American children effectively are often the ones who receive government grants. Grantsmanship has widened the chasm between the pursuit of truth and the intelligent selection among alternatives. Some of the reasons for this are inherent in the system itself.

Those most skillful in securing government grants display their ability to communicate with grant-givers. It should not be necessary to note that there is no automatic relationship between skill in grant design and academic excellence. Too often scholars become smooth operators who maintain themselves by reinforcing the respective misconceptions of the power structure and the community. Not surprisingly, the ethics of some of these individuals relate to the profit motive associated with primitive capitalism; not to the rewards represented by a genuine contribution to either the total sum of human knowledge or the solution of pressing and immediate problems.

The point is that the relationship between the scholar and government is in disarray. At present the academic medicine man converges on Washington with special skills in packaging research programs. To place it in proper perspective the government should diligently and honestly seek scholars with integrity. The validation of truth may be unpleasant—it emphatically will not please all of the public but, if the scholar is not to be politicized, he must feel free to report unpleasant even politically unpalatable truths. Government, on the other hand, must realize that it is no business of the scholar to make American society feel better about itself.

When this necessary change occurs government and scholars can address themselves to the real research needs of the American people.

The President has requested specific guidelines for basic research in this area. The following areas demand urgent attention. Overall, there should be a focus on what has *changed* among Mexican Americans.

One, there is a desperate need for a history of the Mexican-American people which neither serves patriotic sentiments nor panders to the pride of the sub-group.

Two, there is a need for a comparative study of the peoples of the Southwest and their patterns of social interaction. The varying relationships between and among the several minorities and the dominant society in the Southwest must be related and the ongoing process probed in order to assess the viability of American political and social institutions on a broad continuum of past, present, and future trends. The difference between this approach and the more narrow approach is that scholars have conceptualized minorities as if there were no context of a larged society.

Three, the myth of an automatically assumed special relationship between the Mexican-American people and the Republic of Mexico must give way before research into the true relationship that has varied with time, place and generation and is continuously changing. For many scholars the proximity of Mexico has obscured the fact that problems of the Mexican Americans relate to American life. While grandfathers may dream of small villages in Jalisco the majority of the Mexican Americans cannot remember events before World War II.

Four, the border as a concept must be recognized for what it is: a political bludgeon used against Mexican Americans which alternately appears and disappears when agricultural interests dictate.

Five, nostalgic appeal to the rural communitarian past must be challenged by a continuing focus on the present-day urban reality of Mexican American existence, while the problems of the rural present begin to get realistic attention.

Six, and perhaps most important, while most research will remain concerned with things that are there must be substantial support for research that centers on "things that could be." In other words, government, more than anyone else, has a responsibility to support daring, imaginative and possibly outrageous research. Dare to follow with action research the implications of what has been done in Denver by Ozzie Simmons and his colleagues and by Lyle Shannon in Racine, Wisconsin. Dare to trust the poor to direct their own lives; dare to trust them to administer programs, establish direction, and to make decisions. Then study these processes.

Seven, there are two beneficial by-products of research that can justifiably be encouraged by scholars and government. One is research that represents a partnership between the scholar and the community. This not only helps the community to become more aware of itself, as it really is, it also helps the scholar to reformulate his conceptions as he meets real people, not cases. The other is the incorporation of Mexican-American youth into research activities as assistants and managers. This will sensitize these young people to become more confident American citizens; it will also produce scholars of the future who can match compassion and competence with insight.

Finally, a note of caution. There are real limitations to the scope of scholarship and the power of government. Neither can grant dignity to a proud people; for dignity is not granted, it is a product of a personal sense of achievement and esteem. Both the scholar and the government must realize that personal dignity and psychological well-being for the Mexican American cannot be secured through intervention by government. The lady bountiful complex, that has characterized the relationship between scholar, government, and Mexican Americans can only stifle the development of these people, suppress their political socialization and subvert their dignity. To those who have ap-proached the Mexican American people as condescending fathers or anxious hucksters I can only warn you to walk warily for you walk in the dark corners of your own conceits.

DATE DUE